Helping Hands

English

for Nursing and Social Care

von

Ruth Fiand

3. durchgesehene Auflage

Dr. Felix Büchner – Hamburg

Vorwort

Helping Hands
ist ein Englischlehrwerk für „helfende Berufe" im Bereich der Pflege und des Sozialwesens. Insbesondere können mit dem Lehrwerk Klassen der zweijährigen Berufsfachschule Sozialassistenz (Sozialhelfer), der Altenpflege sowie der Heilerziehungshilfe Themenbereiche ihres Berufsfelds in der Zielsprache einüben. Das Buch ist für zwei Schuljahre konzipiert und bietet neben einem Grundkurs (Units 1 – 7) die Möglichkeit, über Basiskenntnisse des Englischen hinausgehend den mittleren Bildungsabschluss im Erweiterungskurs (Units 8 – 14) zu erwerben.
Die wichtigsten Grundlagen der englischen Grammatik werden in den Units aufgegriffen und im beruflichen Kontext eingebunden wiederholt. Dabei werden Basiskenntnisse (A2) aufgefrischt und im Erweiterungskurs die Lernenden auf das Sprachniveau des mittleren Bildungsabschlusses (B1) geführt.

Zunächst stellt das Buch pflegende Berufe und deren typische pflegerische Handlungen im Berufsalltag in den Vordergrund, so die Pflege am Krankenbett, Essen reichen, persönliche Hygiene, Anziehen u. a. Immer wieder werden die Schülerinnen und Schüler in berufliche Alltagssituationen versetzt, in denen sie in der Zielsprache handeln sollen, z. B. bei der Aufnahme eines Bewohners im Pflegeheim, bei der Planung der Pflege, beim Führen einer Pflegedokumentation oder bei Beratungsgesprächen. Neben pflegerischen Handlungen werden die Themen Demenz, die Biografiearbeit sowie die Ernährung im Alter angesprochen. Ein weiterer Fokus liegt auf der Prävention von Erkrankungen durch gesunde Ernährung und Bewegung. Daneben werden Themen wie die Inklusion von Menschen mit Behinderung, Menschen mit psychischen Erkrankungen sowie der Umgang mit dem Tod behandelt.

Helping Hands stellt handlungsorientierte Aufgabenstellungen in den Vordergrund, die berufliche Handlungssituationen aufgreifen und ein fächerübergreifendes Arbeiten ermöglichen. Diese Aufgaben sind mit **„Hands-on task"** gekennzeichnet. Diese zielen auch auf eine Erweiterung der Methoden- und Sozialkompetenz. **Helping Hands** arbeitet mit verschiedensten Aufgabentypen, die dem Europäischen Referenzrahmen entsprechen, auf diese wird entsprechend mit

Reception

Interaction

Production

Mediation hingewiesen.

Jede Unit enthält eine **Listening**-Übung mit weiteren Dialogen aus beruflichen Handlungssituationen.
Im Anhang des Buchs sind **Methodenseiten** zusammengestellt, die weitere Hilfen für den Berufsalltag bieten. Jede Unit endet mit einer Vokabelliste (einige, für Schüler schwer auszusprechende Wörter, wurden separat eingesprochen), am Ende des Buchs befinden sich alle Vokabeln in einer alphabetischen Übersicht zusammengefasst.

So, this book really gives you some **Helping Hands!**

Autorin und Verlag

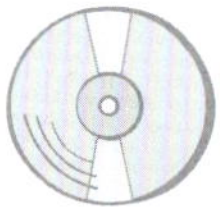

Als Audiotrack erhältlich

Über die Autorin Ruth Fiand
Oberstudienrätin, Englisch, Deutsch, Kinder- und Jugendliteratur an der Käthe-Kollwitz-Schule der Stadt Aachen (Berufsfachschulen Sozialassistenz, Kinderpflege, Assistenz für Ernährung und Versorgung, Fachschule für Sozialpädagogik).
Lehramtsstudium für Englisch und Deutsch, Zusatzqualifikation für Kinder- und Jugendliteratur.
Mitautorin des Englischlehrwerks „Join In – English for Child Care and Education"

Inhaltsverzeichnis

Inhaltsverzeichnis

Anhang

Unit 1 Meeting people

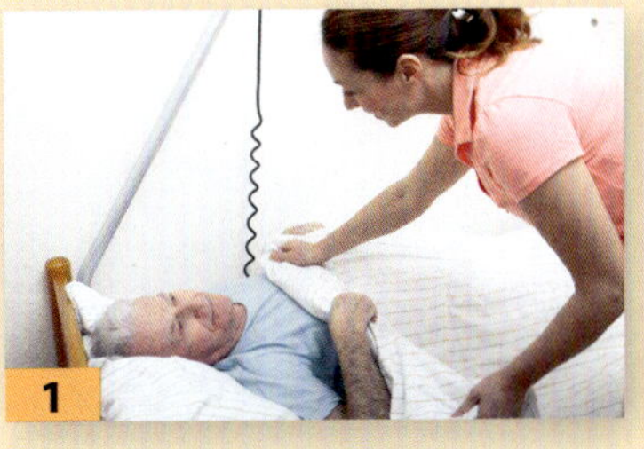
1

a. Work in small groups and find out four things you have in common. Also think of something which is unique about each group member. Tell the class about your findings.

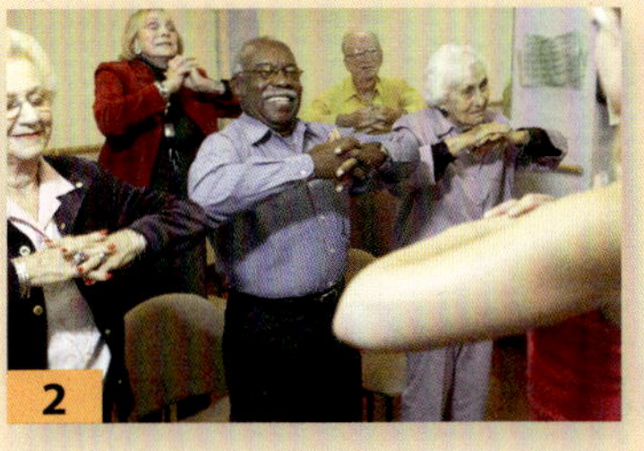
2

b. Complete the following sentence, "If I could have dinner with any person, living or dead, it would be … because …"

3

c. Write two to three statements about yourself on a card. Don't tell anybody what you have written. Collect all cards together and shuffle them. Choose one card, read out the statements and try to guess who the writer is.

4

d. Truth or lie? Write down three statements about yourself. One of these statements should be false. Read out your statements and let the others guess the lie.

5

Talk about the pictures

- What situations do they show? Who is meeting who?
- Do the pictures show situations you have experienced? Describe your experiences. Were they good or bad, pleasant or unpleasant, funny or serious, interesting or uninteresting, exciting or boring, difficult or easy?

Interaction

A **Work in small groups. Choose one of the situations you have spoken about and do a short role-play. How do you start the conversation? How do you introduce yourself to the group or person?**

B **Sometimes, people use icebreakers to get to know each other and "break the ice" when a new work team comes together. Look at the icebreakers in the chart above and choose one to do with your group.**

Meet Helen and Tom

Hi, my name is Helen. I'm 17 years old and I live in Manchester. I live with my father Brian and his wife Corinne. My parents are divorced. We live in a large flat with a balcony in the city centre and I have my own room. I have a stepbrother called Kevin. He is ten years younger than me. My mother Sandra, her husband and Kevin live in London. I often visit them. I love to go shopping in London, but also here in Manchester with my best friend Sandra. When I'm in London, I take the chance to do something with Kevin. We visit the zoo, go to the cinema, play games, or draw pictures. Art is my favourite subject, but I also like biology. I believe working with children is something I could do. I have never had problems with Kevin and I do a lot of babysitting for my neighbours. I like swimming and every year I join an inclusive summer camp at the seaside. I really love these holidays and I always look forward to them. From my experience at summer camp, I know that working with children with special needs is something I want to do in future.

Hello, my name is Tom and I'm 19 years old. My family originally comes from South Africa. Now I live in Manchester with my parents and my sisters Mona and Ronda. My granddad also lives with us. Our house is large enough for all of us and it has a big garden. I finished school last year and right now I'm a social volunteer in an older people's day care centre. I have already had a lot of experience with my grandfather who lives with us. He is a wheelchair user and needs regular care. I help my mother to care for him, and maybe this is why I think that working with older people is something I would love to do as a future job. My year as a social volunteer also gives me the chance to gain some more experience. I enjoy spending time with older people. I love listening to their stories and their warm welcome every morning.
At the weekend, I like to meet my friends and we go to a disco, or we just hang around. I've always enjoyed sport, and nowadays I go to the gym and work out twice a week. You need to be strong to work with older people.

Working with the text

A Are these statements true or false? Correct the false statements.

1. Helen lives in London but Tom lives in Manchester.
2. Tom is older than Helen.
3. Helen's stepbrother Kevin is 4 years old.
4. Both Helen and Tom have some experience with older people.
5. Tom's grandmother lives with his family.
6. Helen has some experience with children with special needs.
7. Tom is doing on the job training in an old people's home.

B Look at the text again and complete the following sentences.

1. Helen believes that she can work with children because …
2. Her yearly summer camp holidays help her to be sure about her future work plans because …
3. In the future, Tom wants to work with older people because …
4. He thinks he has already had a lot of experience with older people because …
5. He thinks it's good to work out regularly because …

Practising grammar

A Fill in the correct form of the verb "be"

Helen and Tom 1. … in their teens. Tom 2. … older than Helen, he 3. … 19 years old and Helen 4. … 17 years old. 5. … they sure about their future job training? Yes, both 6. … interested in working with people. And, 7. … it the same job training they want to do? No, it 8. (not be). Whereas working with older people 9. (not be) something Helen wants to do, Tom 10. … absolutely sure that he loves doing this kind of job.

But, he 11. (not be) interested in working with children. This 12. … very different to Helen. There 13. … an inclusive summer camp each year which Helen goes to. Tom 14. … a social volunteer in an old people's day care centre. He enjoys listening to older people's stories, and the residents 15. … happy to have someone to talk to.

Working at the day care 16. (not be) the only positive experience Tom has had with older people. His grandfather, who 17. … disabled, lives in their household. Both, Helen and Tom 18. … glad to be sure about their future plans. And what about you, 19. … you already sure what you want to do in the future? What 20. … your dream job?

Grammar box: Das Verb "be" in der Gegenwartsform /
Present Simple Tense of be

Aussagen		**Verneinungen**	**Fragen**
Singular / Einzahl			
I am	*I'm*	*I am not / I'm not*	*am I …?*
you are	*you're*	*you are not / you aren't*	*are you …?*
he is	*he's*	*he is not / he isn't*	*is he …?*
she is	*she's*	*she is not / she isn't*	*is she …?*
it is	*it's*	*it is not / it isn't*	*is it …?*
Plural / Mehrzahl			
we are	*we're*	*we are not / we aren't*	*are we …?*
you are	*you're*	*you are not / you aren't*	*are you …?*
they are	*they're*	*they are not / they aren't*	*are they …?*

B When you meet someone for the first time at a new school or work place, you want to know more about this person. Here are some typical questions you may ask but the question word is missing. Fill in the question word.

1. … do you live?
2. … do you come from?
3. … old are you?
4. … else is in your family?
5. … hobbies do you have?
6. … do you do in your free time?
7. … kind of work experience do you have?
8. … are your favourite subjects at school?
9. … do you want to work with people?
10. … future job do you want to do?

Frageworte / Question words

Who?	Wer?
Where?	Wo?
When?	Wann?
What?	Was?
Why?	Warum?
How?	Wie?

Interaction

C Work in pairs.
Use the questions to interview your partner and introduce your partner to the class.

Tom meets his colleagues

It is Tom's first day at the old people's day care centre. Barbara Brown is head of the centre and she wants him to be there at 9 for the daily staff meeting.
Tom looks for the staff room and knocks at the door. Someone tells him to come in and when he opens the door he sees seven people sitting in a circle, discussing something.

Tom: Good morning. I'm Tom, the new volunteer. *(Tom does not enter the room but stays in the doorway)*

Barbara: Oh, hello Tom. Come in. *(she gets up)*. We spoke on the phone, didn't we? *(She shakes Tom's hand.)*

Barbara: Welcome to St Mary's.

Tom: Thank you.

Barbara: You're just in time for the staff meeting. Take a seat! *(She turns to the people sitting around.)* This is Tom. He is going to work as a social volunteer here in our day care. *(the others smile and nod)*

Barbara: Would you like some tea or coffee?

Tom: No thanks, I'm fine.

Barbara: Okay, if you do want a drink, just help yourself. Oh, before I forget, Tom. I would like you to write a personal profile for our staff panel. There are a lot of people going in and out and they are interested in who works in our team. Can you do that for me?

Tom: Yes, sure, I can do that. What should I put in the profile?

Barbara: Well, first of all we need your photo so that people know who you are when they meet you. We can take a photo after the staff meeting. Tell us something about you - your name, age, where you come from. Don't forget to say how long you will be here for, and I think it's also good to know why you have joined our team. I think people should know that you're working as a social volunteer here with us. Maybe you could also say something about your future plans.

Tom: Okay, that's no problem. I can write my personal profile right after this staff meeting, if you like.

If you start a job in Britain, you will probably be introduced to your colleagues by your boss. Your new colleague may say "pleased to meet you", and you can reply "pleased to meet you, too." He may just smile and nod. Some colleagues may shake your hand, particularly if he / she is at a higher level than you.

It is usual to use first names at work, even with your boss. However, if you are talking to one of the residents in a nursing home, use their title and surname unless they offer their first name. This is a sign of respect from the past, when the residents were young. They will use your first name.

When you see your colleagues each morning, you can say "hi", or "(good) morning". You will probably chat a little bit about the weather, what you have done recently, or the area around you. This 'small talk' is important for relationship building. A colleague may ask "How are you?". This is a greeting, and the answer is "fine, and you?". You can give more detailed answers to your close friends.

Working with the text

A Answer the following questions.

1. Who is Barbara Brown?
2. How does she welcome Tom?
   What does she say and what is Tom's answer?
3. When does Tom's first working day start?
4. What does he take part in?
5. What is the first thing he should do?
6. Why should he do that?
7. What does Barbara tell Tom to put into his personal profile?

B This is Tom's personal profile for the staff panel. Look at the unit texts again and fill in the missing words / information.

My name is Tom Sayer and I'm **1. …** years old. My family originally comes from **2. …** . I still live at my parents' home together with my two **3. …** and my grandfather who is a **4. …** . At the beginning of September I startedworking at St Mary's Nursing as a **5. …** for a year. In the future I would like to work with **6. …** . I already have some kind of work experience because I help my **7. …** organise my grandfather's **8. …** . My hobby is doing **9. …** . I go to the **10. …** regularly. At weekends I like to meet my **11. …** and do stuff with them.

Hands-on task

Interaction / Production

C Imagine Helen is also asked to write a personal profile for the inclusive summer camp. Work in small groups and design Helen's personal profile.
If you need some help, look at page129. Here you will find a method card on introducing yourself and writing a personal description.

Hands-on task

Production

D Imagine that you are doing a placement in one of the places below. Choose one and write your personal profile for the staff panel.

old people's home
nursing home
home for children with special needs
hospital
youth club

children's home
inclusive summer camp
day care for children with special needs
old people's day care centre
home care service

Meeting people	
unique	einzigartig
experience	Erfahrung
(to) guess	raten
pleasant	angenehm
unpleasant	unangenehm
serious	ernst
exciting	aufregend
boring	langweilig
(to) choose	auswählen
icebreaker	Eisbrecher, hier: Kennenlern-Aktivität
Meet Helen and Tom	
divorced	geschieden
flat	Wohnung
balcony	Balkon
art	Kunstunterricht
subject	Unterrichtsfach
favourite	Favorit
inclusive summer camp	integratives Ferienlager
children with special needs	Kinder mit einer Behinderung
originally	ursprünglich
large	groß
social volunteer	hier: jemand, der / die ein freiwilliges soziales Jahr macht
old people's day care center	Tagespflege für Senioren
wheelchair	Rollstuhl
regular care	ständige Pflege
(to) care for	sich kümmern um, jmd. pflegen
(to) gain experience	Erfahrung sammeln
sport	Sportunterricht
(to) work out	(Muskeln) trainieren
twice	zweimal
(to) do on the job training	Ausbildung am Arbeitsplatz
Tom meets his colleagues	
colleagues	Kollegen
(to) introduce s. o.	jmd. vorstellen
first name	Vorname
(to) build relationships	Beziehungen aufbauen
(to) nod	nicken
head	hier: Leitung, Leiter / in
staff room	Personalraum
(to) sit in an circle	im Kreis sitzen
volunteer	hier: Praktikant / in
doorway	hier: Türrahmen
(to) shake hands	Hände schütteln
staff	Mitarbeiter
help yourself	Bedienen Sie sich! Bedien dich bitte!
personal profile	Personenbeschreibung, Steckbrief
staff panel	Mitarbeitertafel
(to) be interested in	sich interessieren für
placement	Praktikum
old people's home	Seniorenheim / Seniorenresidenz
nursing home	Pflegeheim
hospital	Krankenhaus
children's home	Kinderheim
home care service	Pflegedienst

Die Aussprache der blauen Vokabeln finden Sie in den Audio-Dateien DA0901055

Unit 2 Giving a helping hand – nursing professions

My name is Maggie.

I've just finished school and my GCSEs. After a three week placement at a hospital, I can imagine working here. A hospital placement is a really good chance to start gaining work experience. You can't do everything, but you help to give medical care. Now I know that I don't get scared when I see blood, but I'm a bit shy and talking to strangers is not easy for me. What vocational training would be the best for me?

Hi, I'm Brett.

My dad is a paramedic. Could I do his job? I find it difficult when I see bad injuries. During my holidays I work in a rehabilitation clinic. I meet people of all ages, young and old. But, I love chatting and spending time with the older patients. I enjoy taking them for a walk or playing cards with them. I'm sure that a nursing profession would suit me, but what could I do?

And you?
What nursing profession do you want to do?
Why?

What nursing profession would suit you?

A care worker is someone whose job is helping people who have health problems, special needs, or social problems.
Care workers work for example at a hospital, in specialist clinics, nursing homes, or in home care services.

Interaction / Mediation

Sit in small groups and answer the following questions.

- What types of care workers do you know? Make a list.
  Use a bilingual dictionary to help you.
  Compare your lists in class.
- Discuss what type of nursing profession Maggie and Brett could do?
- Choose a job for both and tell your class what you have chosen and why.

Working as a care worker

Maureen, aged 27

My patients need support with everyday activities and medical care but they want to stay in their own homes. I work as a home care worker and most of my patients are elderly people. It's not an easy job, because I go into their homes and assist them with such intimate activities as bathing, showering, getting dressed, and even going to the toilet. One of my main jobs is to help people with their personal hygiene and supply them with the medicine they have to take. I also clean the house, prepare meals, or help with transportation to doctor's appointments. Being a good listener and keeping an eye on your patients is very important in my job. You have to watch out for changes in your patients' health and make sure they receive the right treatment.

Isak, aged 35

I work in a nursing home and work with elderly people who need medical care 24 hours a day. I'm a care assistant for elderly people. Our residents need help with their personal hygiene, or can't eat alone and I feed them. My job carries high responsibility. You have to make decisions on behalf of your patients. Do they need a doctor's appointment, or should you call the ambulance? However, the job is also a lot of fun. We become like a family and celebrate birthdays, Christmas, and Easter together. I love to keep everyone occupied and entertained, I sing with them, take them out for walks, or do handicraft with them: anything to keep them busy and active! You have to cheer your patients up because some of them are very lonely. But the hardest aspect of my job is seeing them die.

Sonya, aged 42

Most of my patients undergo an operation. I'm a nurse and my job mainly involves caring for people who are ill, injured or convalescent after an accident or operation. We give the medical care a patient needs to recover. There are typical routine jobs. For example, we give injections and set up infusions; take blood, insert and monitor catheters, dress wounds and daily check and record a patient's temperature, blood pressure, pulse and respiration. You work in a team and alongside the doctors. You give your patients the medicine and care they need. We also clean and monitor medical equipment. You need to be mentally strong to do this job because it's highly stressful. Each patient needs your full attention. I find it important to keep on smiling, even if your patient is bad-tempered. Remember, they are in pain and they depend on your help. It's also very hard to talk to grieving relatives.

Working with the text

A Look at the texts again and match the sentence halves.

1. Maureen doesn't work in a home or hospital …	a. because she helps her patients with intimate activities like she helps them with showering and going to the toilet.
2. Maureen's main job is …	b. at a nursing home for elderly people.
3. Maureen doesn't think her job is easy …	c. but he finds it difficult when his patients die.
4. Isak works …	d. works in a hospital.
5. Isak's patients leave their private home …	e. who are unhappy because they are lonely, in pain, or can't do everything they used to do.
6. Isak loves his job …	f. she visits her patients in their private home.
7. As a nurse, Sonya …	g. because they have an operation.
8. A lot of her patients are in hospital …	h. because they need around the clock care.
9. In every nursing profession you meet patients …	i. to help patients with their personal hygiene.

B Work in pairs. Work through the text again and fill in the table below.

nursing profession	work place	job routines	personal qualification
– home care worker	– nursing home for elderly people	– prepare and give injections, infusions	– good listener

C Imagine Maureen, Isak and Sonya present their job in a class of school leavers who don't know what job they want to do. Here are questions they ask them. Take over the role of Maureen, Isak and Sonya and answer the questions.

What do you love about your job? **What is a real bad aspect of your job?**	I think it's nice to …. A rather pleasant / unpleasant aspect of my job is to (verb) … It's hard to (verb) … / when (sentence) … I like / dislike / love / hate + ing-Form **Beispiel:** I love singing with my patients

Production

D Can you imagine doing Maureen's, Isak's or Sonya's job? Write down your answer.

Grammar box: Simple Present – Einfache Gegenwart

Verwendung

Das Simple Present beschreibt …
- Gewohnheiten und Rituale
- regelmäßig wiederkehrende Handlungen
- Fakten
- berufliche Routinearbeiten

Signalwörter

often, usually, always,
never, sometimes,
every (week), on (Saturdays),
generally, normally,
rarely, seldom

Bildung

Das Simple Present wird gebildet
mit dem Infinitiv (ohne to)
→ **Ausnahme: He, she, it**
→ **das „s" muss mit!**

Beispiel

I work in a hospital.
You care for the elderly.
He/she sings with the residents.
We take them for a walk.
They eat their lunch.

Ausnahmen

- Bei Verben, die auf -o, -sh, -ch, -ss, oder –x enden wird bei he/she/it **–es** angehängt
  Beispiel: go – she goes, rush – he rushes, touch – it touches, kiss – he kisses, mix – she mixes
- Bei Verben, die mit –y enden: **Konsonant + y** → **-ies,** *cry – he cries*
  Vokal + y → **-ys,** *play – she plays*
- **Have → he/she/it has**

Verneinung

- Das Vollverb wird mit **don't/do not** verneint.
  *Beispiel: I/You/We/They **don't like** office work.*
- **Ausnahme:** Bei he, she, it wird mit **doesn't/does not** verneint, dabei wird das „s" nicht mehr an das Vollverb angehängt!
  *Beispiel: He/she **doesn't like** office work.*

Fragen ohne Fragewort

Fragen werden mit **do …, does …, don't …, doesn't …** gebildet.
Beispiel: ***Do** I/you/we/they drink tea or coffee in the mornings?*
***Does** he/she drink tea or coffee in the mornings?*
***Don't** I/you/we/they watch television in the evenings?*
***Doesn't** he/she watch television in the evenings?*

Practising grammar

A Make up positive, negative sentences and questions.

Example:
1. Maggie/do a great job.
   Maggie does a great job.
   Maggie doesn't do a great job.
   Does Maggie do a great job?
2. Brett's father/work as a care assistant.
3. All residents/go on an outing every second month.
4. Nurses/check the patients' blood pressure daily.
5. All hospital patients/suffer from pain after an accident.
6. A home care worker/visit his patients in a nursing home.
7. Most of Maureen's patients/want to go into a nursing home.
8. Isak/only feed the bedridden residents.

B **Here are typical routine jobs Maureen, Isak and Sonya do every morning. Fill in the correct Simple Present form of the verb in brackets.**

Maureen's morning routine

Example:

Maureen's day 1. (start) early in the morning.

Maureen's day starts early in the morning.

Now go on!

Every morning all home care workers 2. (get) together and 3. (have) a short chat and coffee before they 4. (set off) to their patients.

As usual, Maureen 5. (visit) four patients in the morning. All of them 6. (need) help with their morning hygiene. Then they 7. (get) dressed and Maureen 8. (supply) them with their medicine. And she 9. (not leave) any patient without making sure that they 10. (eat) and 11. (drink) something for breakfast. After her morning round, Maureen 12. (drive) back to the team office. Here, all the care workers 13. (meet) once again for their first break before they 14. (collect) some medicine from the pharmacy, 15. (take) a patient to a doctor's appointment, or 16. (go) onto their next round.

Isak's morning routine

Isak's morning shift 1. (start) with waking up the residents. Isak 2. (go) around and 3. (give) them their morning medicine. Some 4. (need) help with their morning toilet and personal hygiene. Together with his colleagues Isak 5. (prepare) breakfast for the residents. All residents 6. (come) together in the dining room but Isak 7. (not join in). He 8. (go) around and 9. (take) breakfast to the residents who 10. (stay) in bed. Isak 11. (feed) those who 12. (not eat) alone. Then he 13. (have) a short rest, 14. (drink) some coffee and maybe 15. (eat) a small snack. After the break all the care workers 16. (get) together and 17. (talk) about their residents and 18. (plan) their care. They also 19. (think) of activities they 20. (want) to do with them. Very often Isak 21. (organise) some handicraft.

Sonya's morning routine

Sonya and her team 1. (go) from room to room in the morning to wake up the patients. The nurses 2. (distribute) the morning medicine and 3. (help) those who 4. (not take) their shower alone with their morning hygiene and toilet. Some of the nurses 5. (change) the bed linen. Sonya 6. (have) a look at the patients' wounds and she 7. (put on) fresh dressings. The nurses also 8. (check) every patient's temperature, blood pressure, pulse and respiration and they 9. (write) everything down. Sonya 10. (make) sure that the infusions and catheters 11. (work). She also 12. (look) after those patients who 13. (undergo) an operation and she 14. (prepare) them before a nurse of the operation team 15. (arrive) to take them into the operating theater. A lot of patients 16. (feel) very nervous and Sonya 17. (speak) to them and 18. (try) to calm them down.

Working with the text

A The verbs in the word box below are missing in the text. Make sure you know their meaning, then fill the gaps.

headlines:
ask – say – treat – show – introduce – explain – make – bring

texts:
encourage – touch – build up – respect – understand – steal – take away – happen – calm down – mean

Bedside care

This is a handout with some basic advice for trainees starting work in a hospital or nursing home.

1. … (1) your patient as your own parent or child.

It's important to put yourself in the other person's shoes. This will help you to … (2) your patient and treat him / her in the way you should.

2. … (3) the patient's name and … (4) eye-contact.

Don't make your patients feel like a "number" by not saying their names or making eye-contact. This is very simple and does not … (5) much time but it shows your patient that you … (6) him / her.

3. … (7) yourself.

Before you come close to a patient's bed, give your name and explain who you are. This will … (8) stress for the patient because you're not a stranger anymore. Don't forget that you are helping your patient with very intimate things. Therefore try to … (9) a relationship.

4. … (10) what you are going to do.

Never do anything without telling the patient what you want to do and why. Imagine how helpless and worried someone could feel who does not know what is going to … (11) next!

5. … (12) interest in the patient and sympathy.

Do you have any children or grandchildren? What job do you do? What are your hobbies? These are simple questions but they show that you are interested in the person and not only in the illness. … (13) your patient's hand or shoulder, or give a hug to show your sympathy. This will help the patient to … (14) and cheer up.

6. … (15) comfort to the patient's room.

Clean the bedside table. Supply your patient with fresh water. Offer to open or close the window or blinds. Take the time to change dirty bed linen. All these simple tasks don't take much time but they … (16) a lot to your patient.

7. … (17) open ended questions.

Ask questions to get information about your patient's health condition and personality. Asking "How does it feel?" is far better than asking "Does it hurt?" because the answer would only be "yes" or "no". Only asking open ended questions … (18) the patient to answer in detail and you find out a lot more about your patient.

Reception

B Peter is a new trainee at St Andrew's hospital.
He enters Mrs Hampton's room to check her pulse rate.
Listen to the dialogue. Here are the beginnings of Peter's questions. How do they end?

1. How are …?
2. Who is …?
3. Have you …?
4. Can I …?
5. And, how …?
6. Can I …?

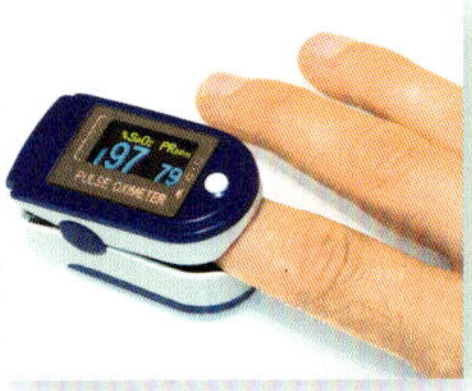

Vocabulary help

fingertip pulse oximeter –	Pulsoxymeter (Sauerstoff- und Pulsmessgerät für den Finger)
have bad hearing –	schlecht hören können
forefinger –	Zeigefinger

C How does the fingertip pulse oximeter work?
Explain.

Hands-on task

Interaction

D Work in small groups and pick one of the situations below.
Work out a role play. Do not forget about the basic rules of bedside care!

Peter fetches Mrs Hampton to take her for an x-ray of her lungs before her operation. Mrs Hampton doesn't know where to go. She can't walk for long and Peter brings a wheelchair along with him.

Peter brings Mr Miller his dinner: soup, steak with peas and potatoes, and chocolate creme. Mr Miller needs help eating as he can only use his left arm and hand. His right arm and hand are in plaster.

The call button rings. Peter is looking after Mr Roberts, who cannot get out of bed alone. He feels too hot. Mr Roberts very often forgets to drink. Because of the sun his room is too bright and he wants to watch TV.

Look at the method card "Talking to patients" on page 130 for help.

Practising grammar

Open ended questions are questions which start with a question word.
Make up questions in the Present Simple.

1. What / you / do in your free time?
2. When / Mrs Hampton / take her pills?
3. How / this infusion / work?
4. Why / Mr Roberts / sit in a wheel chair?
5. When / the nurses / start their morning round?
6. Where / Sonya / work?
7. Who / only eat vegetables?
8. How often / Mr Roberts / ring the call button?
9. Why / Mrs Hampton / need an x-ray?
10. Who / get up early for work?

Grammar box:

Fragen mit Fragewort in der Simple Present Bildung

- **Fragewort + do / does + Rest des Satzes**

Beispiel:
What do you like to eat for dinner?
Where does John take Mrs Hampton?

Ausnahme

"Who?" = Wer?
→ Fragen werden **ohne does** gebildet
Who takes Mr Johnson to the doctor?
Who likes to play some cards?

What nursing profession would suit you?

GCSE General Certificate of Secondary Education	Mittlerer Schulabschluss
medical care	Medizinische Pflege / Versorgung
vocational training	Berufsausbildung
paramedic	Rettungssanitäter
injury / injuries	Verletzung(en)
rehabilitation clinic	Rehabilitationsklinik
nursing profession	Pflegeberuf
(to) suit	passen zu, gefallen
care worker	Pflegekraft
health problems	gesundheitliche Probleme
home care service	häuslicher Pflegedienst; ambulante Pflege

Working as a care worker

home care worker	Pflegekraft im ambulanten Pflegedienst
patient	Patient/-in
intimate	persönlich / intim
(to) assist	helfen, begleiten
bathing	Baden
showering	Duschen
getting dressed	Ankleiden
personal hygiene	Körperpflege
(to) supply with	versorgen mit
transportation	Transport
doctor's appointment	Arzttermin
listener	Zuhörer /-in
(to) keep an eye on	die Augen offen halten auf / für
(to) watch out for	aufpassen auf
treatment	Behandlung
care assistant	Pflegehelfer/-in / Gesundheits- und Pflegeassistenz
resident	(Heim-)bewohner/-in
(to) feed	füttern
responsibility	Verantwortung
on behalf	im Interesse
(to) keep occupied	beschäftigt bleiben / halten
(to) entertain	unterhalten
handicraft	Basteln
(to) keep active	aktiv bleiben
(to) cheer up	aufmuntern
(to) die	sterben
(to) undergo	(sich) unterziehen
operation	Operation
nurse	Pflegefachkraft
(to) involve	beinhalten
ill	krank
injured	verletzt
(to) be convalescent	auf dem Weg der Genesung sein
accident	Unfall
(to) recover	(sich) erholen
injection	Spritze
(to) set up an infusion	eine Infusion legen / jmd. an den Tropf hängen
(to) take blood	Blut entnehmen
(to) insert a catheter	Katheter setzen
(to) monitor	überwachen
(to) dress wounds	Wunden verbinden
(to) check	kontrollieren
(to) record	aufzeichnen, aufschreiben
temperature	Temperatur
blood pressure	Blutdruck
pulse	Puls
respiration	Atmung
alongside	neben, Seite an Seite
medical equipment	medizinisches Gerät
be mentally strong	psychisch stark sein
attention	Aufmerksamkeit
bad-tempered	übellaunig
pain	Schmerz
(to) depend on	angewiesen sein auf
grieving relatives	trauernde Verwandte

Grammar

(to) collect	abholen
pharmacy	Apotheke
(to) distribute	verteilen
bed linen	Bettwäsche
fresh dressing	frischer Verband
(to) arrive	(an-)kommen
operation theater	Operationssaal
(to) calm sb. down	jmd. beruhigen

Bedside care

(to) encourage	ermutigen
(to) touch	anfassen
(to) respect	respektieren
(to) steal	stehlen
(to) calm down	(sich) beruhigen
advice	Hinweis, Ratschlag
(to) put yourself in the other person's shoes	sich in den anderen hineinversetzen
(to) make eye-contact	Blickkontakt herstellen
sympathy	Mitgefühl
illness	Krankheit
(to) give a hug	umarmen
blinds	Rolladen, Jalousie
open ended	offen (gestellte Frage)
health condition	Gesundheitszustand
personality	Persönlichkeit
in detail	im Detail, genau
plaster	Gipsverband
call button	Notrufknopf

Die Aussprache der blauen Vokabeln finden Sie in den Audio-Dateien DA0901055

What help / care does Mrs Hampton need?

After her operation Mrs Hampton can leave hospital but she is weak and needs care. She can't walk or stand for long. She sleeps a lot, but doesn't eat enough to become stronger. She very often forgets to drink. Her operation scar is one more problem because it needs a fresh dressing every day. It's important for Mrs Hampton to take her medicine, but she mixes everything up. Her daughter works full-time and she cannot look after her mother regularly.

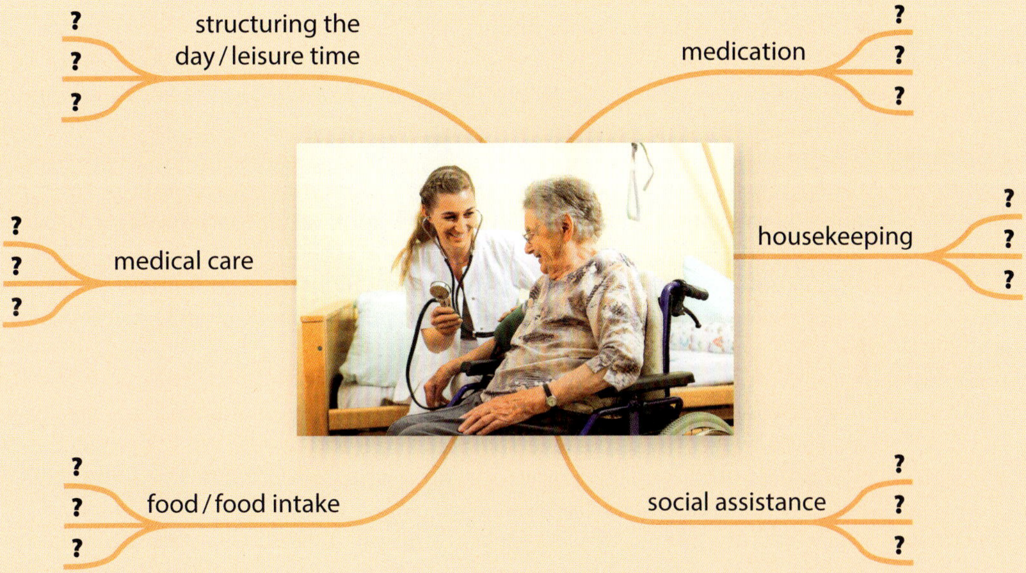

What care does Mrs Hampton need?

A **Work in pairs and think of all the help Mrs Hampton needs during the day. Complete the mind map above.**

B **What do you think? Can Mrs Hampton go back into her own flat?**

C **What can Mrs Hampton and her family do to make sure she receives the help and care she needs?**

Inside St Mary's Nursing Home

Mrs Hampton knows that she still needs a lot of care and she wants to go into a nursing home for short-term care. Her daughter is looking for a suitable nursing home. Today, she and her husband are meeting Barbara Brown, the manager of St Mary's Nursing Home.

Barbara Brown: How do you do, Mrs and Mr Jennings? My name is Barbara Brown. I'm the home manager.

Maria Jennings: How do you do, Mrs Brown? We're looking for a short-term care place for my mother, who is in hospital at the moment.

Barbara Brown: No problem, we quite often have residents for short-term care. They are recovering from health problems, or their normal carer is on holiday.

Maria Jennings: We would like to see if your home is the right place for my mother.

Barbara Brown: Of course. We take our residents' care and well-being very seriously. Do you already know our home?

Ron Jennings: No, not really, only from driving past it.

Barbara Brown: We should go on a tour of the house, then.

Maria Jennings: That would be great. However, we also have some questions about the care you offer.

Barbara Brown: Of course, I would be happy to answer all of your questions. I can also show you the rooms for short-term care residents. I guess, you would be interested in seeing one of those rooms?

Maria Jennings: Yes, sure.

Barbara Brown: Okay, let's start. We're currently standing in our entrance hall with our reception and administration area on the left. On the right, we have a large dining room for the residents in the assisted living unit. We also use this room for events for all the residents, for example for our New Year's party. Right now our home choir is in there and they are practising songs for their next performance.

Ron Jennings: Do you have any private rooms down here?

Barbara Brown: Yes, if we go across this entrance area, we come to the first corridor of residents' rooms. There are ten bedrooms here. Let me show you around! Each level is very similar. However, the upper levels are a bit larger and have some more private rooms. You can go onto each level by lift, for those who have problems with the stairs.

Maria Jennings: Don't your residents get lost easily?

Barbara Brown: No, in fact they can't. The residents' rooms are always in a circle, around a nurse station in the middle. This means that the nurses can see what is happening on their floor. We also have a seating area in front of the nurse station where residents can meet. Each floor has a small kitchen, a dining room, a room for physical and occupational therapy, extra bathrooms with bathtub lifts and toilets near the common areas. And of course there is a staff room and a stockroom.

Ron Jennings: Do the nurses cook for the residents in that kitchen?

Barbara Brown: No, they just prepare snacks, coffee or tea. We have a canteen kitchen right underneath this floor in the basement which I can't show you at the moment because they're preparing today's dinner. Our laundry is also down there.

Maria Jennings: Can your residents go outside?

Barbara Brown: Sure, on this floor you can walk into the garden from the kitchen, dining room and private rooms. There are some nice seating areas there. The upper floors have a large balcony.

Maria Jennings: That's good because my mother loves to sit outside in the sun and read her magazines. Is her room down here, then?

Barbara Brown: On this floor I could offer you either a private or a semi-private room.

Maria Jennings: What does that mean? Can't my mother have her own room?

Barbara Brown: Sure, here in our nursing home we don't have rooms with two or more beds. We have single en-suite rooms, or two single rooms which share one bathroom between the rooms. Those rooms are semi-private rooms.

Maria Jennings: I think a private room near the garden would be the best for my mother. Can I see that room?

Barbara Brown: Yes, come along.

Working with the text

A All these statements are false. Can you correct them?

1. Mrs Hampton is out of hospital.
2. She is going to be in a nursing home for the rest of her life.
3. Maria Jennings is Mrs Hampton's sister.
4. Maria Jennings is at the nursing home because she wants to visit her mother.
5. Maria Jennings already knows the nursing home well.
6. Barbara Brown can only show Mr & Mrs Jennings the home's administration.
7. All residents' rooms have two beds.

B What are the different rooms and areas in a nursing home? Go through the text again and make a list. Compare your list with your neighbour.

C Say what you can do in these rooms and areas. Look at the vocabulary list for help and make sentences.
Example: In the large dining room, the residents eat their lunch and have parties.

nouns

physiotherapy
walker training
exercises
presentations
dinners / meals
performances
visitors
treatment
games

workshops
choir rehearsals
therapy
personal hygiene
bath
handicrafts
staff meetings
magazines / newspapers / books

verbs

take part in
undergo
spend
do
have
talk
meet
play
take
chat
bathe
dine

eat
go for a walk
walk
listen to
watch
relax
sing
gather
come together (for)
receive
read

D This is the map of the first floor of St Mary's Nursing Home.
Compare the map of the first floor with your list. Have you got every room?

Grammar box: Describing directions – prepositions of movement (Richtung)

Grammar box: Prepositions of place – Präpositionen des Ortes

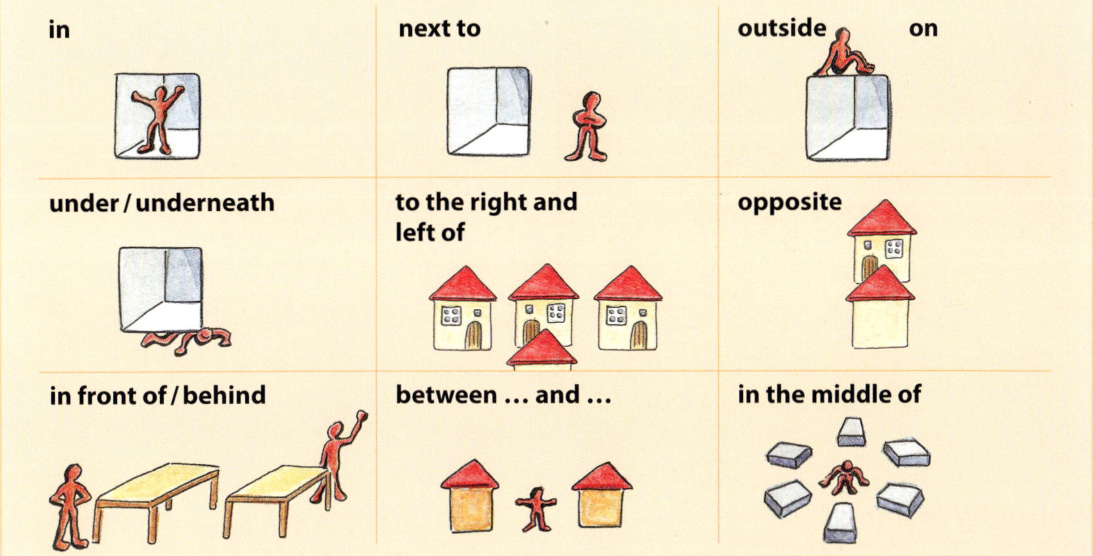

Practising grammar

Back at hospital Mrs Jennings tells her mother about the tour of the house. Look at the prepositions of movement and try to fill the gaps in the text.

1. You come … the entrance hall and enter the first floor.
2. On that floor we could go … one of the short-term care rooms.
3. When you walk … the floor, you can meet other residents.
4. There is a lift and a staircase to go … the other floors.
5. You enter the nursing home … automatic doors.
6. The first rooms on the left hand side are the occupational therapy, physiotherapy and staff rooms. You walk … them to reach 5 private rooms.
7. You can walk …. the garden from nearly every room on the ground floor!
8. Walking … the garden you see some really nice seating areas.

A single private room at St Mary's Nursing Home

Mrs Brown shows Mr & Mrs Jennings one of the single private rooms. You can see this room in the picture. Match the words from the box with the numbers in the picture.

living space
hospital bed with trapeze bar
chest of drawers
TV set
bedside locker
table with chairs
entrance door
shower
shower chair
cupboard
barrier-free bathroom
toilet
washing basin
overbed table

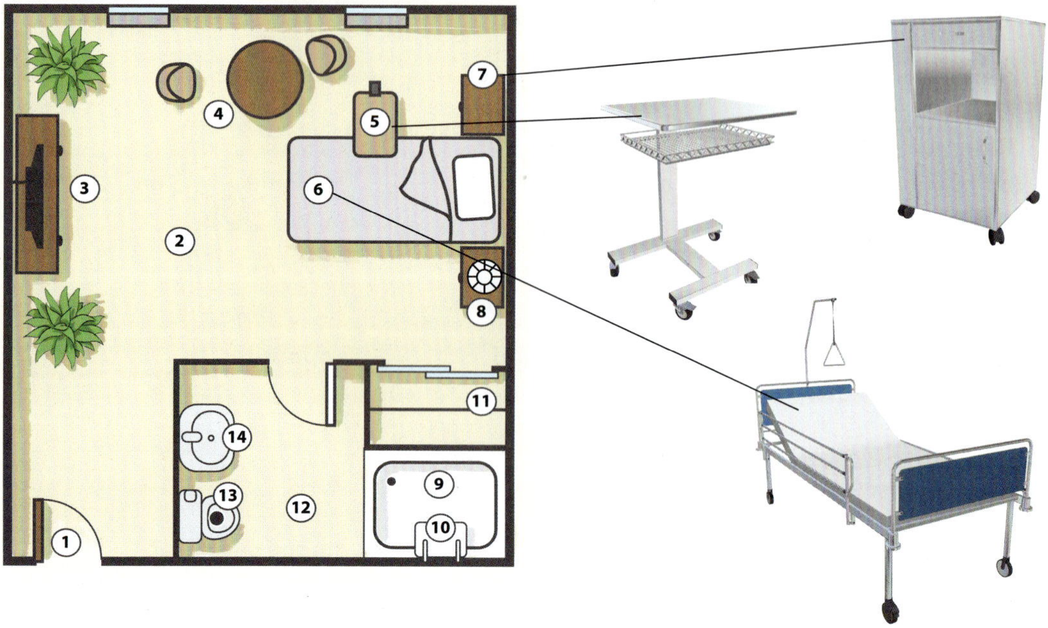

Practising grammar

When Mrs Jennings visits her mother in hospital, her mother is very interested in her private room and asks her to describe it. Now, look at the prepositions of place and fill them in.

Your private room is very spacious. There is a hospital bed **1. …** your room. **2. …** the hospital bed there is a bedside locker and **3. …** the bed there is a chest of drawers. There is also an overbed table which you can use to have your breakfast **4. …** bed for example. **5. …** the hospital bed there is a TV set. The room has two windows in the back wall and **6. …** them there is a table with two chairs. You will have your own private bathroom which is **7. …** the two windows. It's barrier-free and it has a shower. Finally, the room is equipped with a cupboard which is **8. …** a second door next to the bathroom. Your room is on the left hand corridor and **9. …** your windows is one of the nicest seating areas in the garden. When you go out of your room, you can't get lost because the nurse station is right in the **10. …** the floor and the nurses will help you to find your way.

Hands-on task

Interaction / Production

A Have you already done a placement at a hospital or at a nursing home? Draw a picture of a typical room for patients or residents and write a description of the room.

B Work in groups and discuss how a "perfect" single private room in a nursing home or hospital should look? Discuss your ideas and present your room to your classmates. How about drawing a picture of the room on a transparency?

Vocabulary help

There is a private bathroom.
There are some book shelves.
You can **find** a nurse station in the middle of the floor.

All rooms **are furnished / equipped** with a hospital bed.
A typical room **is divided** into a living space and a bathroom.
The toilet(s) **is / are located** opposite the nurse station.

Reception

3 **Most of the nursing home residents put some of their own furniture into their rooms. Listen to Carmen, Keith, Brian and Monica. Say how they want to change their rooms.**

Practising grammar

Look at the grammar box first.
Then fill in the missing personal and possessive pronouns.

1. During the afternoon, Carmen very often sits in … room and … looks at … family album. Look, there is a photo album lying in the waiting area. I think, it's … .
2. Keith loves his old armchair. … prefers to watch TV sitting in … armchair.
3. There is a pair of glasses lying on the dining room table. Carmen and Keith always sit at … to play cards. And … wear glasses. Now, I'm unsure, are these glasses … or … ?
4. Mary, I'm searching for my walker? Oh, there are two walkers in the physiotherapy room. Isn't the blue one …? Yes, sure the blue walker is ….
5. Mrs Brown tells Mrs Jennings: "… nursing home is the best one for … mother".
6. Every Thursday, all the choir members get together and … sing … favourite songs. For two hours on that afternoon the dining room is …
7. "Mrs and Mr Jennings, is that … car in front of the nursing home?" "Yes, that's …"

personal pronoun	**possessive pronoun** (attributiv)	**possessive pronoun** (substantivisch)
I	*my*	*mine*
you	*your*	*yours*
he	*his*	*his*
she	*her*	*hers*
it	*its*	*its*
we	*our*	*ours*
they	*their*	*theirs*

What does care look like in a nursing home?

After the tour of the house, Barbara Brown invites Maria and Ron Jennings to come into her office and ask their questions.

Maria Jennings: Well, your home looks great. But I'm still unsure. Is it the right place for my mother? Can you give her the intensive care she needs?

Barbara Brown: Yes, sure. We have trained nurses and we offer a full medical care service around the clock. We provide all kinds of medical care like checking the pulse, blood pressure and respiration, changing dressings, helping with personal hygiene. Some of our residents are bedridden and need repositioning even during night. We do all that. Our nurses are on-call throughout the night. You see, we have the same medical care as in a hospital.

Maria Jennings: My mother has fractured her thigh bone and she needs help to start walking again.

Barbara Brown: Don't worry. We have a physiotherapist who works with our residents. I guess your mother needs a walker and we can do some walker training. And remember, our nursing home is completely barrier-free and has special equipment for those with a limited movement, like hospital beds, bathtub lifts, wheelchair ramps.

Maria Jennings: Yes, that's true. But my mother also has to see a doctor regularly.

Mrs Brown: That's no problem at all. We work with some doctors who visit our residents regularly and we can get your mother to any consultation she needs.

Ron Jennings: There is one more thing we are worried about. My mother-in-law has become very thin and weak.

Mrs Brown: Our kitchen crew can prepare a special diet for her to build up her strength. We always make sure that our residents eat and drink enough.

Maria Jennings: I think your home is just perfect for my mother. I only hope she will feel at home soon.

Mrs Brown: It always takes some time. We will encourage her to take part in our "coffee and cake Friday" when all residents get together to meet and chat. She can also spend some afternoons at one of our workshops like painting, handicraft, or seasonal activities. Maybe she likes singing; our home choir always needs new members. Not to forget the gambling afternoons. You see, there are a lot of opportunities to make friends and enjoy yourself.

Maria Jennings: My mother loves cake and I think she will like your "coffee and cake Friday".

Working with the text

A The underlined word / words are false. Look through the text and find the right word / words.

1. After the tour of the house Mrs Jennings is still <u>sure</u> that the home is the right place for her mother.
2. The home offers <u>limited</u> medical care.
3. The nursing home offers <u>different</u> medical care to hospitals.
4. There is special equipment for those with <u>full</u> movement.
5. Mrs Hampton needs help to <u>stop</u> walking.
6. She needs a <u>walking stick.</u>
7. Mrs Brown wants her to do <u>sports training.</u>
8. After her operation, Mrs Hampton has become very <u>strong.</u>
9. The nurses always make sure that the residents eat and drink <u>as little as possible.</u>
10. The home is <u>partially</u> barrier-free.

B Answer the following questions.

1. Why does Mrs Brown think that she can offer Mrs Hampton the same care as in a hospital?
2. What health problem does Mrs Hampton, Mrs Jennings' mother, have?
3. How does Mrs Brown want to help her to start walking again?
4. Why is Mrs Brown sure that Mrs Hampton will build up her strength?
5. Who comes into the nursing to help with medical care?
6. What does Mrs Brown think could help Mrs Hampton to soon feel at home?
7. Why does her daughter think that she is interested in the Friday programme?

Interaction

C Imagine that Mrs Hampton tells her daughter that she is worried the nursing home is maybe not the right place for her.
What could she be worried about and how could Mrs Jennings answer?
Work in small groups and write a role play.

Production / Interaction

D There is an open day at St Mary's nursing home and some visitors have the wrong idea about life in a nursing home. Take on Barbara Brown's role and reply to their opinions.

visitor	Barbara Brown
I think that in a nursing home the private rooms look much the same as in a hospital. Two to three hospital beds, maybe bedside lockers and a small cupboard and that's it.	No, on our tour of the house you can see that each resident has … and …
I guess you just give your residents medical care let them lie in bed watching TV for the rest of the day.	Sure, we give our residents medical care but we do a lot more. …
Food and drink always tastes pretty bad in hospitals and nursing homes.	That's not true. We try to ensure that every resident …

E This unit gives you a lot of information on nursing homes. Sit in small groups and sketch the most important aspects on a mind map. Present it in class.
Have a look at page 132 for a method card on mindmapping.

Grammar box: **Present Continuous / Progressive** – Verlaufsform der Gegenwart

Verwendung

Present Continous wird genutzt …
- für Handlungen, die im Moment, also zum Zeitpunkt des Sprechens stattfinden
- vorläufige Handlungen
- für die Beschreibung von Bildern und Fotos:

Beispiel: In the photo, John is taking a walk with Mrs Hampton.

Signalwörter

now
at the moment
at present
right now
Listen!...
Look!...

Bildung

→ **am / is / are + ing-Form des Vollverbs**

Beispiel

*I'**m** feed**ing** Mrs Johnson.*
*You **are** prepar**ing** the dinner.*
*He / she **is** sing**ing** a song.*
*We **are** prepar**ing** today's dinner.*
*They **are** play**ing** cards.*

Ausnahmen

- Endet die Grundform des Verbs auf –e, fällt das –e weg:
  make → making, dine → dining, take → taking
- Bei einigen Verben wird der Endkonsonant verdoppelt:
  run → running, stop → stopping, plan → planning
- -ie wird zu „-y": lie → lying, die → dying
- Verben mit statischer Bedeutung und Verben des Denkens / Erkennens bilden keine Verlaufsform. Dazu gehören z. B.:

be – sein	have – besitzen	belong – gehören
contain – enthalten	believe – glauben	think – denken
want – wollen	prefer – bevorzugen	mean – bedeuten

Verneinung

I'm not feeding Mrs Johnson.
You aren't preparing the dinner.
He / she isn't singing a song.
We aren't preparing today's dinner.
They aren't playing cards.

Fragen ohne Fragewort

Fragen können mit **Am** …? **Is** …? **Are** …? gebildet werden.

Beispiel:
***Am** I feed**ing** Mrs Johnson?*
***Are** you prepar**ing** the dinner?*
***Is** she sing**ing** a song?*
***Are** we prepar**ing** today's dinner?*
***Are** they play**ing** cards?*

Practising grammar

A Look at the pictures and say what the people are doing.

Example:
What Janet (do) right now? She (take) Mr Brian's blood pressure.
What is Janet doing? She is taking Mr Brian's blood pressure.

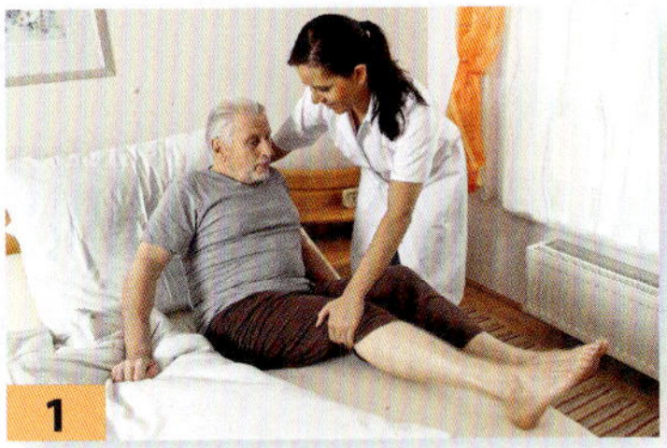

1 Mr Harper can't get out of bed alone. Look, Miriam (lift) him out of bed.

2 Mrs Taylor has some problems with her eyes. Listen, Helen (read) a book to her.

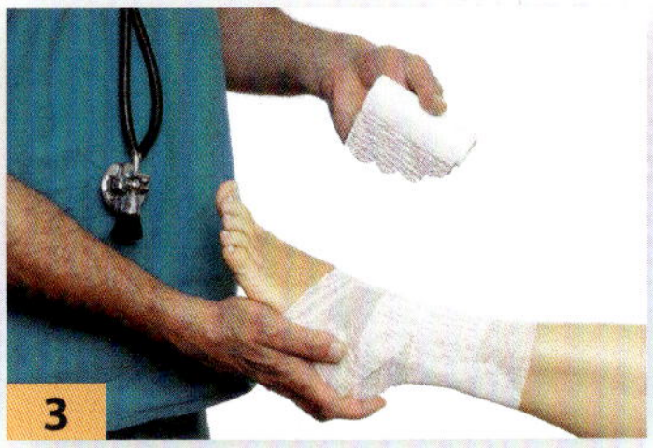

3 Mrs Bowler needs a new dressing. Ronny (put) on a fresh dressing.

4 Mrs Taylor can't walk but the sun (shine) and she wants to go out. Look, Sammy (take her out) with her wheelchair.

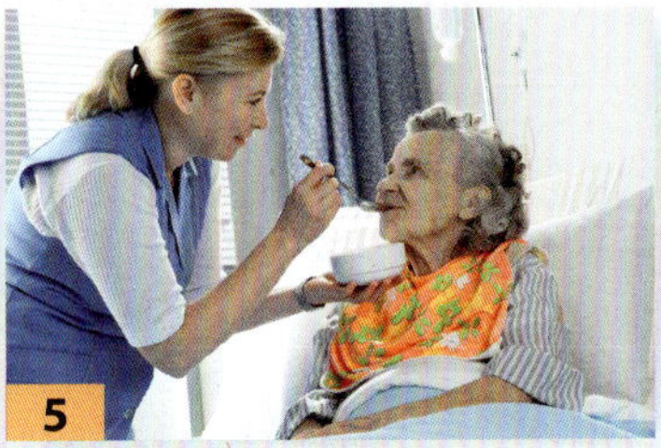

5 Mrs Johnson can't eat alone. Right now, Sandra …

6 Today is "gambling time". At the moment Thelma and Louise …

B Fill in the present continuous form of the verb in brackets. Be careful, there are negative and positive sentences.

Example:
John (not feed) Mrs Meyer right now. He (change) her dressing.
John isn't feeding Mrs Meyer right now. He is changing her dressing.

1. Mrs Miller (not paint) at the arts workshop, she (go) for a walk with Mr Brian. Listen! They (chat) and (laugh).
2. At the moment the home choir (not sing) any songs, they (take) a break and everyone (drink) a cup of tea or coffee.
3. Mary (not distribute) the morning medicine, she (prepare) breakfast with Michael and they (serve) the first residents in the dining room.
4. Mrs Brown (not phone) Mr and Mrs Jennings, right now she is on a tour of the house and she (show) them the first floor.
5. It (no rain) anymore and the first residents (sit) in the outdoor seating area because the sun (shine) again.
6. Today Mrs Hampton (not sit) in her wheelchair. She (do) her walker training with the physiotherapist. Right now, they (walk) through the park.
7. The kitchen crew (not prepare) today's dinner. It's already late afternoon and they (clean) the kitchen.

Inside a nursing home	
operation scar	Operationsnarbe
dressing	hier: Verband
medication	Medikation / Tablettenversorgung
food intake	Nahrungsaufnahme
housekeeping	Haushaltsführung
leisure time	Freizeit

Inside St Mary's Nursing Home	
nursing home	Pflegeheim
short-term care	Kurzzeitpflege
suitable	passend
(to) recover from	sich erholen von
carer	Person, die sich um die Pflege kümmert
(to) offer	anbieten
currently	zurzeit
tour of the house	Hausrundgang
entrance hall	Eingangshalle
reception	Rezeption, Empfang
administration	Verwaltung
area	Bereich
assisted living	betreutes Wohnen
choir	Chor
performance	Auf- / Vorführung
private rooms	Privaträume
corridor	Flur
level	Ebene, Stockwerk
lift	Aufzug, Lift
stairs	Treppe
(to) get lost	Orientierung verlieren / sich verlaufen
(to) form a circle	einen Kreis bilden
nurse station	Stationszimmer
seating area	Sitzbereich / Aufenthaltsbereich
physical therapy	Physiotherapie
occupational therapy	Beschäftigungs-therapie
bathroom	Badezimmer
bathtub lift	Badewannenlift
toilet	Toilette
staff room	Personalraum
stockroom	Lagerraum
canteen kitchen	Großküche
laundry	Wäscherei
balcony	Balkon
semi-private room	privater Raum mit geteiltem Bad
wheelchair ramp	Rollstuhlrampe

A single private room at …	
en-suite room	Zimmer mit eigenem Bad
hospital bed	Krankenbett
chest of drawers	Kommode
bedside locker	Krankenbettspint
overbed table	Rolltisch / Beistelltisch
shower chair	Duschstuhl
barrier-free	barrierefrei
cupboard	(eingebauter) (Kleider)schrank
wash basin	Waschbecken
be equipped with	ausgestattet sein mit
be furnished with	möbliert sein mit
be divided into	aufgeteilt sein in
walker	Rollator

What does care look like…	
around the clock	rund um die Uhr
bedridden	bettlägerig
repositioning	Neupositionieren
be on call	abrufbereit sein
fractured	gebrochen
thigh bone	Oberschenkelknochen
walker training	Rollatortraining
limited movement	eingeschränkte Bewegung
consultation	Konsultation, hier: ärztliche Behandlung
(to) build up strength	Kraft gewinnen
(to) encourage to	ermuntern zu
gambling afternoon	Spielnachmittag
opportunity	Möglichkeit
walking stick	Gehstock

Die Aussprache der blauen Vokabeln finden Sie in den Audio-Dateien DA0901055

Are you a good team player?

A **Look at the picture and pick out one of the sentence beginnings and finish it.**
1. The picture shows a good team because …
2. The team in the picture is a rather bad team because …

B **Are you a team player? Do you get along with others when working in a team?**

C **Can you say what you need to be a good team player?**

D **Think of why care can only be managed as team work.**

join a team	sich einem Team anschließen
exclude oneself from a team	sich aus einem Team ausschließen
row in the same / different direction	in die gleiche / verschiedene Richtung rudern
win / succeed as a team	als Team gewinnen / erfolgreich sein
accept the team leader / team members	den Teamleiter / die Teammitglieder akzeptieren
be able to work in a team	im Team arbeiten können / teamfähig sein

Why is teamwork important at work?

We are all members of different teams, at work, in school, or in our free time, for example in a sports team. Working in a team very often means dealing with all sorts of personalities and many people say that it is really hard work to do this and get good results. There are people who prefer working alone and do not like being in a team, but at work the concept of "**T**ogether **E**veryone **A**chieves **M**ore" is very important. Teamwork gives us a good opportunity to get to know other people and learn how to work together. Here are some simple rules which help create a great team.

Delegation
To achieve the best results, you should know who is good or bad at a certain task. Tasks should be divided up so that they are done by the most suitable people.

Efficiency
A team can get things done faster than a single person because a task can be delegated to the team member who is the best – and quickest! – at that task.

Variety of ideas
Teams can discuss problems and develop different ideas by brainstorming information. As a result, a team can produce a larger variety of ideas than a single person.

Support
In a good team, everyone can rely on each other and trust each other. Members can help each other and work together to improve their work. This means that a good team can keep working and being productive - even if someone leaves the team or is off sick.

Communication and Feedback
Good communication is important for good team work. You can hold meetings, send e-mails, call each other, or write each other notes or memos. Constructive feedback helps the whole team to improve.

Working with the text

A Look through the text again and finish the following sentence beginnings. Work with the text but try not to copy whole sentences.

1. We are all members of different teams, for example …
2. It's hard work to get good results in a team because …
3. Team work gives you a good opportunity to …
4. You should know who is the best person to do a certain task so …
5. A team always works faster than a single person because …
6. Brainstorming in a team is very effective because …
7. A team needs feedback to …

B What is your experience with team work or group work at school? Give examples of good or rather bad team work.

C **Here are four negative opinions about team work. Work in pairs to write a positive answer to each negative opinion. What can these people do to improve their negative team experience?**

People only pick out the tasks they like doing and the unpopular tasks are left undone.

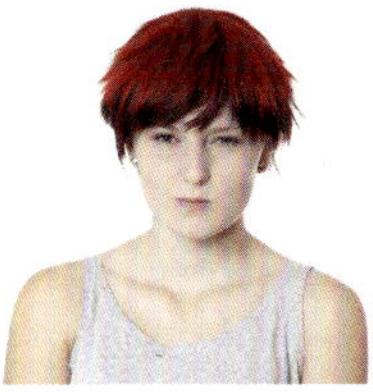

I hate team work because there is always someone who does not do any work at all.

I'm always the one who does the lion's share of the work, and it's disappointing that noone appreciates the work I do.

I can only work with a good friend I can rely on. You can't trust everybody.

Convincing someone of team work

It is always better to …

Teamwork is much better than working alone because …

Don't forget that working in team can be better because …

Don't forget the positive aspects, such as (-ing) …

Next time you join a team avoid (+verb-ing) … and you will see that …

If you make sure that …, … will not happen.

Teamwork can work really well, if you …

Teamwork can be really positive if you …

You can achieve a lot more in a team if …

Working with language

A **Work on the following tasks in pairs. You can use a bilingual dictionary to help you. First find nouns which go with the following verbs.**
1. to deal with 2. to exclude 3. to be efficient 4. to support 5. to communicate

B **Find the verbs which go with the following nouns.**
1. development 2. achievement 3. meeting 4. success 5. improvement

C **Now find adjectives which go with the following nouns.**
1. personality 2. success 3. difference 4. importance
5. simplicity 6. qualification 7. skill 8. information

D **Work in pairs and explain the following expressions in your own words. Write down your explanations and compare them with your class. Look at page 133. Here you will find some help in how to explain words.** Production
1. team 2. to delegate 3. efficiency 4. feedback 5. to get to know

Grammar box: **Comparison of adjectives** – Steigerung der Adjektive

Mit „-er" (Komparativ) und „-est" (Superlativ) werden folgende Adjektive gesteigert …

→ **einsilbige Adjektive**

Beispiele: *quick – quick**er** – quick**est***
*high – high**er** – high**est***
*low – low**er** – low**est***

→ **zweisilbige Adjektive auf „-er", „-le", „-ow", „-y"**

Beispiele: *clever – clever**er** – the clever**est***
*simple – simpl**er** – the simpl**est***

Bei dieser Art der Steigerung sollte man folgende **Rechtschreibbesonderheiten** beachten …

→ **y wird zu i**

Beispiel: *eas**y** – eas**ier** – eas**iest***

→ **Wegfall von stummem End-„e"**

Beispiel: *larg**e** – larg**er** – larg**est***

→ **Verdoppelung des Endkonsonanten nach kurzem, betonten Vokal (a, e, i, o, u)**

Beispiel: *thin – thin**ner** – thin**nest***

Mit more (Komparativ) und most (Superlativ) werden folgende Adjektive gesteigert …

→ **zweisilbige Adjektive, die nicht auf „-er", „-le", „-ow", „-y" enden**

Beispiele: *useful – more useful – most useful*
famous – more famous – most famous

→ **drei- und mehrsilbige Adjektive**

Beispiele: *important – more important – most important*
successful – more successful – most successful

Ausnahmen / unregelmäßige Steigerungen der Adjektive

good	better	best
bad	worse	worst
ill	worse	worst
little (wenig)	less	least
much	more	most
many	more	most
far	further / farther	furthest / farthest (Bedeutung: weiter, räumliche Entfernung)

Practising grammar

A Write down the comparative and superlative of the following adjectives.

1. clean	2. bad	3. beautiful	4. soft
5. big	6. difficult	7. much	8. famous
9. thick	10. fat	11. nice	12. hot
13. lucky	14. great	15. good	16. happy

B Now fill in the correct form of the adjective.

Examples

Mike is taller **than** Henry.	… größer **als** …
But Henry is **as** tall **as** Tom.	… **so** groß wie …
Mike is **the** tallest of them all.	… **der** größte **von** …
Mike is **very** tall.	… **sehr** groß …
It is **too** late.	… **zu** spät …

ill	Jonathan cannot come to work because he is **1. …** He has been at home for a week now, but he feels even **2. …** than he did at the beginning of the week.
skilled	Sure, I can take over Jonathan's tasks. But I think Maria is **3. …** than me. In fact I think she is the **4. …** person of the whole team.
simple	There are some really **5. …** rules which make teamwork easy and effective. One of the **6. …** rules is to divide up tasks.
quick	We can be a **7. …** team if everyone does the tasks he is best at. I think I'm **8. …** than Maria in preparing the patients' medicine. And she is the **9. …** at changing dressings.
little (wenig)	I only had a **10. …** sleep last night because one of the residents, Mr Harper, was ill. However, I think he had even **11. …** sleep than me, and the **12. …** sleep had my colleague on watch in the nurse station.
pleasant	It's nice and sunny today, so our outing is **13. …** than the last one, when it rained. All the residents are enjoying the sun on a boat trip and it's a very **14. …** atmosphere here.
important	In a care job, it is very **15. …** to listen to your patients and to spend some time chatting to them. Having a good chat is sometimes **16. …** to patients than talking about their health. Making patients feel happy can play an **17. …** role in their convalescence.
old	I am one of three children. I have got a brother who is **18. …** than me. But he is not the **19. …** I also have a sister, and she is the **20. …**
young	And I'm the **21. …** child.

A care team

A This is a care team at St Mary's Nursing Home. Look at their tasks and fill in their jobs.

nursing assistant
registered nurse
general practitioner / doctor
psychologist
occupational therapist
physiotherapist

Amanda Miller and Brenda Summers

job: ??
in charge of one floor
in shiftwork
tasks:
- perform medical care
- authorised to give some medication
- observe and report physical, mental, and emotional condition
- report and monitor vital signs, food and fluid intake and output
- consult specialists
- …
- …

Helen Bowls and Seyman Soumar

job: ??
in charge of one floor
in shiftwork
tasks:
- report patient's vital signs, food and fluid intake and output
- feed residents and supervise liquid intake
- prepare hot drinks and small snacks
- lift and reposition residents
- go for walks with the residents
- take residents to appointments / to have treatment
- …

Roberta Baker and Malabar Asuma

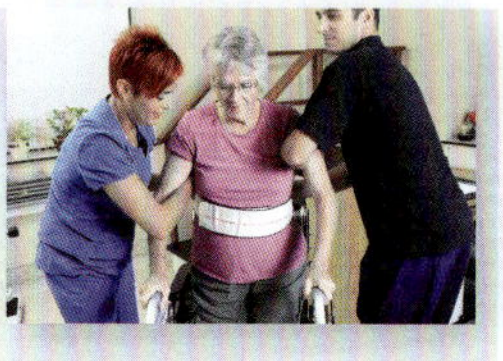

job: ??
work with all the residents
tasks:
- carry out individual physiotherapy to regain and maintain mobility
- carry out individual physiotherapy to avoid muscular weakness
- …

Mandy Jameson

job: ??
works with all the residents
tasks:
- carries out and organises workshops
- organises parties and outings
- …
- …
- …

Hillary Bonham

job: ??
external, works with all the residents
tasks:
- carries out medical treatments
- fully authorised to give medication
- advises nurses / care assistants how to care for the residents
- …

David Mc Allison

job: ??
external, works with all the residents
tasks:
- responsible for carrying out neurological and psychological treatments
- carries out and analyses neurological tests, particularly dementia tests
- …

B In the box below, you can find some of the typical tasks these care workers contribute in a nursing home. Can you say who carries them out?

- create and modify care plans
- perform routine tasks under the supervision of a registered nurse
- refer residents to hospital
- give therapy to residents with dementia, depression, mental health problems
- run exercise classes
- do individual walking and walker training
- refer residents to specialists
- counsel residents and work out ideas for their personal development
- assist with personal hygiene and dressing
- authorised to give full medication, mainly for neurological conditions
- supervise nursing assistants
- distribute medicine
- carry out and evaluate the full range of medical tests, e.g. laboratory tests

Reception

C Listen to different members of the care team and say what they believe they are each good at.

Care planning in a team

At St Mary's Nursing Home, the registered nurses on each floor also act as care coordinators and chair care team meetings. In these meetings, records of care are very important to plan further care. Today, Brenda Summers is in charge of the meeting and she wants to talk about Mrs Hampton. Here is one of Mrs Hampton's recent records of care.

Record of Care

Name:	*Valery Hampton*
Date:	*February, 18th, 20..*
Time:	*7:25 a.m.*
Care worker:	***Helen Bowls***

Vital signs:

blood pressure:	60/110
pulse:	65
respiration:	14
weight:	62 kilos

Care activities:
personal hygiene, toilet, change of operation scar dressing, closed wound, crust, but also pus
medication: according to medication plan
extra painkiller during night, dose: 500 mg

Health condition:
weight loss, good vital signs
says she is in pain, despite painkiller

Mental condition:
shows some depression, slow and lethargic body language, inactive

A care team meeting

Brenda Summers: Okay, Mrs Hampton has been in our home for three weeks now. From her record of care I can see that there are still some problems with her operation scar. It's closed, but is not healing as expected. Mrs Hampton keeps on saying that she is in pain. The painkiller she takes at night is not helping, but I can't give her a higher dose without a doctor. Her vital signs are okay, despite her weight - it's lower than when she was admitted.

Seyman Soumar: She is also showing signs of depression. She is very quiet, does not talk much.

Brenda Summers: Maybe she still needs some time to get used to our home?

Helen Bowls: Well, when you ask her she says that everything is fine, but her body language is giving a completely different message. I think it's more than that.

Seyman Soumar: We should first try different wound management. The ointment we have got here isn't working. When you change her dressing, you can still see pus on the wound.

Amanda Miller: And, there's another problem. More and more, she's refusing to come out of bed. She says it's too painful. I'm worried that her muscles will become weak.

Brenda Summers: Yes, you're right. We need to do something. First of all I suggest taking a new x-ray of her hip bone to make sure everything is okay. That means we need to refer her to hospital before considering new painkillers.

Helen Bowls: That's a good idea. But what about her weight loss and depression. They could also be first signs of dementia.

Brenda Summers: You're right. What else should we do and who should do it?

Working with the text

Work in small groups and complete the following tasks to prepare Mrs Hampton's further care.

1. Make a list of the health problems Mrs Hampton still has.
2. What has the care team observed and recorded about her mental condition? Add these observations to your list.
3. What has the care team done so far?
4. What does Brenda suggest doing next?

Interaction

Hands-on task

In your small groups, plan Mrs Hampton's care. What are next steps you want to take and which team member should do it? Present your care plan in class.

Making suggestions

- We suggest (verb+ing) … because she needs …
- (Person) is in charge of (task – noun / verb+ing) …
- (Person) should make sure / keep an eye on …
- We should do something about (noun / verb+ing) …
- We should take care that …
- We should ask (person), if he / she can / is able to …

Working with language

Body language

Being able to read body language is a very useful skill in care and should also be included in a record of care. Signs of depression and a blank facial expression may be signs of dementia. And there are a lot of patients who tell you that everything is fine, but their body language shows you that this is not true.
Looking at facial expressions is very important. What mood does the face show you? Does your patient make eye-contact or avoid it? Exchanging glances with a raised head shows openness and liking. If someone is not looking at you and maybe has a lowered head, he may be lying to you or hiding something like guilt. Some people tend to look down because they are shy or upset. But there are also cultural differences. Some cultures believe that direct eye-contact is a sign of disrespect, and only look at intimate friends or family. Someone who widens his eyes and raises his eyebrows may be surprised or shocked. Someone who has his eyes more or less shut may be trying to concentrate. If someone screws up his forehead, he may be angry.
A person's stance may be open or closed. Is your patient creating a barrier with his arms or legs, or is his stance open? Very often, people with crossed arms are shutting themselves off from social influence.
Pay attention to how physically close someone stands to you. The closer and more open their body position is, the more likeable they find you.
Also, be aware of nervous gestures. Foot tapping, rocking from side to side or uncontrolled laughing suggest that the person feels uncomfortable, impatient, or even intimidated.

A Look through the text to fill in the table below.
Compare your lists in class.

What is the body language?	What does it show you?
• show blank facial expression	• start of dementia
• make eye-contact / exchange glances …	• openness and liking

B *All people have the same body language.*
Is this statement true or false? Give reasons

Production

C As a care worker you should observe your patients and learn to "read" their body language. Here are three photos showing residents at St Mary's Nursing Home.

1. Work in pairs and discuss what each person's body language may be saying about his / her mood.
2. What do you want to take down for the care report? Write it down.

1

2

3

Adjectives for a good mood

alert	aufgeweckt
amused	amüsiert
bright	strahlend / wach
cheerful	fröhlich / vergnügt
calm	ruhig / friedlich
content	zufrieden
energetic	lebhaft / energievoll
interested	interessiert
lively	lebendig / lebhaft
optimistic	optimistisch
relaxed	entspannt

Adjectives for a bad mood

angry / annoyed	wütend / verärgert
apathetic / blank	apathisch / ausdruckslos
bored	gelangweilt
confused	verwirrt
depressed	depressiv
disappointed	enttäuscht
frustrated	frustriert
grumpy	mürrisch / brummig
lethargic	lethargisch
pessimistic	pessimistisch
restless	ruhelos
shocked	schockiert

Grammar box: Comparison of simple present and present continuous tenses

– Vergleich der einfachen Gegenwart und der Verlaufsform der Gegenwart

Present Tense Simple

*Who **does** the night shift every Saturday?*
***Does** Helen sometimes **do** the night shift?*
***Do** Malabar and Roberta **run** exercise classes?*
*Brenda **does** the night shift every second month.*
*Helen and Brenda **organise** care.*
*Malabar and Roberta **don't organise care,** they **run** the exercise classes.*
*Mandy **doesn't** distribute medicine, she **organises** workshops.*

→ **Beschreibung beruflicher Routine**
→ **wiederkehrende Handlungen**
(siehe Seite 10 zur Wiederholung)

Present Tense Continuous

*Who **is doing** the night shift right now?*
***Is** Helen **doing** the night shift?*
***Are** Malabar and Roberta **running** exercise classes at the moment?*
*Brenda **is doing** the night shift now.*
*Helen and Brenda **are leading** today's care team meeting.*
*Malabar and Roberta **aren't running** exercise classes today, they **are doing** walker trainings.*
*Mandy **isn't painting** with the residents, she **is taking** them on an outing.*

→ **Beschreibung momentaner und / oder vorläufiger Handlung**
(siehe Seite 24 zur Wiederholung)

Life in a nursing home – hour by hour

7:00 a.m.	vital checks, medication, and morning personal care
8:00 a.m.	breakfast
9:00 a.m.	optional activities (for example: art, handicraft, music, exercise classes, etc.) or healthcare treatments
10:30 a.m.	walks with physiotherapist or nursing assistants
12:00 a.m.	lunch
1:00 p.m.	optional activities (classes or outings) or healthcare treatments
2:30 p.m.	afternoon naps or free time
4:00 p.m.	optional programmes (performances, movies, games, workshops, etc.)
5:30 p.m.	dinner
6:30 p.m.	shower, medication, evening personal care
8:00 p.m.	bed time
throughout the night	vital checks, repositioning, medical staff on-call

Die Uhrzeiten

a.m. = ante meridiem = vormittags, z. B.
2 a.m. = 2 Uhr morgens,
11 a.m. = 11 Uhr morgens oder vormittags,
12 a.m. = noon,

p.m. = post meridiem = nachmittags und abends, z. B.
1 p.m. = 1 Uhr mittags,
8 p.m. = 8 Uhr abends

0:00 Uhr = midnight

Practising grammar

This is the daily schedule at St Mary's Nursing Home. The team tries to keep to it, but today there are some deviations. Fill in the correct form of the verb. Example:

Normally Helen (do) check ups in the morning but right now she (help) Mr Harper with his morning hygiene.
Normally Helen does check ups in the morning but right now she is helping Mr Harper with his morning hygiene.

1. Usually, Malabar (run) an exercise class every Friday at 9 a.m. but today all the residents (go) on an outing.
2. Every morning, Mr Ronald usually (go) for a walk with the physiotherapist but today he (visit) the doctor.
3. Amanda and Brenda (be) usually in charge of care planning, but today they (take) part at a body language training so Helen (plan) today's care.
4. Dr. Hillary Bonham (visit) the nursing home every Tuesday and Thursday. But this week she (lie) on a beach, on holiday. Therefore, Dr. Brian Holland (look) after Mrs Miller, who (not feel) well.
5. Normally, Mr Hollander (not need) a nurse for repositioning during night but right now he (suffer) from a bad back and he can't turn over on his own.
6. Usually Seyman (help) feed the residents but right now he (transport) Mrs Hampton to hospital because the care team (want) to have a new x-ray of her hip bone.
7. Mrs Johnson (take) a nap every afternoon but today (be) her 80th birthday and she (sit) in the dining room with her family and they (eat) birthday cake.
8. On Friday at 4 p.m. there (be) usually a game afternoon where the residents (play) bingo but today a dance group (give) a performance instead.

Are you a good team player?	
(to) set oneself goals	sich Ziele setzen
competitive	konkurrierend
cooperative	kooperativ
(to) require	brauchen, benötigen
(to) appreciate	zu schätzen wissen
Why is teamwork important …?	
personality	Persönlichkeit
(to) achieve	erreichen
result	Ergebnis
(to) get to know	vertraut werden mit
(to) delegate	delegieren / übertragen
suitable	geeignet, qualifiziert
efficiency	Effizienz
variety	hier: Vielfalt,
(to) brainstorm	hier: Ideensammlung
(to) rely on	sich verlassen auf
(to) trust	vertrauen
(to) improve	verbessern
productive	produktiv, schöpferisch
(to) be off sick	wg. Krankheit fehlen
memo	Notiz
constructive	konstruktiv, hilfreich
(to) improve	verbessern
left undone	liegen bleiben, nicht erledigt werden
(to) do the lion's share	den Löwenanteil machen
skilled	qualifiziert, erfahren
(to) be on watch	hier: Nachtwache haben
convalescence	Genesung
A care team	
nursing assistant	Pflegehilfe / Gesundheits- und Pflegeassistenz
registered nurse	Pflegefachkraft
general practitioner	Arzt / Ärztin für Allgemeinmedizin
authorised	autorisiert, befugt
(to) observe	beobachten
(to) report	berichten
physical	körperlich
mental	mental, geistig
fluid intake	Flüssigkeitsaufnahme
(to) consult	konsultieren, sich besprechen mit
vital signs	Vitalzeichen
(to) lift	heben
(to) reposition	positionieren bzw. neu positionieren
(to) regain	wiedererlangen
(to) maintain	erhalten
mobility	Mobilität, Beweglichkeit
muscular weakness	Muskelschwäche
external	jemand, der von außen in ein Team kommt
(to) carry out	durchführen
neurological	neurologisch
psychological	psychologisch
treatment	Behandlung
dementia	Demenz
(to) contribute to	beitragen zu
(to) create	erstellen
(to) modify	ändern, modifizieren
(to) refer sb. to hospital	jmd. ins Krankenhaus überweisen
(to) counsel / advise	beraten
(to) distribute	austeilen
(to) evaluate	bewerten, auswerten
Care planning in a team	
care coordinator	Pflegekoordinator
(to) chair	leiten, den Vorsitz haben
record of care	Pflegebericht
crust	hier: Wundschorf
pus	Eiter
painkiller	Schmerzmittel
dose	Dosis
lethargic	träge
inactive	inaktiv, ruhig
A care team meeting	
healing	Heilung
admitted	hier: eingeliefert
wound management	Wundversorgung
ointment	Salbe
(to) refuse to	sich weigern zu
muscles	Muskeln
x-ray	Röntgenaufnahme
hip bone	Hüftknochen
(to) consider	in Betracht ziehen
Body language	
skill	Fähigkeit
(to) notice	hier: erkennen
facial expression	Gesichtsausdruck
mood	Laune, Stimmung
(to) make eye-contact	Blickkontakt herstellen
(to) exchange glances	Blicke (aus)tauschen
(to) raise	heben
(to) lower	senken
openness	Offenheit
guilt	Schuld
(to) tend to	neigen zu
disrespect	Respektlosigkeit
(to) widen	weiten, öffnen
eyebrows	Augenbrauen
(to) screw up the forehead	„die Stirn runzeln"
stance	Körperhaltung
(to) create a barrier	eine Barriere aufbauen
cross arms	Arme verschränken
physically	körperlich
(to) shut off	sich verschließen, sich abgrenzen
gesture	Geste
foot tapping	mit dem Fuß wippen
(to) rock from side to side	Hin- und Herschaukeln
deviations	Abweichungen

Die Aussprache der blauen Vokabeln finden Sie in den Audio-Dateien DA0901055

Unit 5 Stress at Work

What are typical stress situations?

1. Look at the pictures and describe the situation you see.
2. Why are the people in the pictures feeling stressed?
3. What do you do to avoid stress?
4. What could the people in the pictures do to avoid stress?

Home care – a typical morning shift

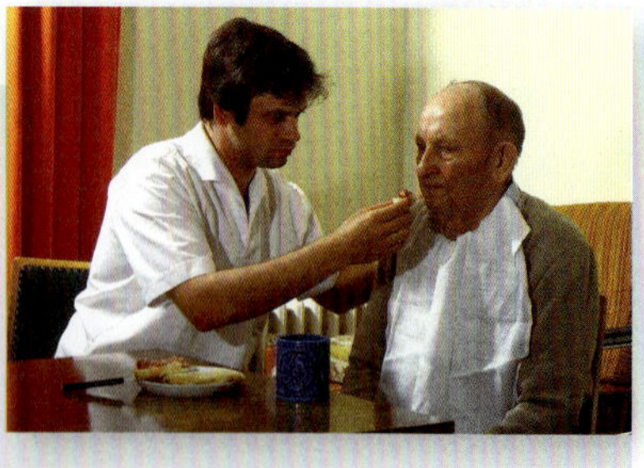

6:00 a.m. The alarm clock rings. Henry jumps out of bed, takes a shower, puts on his uniform and after a quick breakfast he drives to the home care office.

6:30 a.m. He looks through his list to prepare the tablet boxes. On his way out he hastily grabs his gloves, apron and new bandages and sets off.

7:00 a.m. He arrives at his first call. He only has 20 to 25 minutes to assist Mr Brian with his morning hygiene, have breakfast and make sure he takes his tablets. He must do this quickly to stay on schedule. Before he leaves, he quickly fills in the record of care and the medication chart.

7:45 a.m. Mrs Morrison is already on her feet and Henry helps her into the shower. She can manage the rest alone. He dashes around, makes the bed, empties the night commode, always keeping one ear open in case she needs help. She dresses alone, but Henry has to fasten the buttons and put on her thrombosis stockings. Then he makes sure she eats her breakfast and takes her tablets. She wants him to stay for a chat but he can't. He should already be on his way to Mr Jones.

8:10 a.m. He pops into Mr Jones' home. He suffers from slight memory loss and needs reminding to take his medication. Mr Jones likes to talk about the England football team but mornings are very busy and Henry needs to keep to his schedule. Searching for a parking space and traffic jams are also time-consuming.

9:00 a.m. Mr Miller likes to have a lie-in and doesn't mind Henry coming later. He suffers from painful arthritis and Henry assists him going to the toilet and getting ready. Caring for Mr Miller isn't easy because he can be very grumpy. He takes his frustration out on Henry. Henry does not take it personally. He knows it is not because of him but because of his situation and he sits down to talk despite his busy schedule.

9:40 a.m. Back in the car, Henry decides to call Mr Miller's doctor, maybe he needs new painkillers. His next call is Mrs Smith. She is blind but can wash and dress herself. She only needs help with her medication.

10:15 a.m. The morning flies by. Henry sets off to Mrs Martinez who has an open sore and Henry changes her leg bandage.

10:45 a.m. Henry's mobile rings. Mr Miller's doctor wants to see him and he drives to the practice to have a quick chat. He leaves with a new prescription.

11:00 a.m. He drops into the pharmacy but the medicine is not available, he has to come back again in the early afternoon. He looks at his schedule, how is he going to manage that?

11:15 a.m. Henry should have his 30 minute break, but he spends it in the car with a sandwich in his hand driving to the meal service. He collects lunches for his clients and quickly packs them into the "hot-boxes".

11:45 a.m. He delivers 6 meals. Most clients want their meal at 12noon. Henry hurries to serve them whilst they're hot. He can't sit down to keep his clients company, although many of them ask him to do so. Very often, Henry is the only person they see all day.

1:00 p.m. Mr Hollander is his last lunch delivery. He has had a stroke and Henry must cut his food into small pieces to make sure he can swallow it. This takes a long time; too much time to allow him keep to his schedule.

1:30 p.m. There is one last call. Mrs Summers is a cancer patient in the terminal stage. Henry has to give her a new infusion. This is a hard call for him because she is his age, 36.

2:00 p.m. On his way back home he stops at the pharmacy again to fetch Mr Miller's new painkillers. At last, Henry can finish work.

Working with the text

A Say where Henry probably is and what he is doing at these times.

1. 7:10 a.m.
2. 8:00 a.m.
3. 8:15 a.m.
4. 9:45 a.m.
5. 10:20 a.m.
6. 10:50 a.m.
7. noon
8. 2:05 p.m.

B Match the sentence beginnings with the correct sentence endings according to the text.

1. Every morning Henry's alarm clock rings at 6.a.m. …	a. because he knows that he is frustrated because of his arthritis.
2. Before he visits his clients, he drops into the home care office …	b. because he suffers from memory loss and forgets to take his tablets.
3. Mrs Morrison tries to remain as active as possible …	c. because he is in almost constant pain.
4. Henry brings Mr Jones his tablets …	d. and he takes a shower, puts on his uniform and leaves home after a quick breakfast.
5. Mr Miller is a very grumpy client …	e. why Mr Miller prefers to stay in bed.
6. This pain is also one of the reasons …	f. because his clients want to have a hot meal at noon.
7. Henry doesn't take Mr Miller's grumpiness personally …	g. but she needs help putting on her thrombosis stockings and fastening buttons.
8. Henry hurries to pack the lunches …	h. to have a look at the schedule and prepare everything for his calls.

Mediation / Interaction

C Work in pairs and do the following tasks.

1. "The morning flies by".
   Can you translate this expression into German?
2. Time pressure is one of the biggest causes of stress. Look through the text again and collect words and expressions which show Henry is under time pressure. Translate them. You may use a bilingual dictionary or the internet to help you.

D Answer the following questions.

1. Henry is under such time pressure, there are some things Henry can't do for his clients or for himself. What are they?
2. What problems does Henry have with Mr Miller?
3. Why is Henry's call at Mrs Summer's not easy for him?

Reception

E Listen to four dialogues between Henry and one of his clients. Find out …

1. where he is and …
2. what he is doing.

Grammar box: "Going-to"- Future – "Going-to" – Zukunft

Bildung

am / is / are + "going to" + 1. Form des Verbs (Infinitiv)

Achtung: "be going to" + 1. Verbform hat hier nicht die Bedeutung von „gehen", in diesem grammatikalischen Zusammenhang bedeutet dies „werden",
z. B. Henry is going to visit Mr Jones. – Henry wird Herrn Jones besuchen.

Beispiele

Aussagesatz	Verneinung	Frage
I'm going to pack *lunches.* *You / We / They* ***are going to pack*** *lunches.* *He / She* ***is going to pack*** *lunches.*	***I'm not going to pack*** *lunches.* *You / We / They* ***are not / aren't going to pack*** *lunches.* *He / She* ***is not / isn't going to pack*** *lunches.*	***Am I going to pack*** *lunches?* ***Are you / we / they going to pack*** *lunches?* ***Is he / she going to pack*** *lunches?*

Fragen mit Fragewort

*Who **is going to fetch** Mr Miller's pain killers?*
*What **are** we **going to do** about Mr Miller's pain?*
*Where **am** I **going to be** at 8:00 a.m. according to my new schedule?*
*When **are** the lunches (they) **going to be** ready?*
*How **is** she **going to organise** the evening calls?*
*Why **are** you **going to call** Mr Miller's doctor?*

Verwendung

Der Sprecher nutzt "Going-to"-Future, um damit …

→ eine logische Schlussfolgerung auszudrücken
Henry's going to be late for his next appointment because it's taking a long time to cut up Mr Hollander's food.

→ um ein Vorhaben auszudrücken, das man bereits gefasst oder länger geplant hat (keine spontane Entscheidung)
I'm going to stop at the pharmacy to fetch the new painkillers after work.

Practising grammar

A The home-care team meets to talk about next week's schedule. Fill in the going-to future

1. Henry's schedule / change because he / start calling at Mrs Gabriel.
2. Mrs Gabriel suffers from dementia and Henry / take over her morning medication and personal hygiene.
3. He / go to visit her at 8:30 a.m.
4. Miriam / visit Mrs Gabriel in the evening and she / give her tablets for the night.
5. Furthermore, Miriam / undress Mrs Gabriel and she / put her to bed.
6. On Monday Mr Miller / see a doctor and he / have some neurological tests.
7. Henry and Miriam / take Mr Miller to and from his appointment.
8. Henry / drive Mr Miller to the practice and Miriam / fetch him.

B Here are some questions about next week's schedule.

1. Who / transfer / Mr Miller to the doctor?
2. I / fetch him after his neurological test?
3. You / visit Mrs Gabriel this evening??
4. How / you / organise Wednesday morning?
5. When / Henry / give Mrs Summers her infusion?

Grammar box: Need, needn't – must, mustn't

I / You / We / They	***need***	*regular breaks to stay healthy.*
He / She	***needs***	*a holiday to refresh from stress.*
Henry	***needs to***	*hurry to keep to the roster.*
I / You / We / They	***needn't***	*hurry to the next call.*
	don't need to	*be quick. There is still enough time.*
He / She	***needn't***	*feed Mr Miller. He can eat alone.*
	doesn't need to	*dress Mrs Mayer. She can manage alone.*

→ *need to* = „brauchen"
→ *needn't* **in Verbindung mit Verb** = „nicht brauchen"

I / You / We / They	***must***	*check Mr Miller's blood pressure.*
He / She	***must***	*monitor Mr Hollander's food intake.*
I / You / We / They	***mustn't***	*forget to fill in the record of care.*
He / She	***mustn't***	*forget to put on a new dressing because Mrs Martinez has an open sore.*

→ *must* = „müssen" (strenges Gebot)
→ *mustn't* **in Verbindung mit Verb** = „nicht dürfen" (strenges Verbot)

Practising grammar

A Henry is going on a holiday, so Miriam is going to take on his calls and Henry gives her some information. Fill in need, need to, needn't, must, mustn't.

Okay Miriam, there are some things you **1. …** forget. Every morning you **2. …** check the medication chart. This is very important because sometimes the medication changes and our patients **3. …** have new tablets. For example, Mr Miller suffers from arthritis and he **4. …** have new painkillers quite often. He is a bit grumpy but you **5. …** be afraid, he is very frustrated with his situation but not angry at you. Don't forget to take new bandages with you because some of the clients have open sores and you **6. …** change their bandages every day to prevent infections. You **7. …** help Mrs Morrison into the shower because she can't lift her feet very high but you **8. …** stay with her in the bathroom, she can manage and prefers to shower alone. She gives you a call when she is ready. She picks her own clothes but she **9. …** your help with the buttons. Don't forget to help her with her thrombosis stockings, she **10. …** wear them! You **11. …** monitor every client at their meals but Mr Hollander. He has had a stroke and you **12. …** leave him alone with his meals. That's all I think, or do you **13. …** any more information?

Grammar box: Word Order – Satzstellung

Subject	***Verb***	***Object***	***Place***	***Time***
Henry	*checks*	*his schedule*	*at the home-care office*	*at 6:30.*
Time	***Subject***	***Verb***	***Object***	***Place***
Every morning	*Henry*	*packs*	*the medication boxes*	*at the office.*

B Reconstruct the following sentences

1. every – bed – takes – morning – and – out – Henry – jumps – shower – a – of – he
2. seven – arrives – at – call – about – his – o'clock – he – at – first
3. Mr – night – Miller – in – pain – at – is
4. in – for – fetches – Mr – Henry – Miller – at – painkillers – pharmacy – afternoon – new – the – the
5. hot-boxes – Henry – at – 11am – the – into – packs – lunches – the
6. delivery – Hollander – is – day – lunch – of – the – Mr – last – the

Grammar box: **Genitive** – Genitiv

s-genitive	*of-genitive*
→ **bei Personen, Tieren** *Henry'**s** clients* • *Mr Jones' record of care* • *people'**s** health* • *the clients' medication* • *the dog'**s** bone*	→ **bei Sachbezeichnungen** • *the new colour **of** the uniform* • *the pages **of** the work report*

C Write the s- or of-genitive.

1. (Mr Miller) record of care
2. (Mrs Morrison) thrombosis stockings
3. (cup) tea
4. (home care workers) uniform
5. (Henry) schedule
6. (home-care service) office
7. (doctor) prescription
8. (clients) tablet boxes
9. (my cat) toy

Stress factors in care work

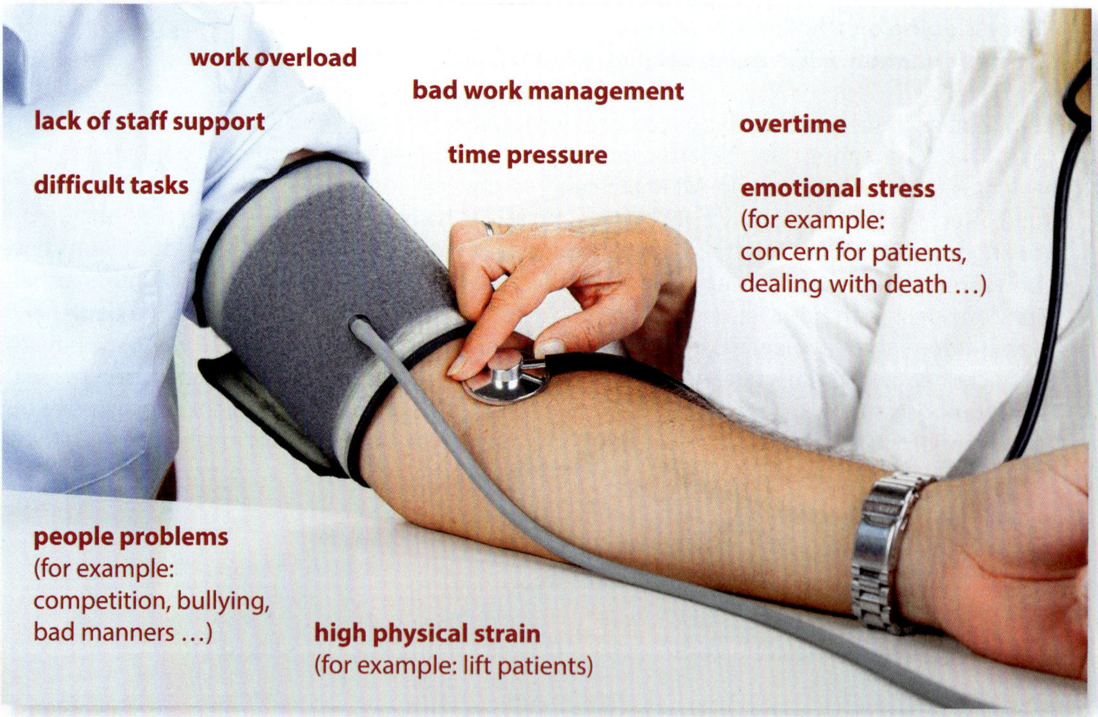

Two care workers speak about their problems and stress at work

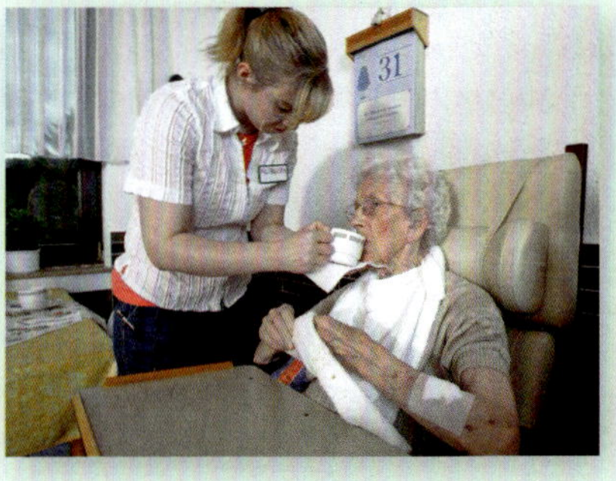

Sonja – a home care worker

Very often I work 10 days without a break and getting out of bed is a real struggle for me. Even after a long night's sleep I do not jump out of bed feeling refreshed. But there is no time to feel ill. There are 6 people waiting for me to get up and dressed. In order to stick to my schedule, I rush into and out of my clients' homes as quickly as possible. Despite all that hurry, I'm always behind schedule, which means that I run into my noon call's home, prepare a cup of tea and microwave her lunch, and run out without having chatted to her or monitored her food intake. A lot of my clients don't eat properly. All this makes me feel very guilty.

Timekeeping is a constant problem and there are clients who get angry with me. I have to apologise again and again. I also wish my home-care office would consider people's wishes instead of packing my schedule with as many calls as possible. For example, I arrive at the first job on my schedule at 7:15a.m but that lady actually wants a 9a.m call. She refuses to let me in and shouts at me.

In the evening, the situation can be worse. Today I have three meal calls, a catheter bag to empty and four people to undress and get to bed, and "only" two medication prompts.

Very often, people don't get the care and support they need and I feel extremely disheartened. Many of my clients have very little social contact and they beg me not to leave but I have to because there is always someone else waiting. We are always overburdened with calls. As a consequence this way of working has become the norm. There are days when I consider getting another job with a better salary and regular breaks.

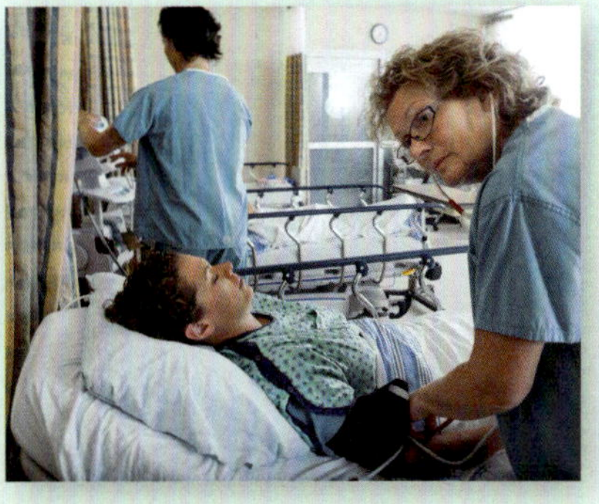

Melissa – a nurse

I often cry because I'm so exhausted. There are lots of nights I lie awake because the decisions I always have to make are going around my head. I'm in charge of a hospital ward and as a registered nurse I am responsible for everything. Sure, I can ask the doctors for advice, but they are overwhelmed by their operations. I get yelled at for asking questions and they tell me to stop calling so much and to try to manage on my own. Most of the time I am run off my feet. There is medication to give, vital checks to do, patients who've had operations, admissions and discharges all at once and of course lots of paperwork and doctors shouting orders at me. When I arrive I immediately start giving medication and monitoring vital signs.

I chart them and make sure I'm aware of any changes. But again and again I have to stop because I get calls from patients who need my help or doctors ask me to treat a patient. I'm constantly on the go, and there are still total care patients who haven't been turned in over 2 hours. I'm utterly ashamed of this. When we complain about the lack of trained staff they blame nurses for their poor time management skills. People have to pay a lot for their health insurance, so why can't we have enough nurses? They are pretty much the core of the health care system. I wanted to be a nurse to be able to comfort patients, hold their hands and explain everything to them without being under constant time pressure. It's high time things changed!

Working with the text

Mediation

A Translate the following sentences and expressions from the text into German. You may use a bilingual dictionary to help you.

1. "... getting out of bed is a real struggle for me." (l. 1 – 2)
2. "... I feel extremely disheartened." (l. 20)
3. "We are always overburdened with calls". (l. 22)
4. "... the decisions I always have to make are going around my head." (l. 4 – 5)
5. "Most of the time I am run off my feet." (l. 9 – 10)
6. "I'm utterly ashamed of this." (l. 16 – 17)
7. "They (= nurses) are pretty much the core of the health care system." (l. 19)

B Choose one of the care workers, either Sonja or Melissa and do the following tasks.

1. Look at the stress factors and go through the statements again. Find out what stress factors Melissa and Sonja have in their jobs. Give examples from the text.

<u>*Example:*</u>
Sonja has time pressure in her job because she very often says that ...
One example of time pressure in Sonja's job is that she ...
Time pressure is a stress factor at Melissa's workplace because she says / explains / reports that ...

2. How do Sonja and Melissa react to the stress they have every day? Find examples in the text.
3. How do clients and patients suffer when the care worker is under stress?
4. How do Sonja and Melissa feel about that?
5. How do they want to change their situation?

Interaction

Hands-on task

C What are the consequences of stress for the individual?

1. Use this question as the headline for a poster. Work in small groups and design the poster. Use a bilingual dictionary to help you.
2. Display your posters in class and compare them.

Look at page 134 for information on how to design posters.

Grammar box: Quantifiers – Mengenangaben

Nicht zählbar	Zählbar
*Sonja doesn't have **much** time.* = **viel**	*She doesn't have **many** breaks.* = **viele**
*There is **little** time to spend with a client.* = **wenig**	*There are **few** opportunities to have a break.* = **wenige**
*Sonja sometimes has **a little** time for herself.* = **ein wenig**	*There are **a few** people she really loves visiting.* = **einige**
***How much** time does she have?* = **wie viel**	***How many** calls does she have?* = **wie viele**

Steigerungsformen

much (viel)	– more (mehr)	– the most (der / die / das meiste)
little (wenig)	– less (weniger)	– the least (der / die / das wenigste)
many (viele)	– more (mehr)	– the most (am meisten)
few (wenige)	– fewer (weniger)	– the fewest (am wenigsten)

Beachte

In bejahten Aussagesätzen kann auch
a lot of, lots of, plenty (of), a great quantity of, a large quantity of, a great / good deal of (nur für much) und a large number (nur für many) eingesetzt werden
(z. B. She has got a lot of time / plenty / a great deal of time. There are a large number of people here.).

Practising grammar

A Fill in much or many.

1. There aren't … people who could be a good carer
2. It's not … fun changing a catheter.
3. How … children does Sonja have?
4. Very often she spends so … hours on the road that there isn't … time left to do the calls.
5. Sometimes she is too tired to write … in the record of care.
6. How … money does a home care worker earn?

B Little or few?

1. Sonja has very … time for her family.
2. She eats … food during the day – she doesn't have any time!
3. Very … men work as carers.
4. They pay too … money for that job.
5. A lot of elderly people drink … water
6. Mr Hollander eats a … bites of his sandwich before throwing it in the bin.

Mediation

C Translate the following expressions.

1. mehr Geld
2. am wenigsten Zeit
3. die meisten (Pflege)Besuche
4. mehr Urlaub
5. am wenigsten Ferien
6. die wenigsten Männer
7. weniger Hilfe
8. mehr Kunden / Klienten
9. weniger Freude

What are typical stress situations?	
(to) fire	entlassen
Home care – a typical morning shift	
schedule	Einsatzplan / Zeitplan
gloves	Handschuhe
apron	Schürze
bandage	Bandage, Verband
record of care	Pflegebericht
medication chart	Einnahmeplan / Medikamente-übersicht
night commode	Nachtstuhl (Toilettenstuhl)
(to) fasten	hier: zuknöpfen
button	Knopf
thrombosis stockings	Kompressions-strümpfe
slight	hier: leicht
memory loss	Gedächtnisverlust
(to) keep to schedule	den Einsatzplan / Zeitplan einhalten
(to) have a lie in	ausschlafen
painful	schmerzhaft
arthritis	Arthritis
(to) take frustration out on s. o.	Frustration an jmd. auslassen
(to) take s.th. person-ally	etw. persönlich nehmen
(to) change bandage	Verband wechseln
prescription	(ärztl.) Rezept
be available	hier: vorrätig sein
hot-box	Warmhaltebox
whilst (=while)	während
(to) keep sb. company	jmd. Gesellschaft leisten
stroke	hier: Schlaganfall
(to) swallow	schlucken
cancer	Krebs
terminal stage	Endstadium

Stress factors in care work	
stress factor	Stressfaktor, Stressverursacher
work overload	Arbeitsüberlastung
lack of	Mangel an
staff support	Unterstützung durch Mitarbeiter
people problems	persönliche Probleme
work management	Arbeitsorganisation
time pressure	Zeitdruck
emotional stress	emotionaler Stress
concern for	Sorge um
(to) deal with death	mit dem Tod umgehen
physical strain	körperliche Anstrengung
(to) lift out of bed	aus dem Bett heben
Two care workers speak	
refreshed	erfrischt, hier: erholt
(to) stick to schedule	den Einsatzplan / Zeitplan einhalten
(to) be behind schedule	hinter dem Zeitplan zurück sein / liegen
(to) feel guilty	ein schlechtes Gewissen haben
timekeeping	Einhalten / Einhaltung der Zeit
(to) refuse	(sich) weigern
catheter bag	Katheterbeutel / Urinbeutel
overburdened	überlastet
be overwhelmed	überfordert sein
hospital ward	Krankenhausstation
(to) yell at	anschreien
admission	(Krankenhaus-) Aufnahme
discharge	(Krankenhaus-) Entlassung
paperwork	Papier- / Büroarbeit
orders	hier: ärztliche Anweisung
(to) treat a patient	Einen Patienten behandeln
time management skills	Zeiteinteilung Fähigkeiten

Die Aussprache der blauen Vokabeln finden Sie in den Audio-Dateien DA0901055

Unit 6 Keeping fit and healthy

1

2

3

4

5

6

7

8

9

Talk about the pictures

Production

- What healthy habits do the pictures show?
- What unhealthy habits do the pictures show?
- Explain why these habits are healthy or unhealthy.

Work in pairs and discuss healthy and unhealthy habits.
What should or shouldn't you do to stay fit and healthy?
Make a list of "dos" and "don'ts" and present your list in class.

This is how your list may look:

Dos	Don'ts
Examples: **Go** for a walk every day. **Choose to** go for a walk **instead of** sitting in front of the TV. …	Examples: **Don't sit** in front of TV all day. **Avoid sitting** in front of TV all day. …

How to keep fit and healthy

Staying fit and healthy is surely something everyone wants. We all know how important health is. Here are some basic rules to stay fit and healthy.

1. **Eat healthy food and keep your weight under control.**
   Being overweight increases the risk for diseases like diabetes, high blood pressure, certain cancers and heart disease. Therefore, it's important to eat healthy food. Eat a lot of vegetables and fruit and avoid eating fatty food. Say no to fast food. It's full of fat and will only make you put on weight. Also watch the amount of sugar in the food you eat. Not eating too much sugar is also important to maintain good health.
2. **Exercise regularly.**

   You need to exercise twice a week. Go to the gym, go jogging or play ball games with your friends. All these kinds of activities can make you fitter. But even if you don't have any time to exercise, try to move as much as you can. For example, go by foot instead of taking the car, go for a walk or do some gardening. Even small, everyday changes can improve your strength and fitness.
3. **Don't smoke.**

   Smoking kills. That's a fact, so just don't start. If you already smoke, stop. Even smoking a few cigarettes a day affects your health. It affects your heart and can also cause cancer, particularly lung cancer.
4. **Don't take drugs.**
   Even legal drugs are unhealthy. For example, drinking too much alcohol damages your liver. Only drink alcohol in moderation.
5. **Reduce stress.**

   Some stress can be positive, but too much stress is bad for your health. It makes you feel nervous and causes sleep problems. It is also responsible for headaches, stomach pains and not being able to concentrate. Stress also weakens your immune system. It is very important to relax regularly. Try to do something which you like and which can take off your mind from work and worries. How about taking a long, hot bath; listening to music; reading a book; meeting friends; laughing, or doing yoga. All these activities are good stress busters.
6. **Be clean & hygienic.**

   Good hygiene is not only important in times of high infection like in winter. Wash your hands regularly and free your body from bacteria by taking a bath or shower regularly, wearing clean clothes and keeping your teeth clean and healthy.

If you follow these six rules, you will have a long and healthy life!

Working with the text

A These sentences give you bad advice. Look at the fitness rules again and correct the sentences to give good advice.

1. Diabetes, low blood pressure and even cancer can be the consequences of eating unhealthy food.
2. Eating fast food makes you lose weight.
3. Eat fatty and sugary food to stay fit and healthy.
4. Improve your health and start smoking.
5. Drinking supports your liver function.
6. Stress stabilises your immune system.
7. Yoga is a good activity to cause stress.
8. Only wash your hands once a week.

B The end of each sentence is missing. Look at the fitness rules and add reasons for each piece of advice.

1. It's important to keep your weight under control because …
2. You should do some kind of sport regularly because …
3. Smoking kills because …
4. Drink alcohol in moderation or not at all be-cause …
5. Too much stress is unhealthy because …
6. Wash your hands regularly because …

Working with language

A Find words in the text which fit the following definitions.

1. Something in your body which helps you to fight against infections.
2. Keeping clean in order to stay healthy.
3. A word for tomato, bean, potato, onion etc.
4. A word for apple, banana, orange, cherry etc.
5. When these attack your body you can become ill.
6. Not going by car, bus or bike.
7. Stop doing something, give up a bad habit.
8. Only taking small bites or only drinking a drop.

B Fill in the noun or adjective.

noun	adjective	
health	**healthy**	I think my **1.** … is good because I only eat **2.** … food.
dentist	**dental**	I have healthy teeth because I brush my teeth after every meal. I always take great care in **3.** … hygiene and I see my **4.** … once a year.
immune system	**immune**	These days, there are a lot of infections and it's not easy to stay **5.** … against all the bacteria. You have to do a lot to keep your **6.** … stable and stay **7.** … against aggressive infections.
infection	**infectious**	Last year there was a bad cold going around. This was a real serious **8.** … Almost everyone in my family was ill. And I thought I had got away without an **9.** …, but then I got it, too. You can't avoid such an **10.** … illness if everyone around you is ill.
hygiene	**hygienic**	I work in a kitchen where **11.** … is really important. But after a while, the **12.** … handling of food becomes a routine.

People talk about their living habits

Stephen, aged 24

Well, I will never be really sporty, but I go to the gym now and then. Ok, I only go when I notice that I have put on weight. Then I start working out again until I get lazy and start staying at home again. I know myself! I weigh myself and try to keep my weight under control. I don't eat fast food. Well, only sometimes. Once a month or every two months, I go out with some of my friends and we eat pizza or hamburgers and chips. I eat a lot of fruit and I cook a fresh dinner almost every day. I am not really good at avoiding sweets. I have a lot of stress at work and to stay calm I eat chocolate. Sometimes a bar a day. I shouldn't, I know. I always tell myself that in future I won't do that again but I do.

Maria, aged 82

I don't do any kind of exercise. Until I was 70 I went to the swimming pool with one of my friends once a week and I did gardening. But then I had a stroke, now it's much better but I did not recover fully and I had to give up my house and garden. Today I live in a small flat. I try to do some of my housework alone and I won't give up this habit. It keeps me active. But I also have a cleaning lady to help me. I rarely cook anything fresh. Most often I eat sandwiches or yoghurt and some cake. Maybe I will order meals on wheels in some months or next year. One of my grandchildren does the shopping for me. I rarely leave my flat or go for a walk because I soon get out of breath. I like sitting on my balcony and reading a magazine. If I can't, I watch TV. But I will try to be more active in the future.

Sandra, 17

Yes, I know I am a bit overweight. I tried to do some jogging but I soon gave up. In school we have PE* once a week and this is enough for me. My Mom wants us to eat healthily. She cooks a fresh dinner and she buys a lot of fruit and vegetables. At home, sweets are not allowed but when I go out with my friends we often eat some. We also often go to a fast food restaurant. I don't eat hamburgers or chips very often but I like to drink a chocolate milkshake. At parties and when I am with my friends I smoke, but not at home. All of my friends do this. At weekends we drink some alcohol, sometimes I get drunk. My parents will be angry if they see me drunk. It's difficult to control how much you drink when you're with your mates. If someone brings a bottle of alcohol, it is passed around and everyone takes a mouthful.

*PE – physical education – Sportunterricht

Working with the text

A All these statements are wrong. Give the correct answer.

1. Stephen regularly does a lot of sports.
2. He prefers eating ready meals or fast food.
3. None of the food he eats contains any vitamins.
4. Maria still loves swimming to keep fit.
5. She cooks a fresh dinner every day.
6. Sandra keeps her weight under control by jogging.
7. She also avoids eating sweets.
8. She never drinks or smokes.

B Now work on the following tasks.

1. Highlight the healthy habits Stephen, Maria and Sandra have.
2. How do these habits keep them healthy? Give reasons.
3. What unhealthy habits do they have?
4. Explain why these habits are unhealthy.

Hands-on task

Interaction

A Imagine you are a fitness trainer. Stephen, Maria and Sandra come to you because they want to change their lifestyles to get fit and healthy.

1. Work in small groups and pick one person. Work out a "healthy living plan" for this person. How can this person change his or her lifestyle? What can this person do or eat in order to become and stay fit and healthy?
2. Present your "healthy living plan" in class.

Production

B How do you try to stay fit and healthy? Write a statement of about 100 words and read it out in class.

Reception

C First listen to what Robert (aged 90)**, Mark** (aged 38) **and Andrea** (aged 32) **tell you about their life.**

stop eating meat
ride a bike to train coordination
do kite surfing
do crosswords
go climbing
quit smoking

train muscles
join a yoga and stretching group
read a daily newspaper
drink one glass of wine
jog regularly
eat a lot of fruit

1. After listening say who keeps to the activities listed above.
2. Listen to the recording once again and say what else Robert, Mark and Andrea do to keep fit and healthy.

Grammar box: Zukunft – Future: will-future

Bildung

will + Verb im Infinitiv

He will regret making that decision.

Abkürzung

He'll regret that.

(ebenso: I'll, you'll, she'll, it'll, we'll, they'll)

Verneinung:

It's started snowing, I will not go jogging.

Abkürzung

It's started snowing, I won't go jogging.

Fragebildung

Will the exam be hard?

Frage mit Fragewort

When will I meet Mr Right?

über ein zukünftiges Geschehen zu äußern, auf das man keinen Einfluss nehmen kann.

You look very pale.

Wait a minute, I will get you a class of water.

→ um einen Entschluss zum Ausdruck zu bringen, der im Moment des Sprechens spontan gefasst wird.

I think Stephen will have no time for a holiday, because he's too busy.

→ um eine Vermutung zu äußern.

Signalwörter

next …,
the following …,
in 2020,
in the future …,
tomorrow,
in 4 days …,
in 3 weeks …

Vorsicht vor einer typischen Fehlerquelle !!!

I will = Ich werde,

aber

I want = Ich will !!!

Falsch	Richtig
I think this party is boring. I will go home.	I think this party is boring. I want to go home.
In future I will work as a care assistant.	In future I want to work as a care assistant.
I avoid eating chocolate because I will not put on weight.	I avoid eating chocolate because I don't want to put on weight.

Practising grammar

A Stephen, Maria and Sandra have decided to make some changes.
What do you think will happen as a result?
Make sentences using the will-future.

Example:

1. *Stephen has decided to stop eating pizza. He – become - healthy*
   Stephen has decided to stop eating pizza. He will become healthier.
2. Stephen has decided to work out twice a week.
   He – become – strong
3. Maria has decided to join a senior citizens' exercise group instead of sitting in front of the TV.
   She – meet – new people
4. Sandra has decided not to drink any fatty or sugary drinks like chocolate milkshakes.
   She – lose – weight
5. Sandra has decided not to touch alcohol again. Instead – she – drink mineral water

B If you want to live a healthy lifestyle, you need to make the right decisions.
However, it can be difficult to make the right decision all the time.
Stephen, Maria and Sandra are all in difficult situations.
They wanted to do the right thing, but spontaneously make the wrong decision.
Write what they decide, using 'will'.

Example:

1. *Stephen wanted to eat a salad, but the pizzas look delicious.*
   "I – eat – a large Meat Feast pizza – instead"

"I will eat a Meat Feast pizza instead."

2. Sandra didn't want to drink any alcohol tonight, but a friend has bought her favourite vodka.
   "I – only – have – a mouthful"
3. Maria wanted to go to her exercise group, but her favourite programme has just started.
   "I – stay – here"
4. Stephen wanted to go to the gym, but he's enjoying his playstation game too much.
   "I – play – one more game"

C Form questions with will.

Example:

1. *Stephen - go jogging - regularly?*
   Will Stephen go jogging regularly?
2. Maria – join a senior citizens' exercise group?
3. Sandra – stop drinking alcohol?
4. Stephen- work out twice a week?
5. All three – keep to their new habits to stay fit and healthy?

D What do you think?
Write your predictions for all the questions in C.

Example:

1. *Will Stephen go jogging regularly?*
   No, he won't. He'll play his playstation instead.

Talk about the pictures

(to) avoid (+ing-Form)	vermeiden

How to keep fit and healthy

health	Gesundheit
weight	Gewicht
overweight	übergewichtig
(to) increase	zunehmen
diabetes	Diabetes, Zuckererkrankung
blood pressure	Blutdruck
(heart) disease	(Herz-)Erkrankung
amount	Menge
(to) maintain health	die Gesundheit erhalten
(to) exercise	hier: sich bewegen, trainieren
twice	zweimal
(to) improve	verbessern
(to) affect	beeinflussen
(to) cause	verursachen
lung cancer	Lungenkrebs
drugs	Drogen
(to) damage	zerstören
liver	Leber
in moderation	in Maßen
(to) reduce	reduzieren
responsible	verantwortlich
headache	Kopfschmerzen
stomach pain	Magenschmerzen
(to) weaken	schwächen
immune system	Immunsystem, Körperabwehr
(to) relax	sich entspannten
(to) take your mind off sth	auf andere Gedanken bringen
stress busters	Stresskiller
hygiene	Hygiene
infection	Infektion, Ansteckungserkrankung
bacteria	Bakterien
dental	adj. Zahn-…, zahnmedizinisch
infectious	ansteckend, infektiös

People talk about their living habits

habits	Gewohnheiten
sporty	sportlich
(to) put on weight	zunehmen, Gewicht zulegen
stroke	Schlaganfall
(to) recover	genesen, sich erholen / regenerieren
meals on wheels	Essen auf Rädern
out of breath	außer Puste / Atem
(to) pass around	(herum-)reichen
(to) take a mouthful	einen Schluck nehmen
(to) prefer	bevorzugen
(to) be interested in	sich interessieren für

Die Aussprache der blauen Vokabeln finden Sie in den Audio-Dateien DA0901055

Unit 7 Caring for the elderly

Look at the cartoon first, then work on the following tasks

A Describe what you can see in the picture. How does the person change with advancing age? Look at the word box below which may give you some vocabulary help.

body changes like … / appear
lose strength / energy / physical strength
become unsteady / slower / less flexible
need the help / support of …
not be able to walk / stand upright …

B Do you still have your grandparents or do you know other elderly people? Describe your experience with old people.
Look at the following questions which can help you to gather your ideas.

1. Have you noticed other changes than those shown in the picture?
2. Do these elderly people lead a different kind of life to yours?
3. Do they need help because of their age? What kind of help?

How does being old feel?

Matilda Freemaker trains young people who want to work with the elderly. At the beginning of the training course she asks the students to wear an age suit in typical daily situations. The suit has weights which make the students' bodies change into that of someone of 75 or older. Splints restrict the movement of joints such as hands, elbows, neck, upper and lower torso, knees and ankles. The suit simulates the loss of mobility. A pair of glasses blurs the vision and ear muffs make the wearer nearly deaf. When wearing the suit, the wearer can feel the body changes and restrictions of advancing age.

Matilda: "When we ask our new students what old age means, most often they mention memory problems and list the obvious body changes like wrinkles, grey hair, hardness of hearing and the need to reach for reading glasses. But these are symptoms which you see on the surface. What is going on underneath, how does it really feel to be old? With the suit young people can discover the restrictions of old age. Those students who have worn the age suit have a much better understanding of what it is like to be old and what help the elderly need".

Two students report on their experience.

Sandra: "I will never forget the day I wore the age suit. When I put it on and felt the back splint I first thought that being old is just painful and unbearable. I went out food shopping. I went into a supermarket and felt helpless. I could see the shelves but not what was on them. My legs and hands were so stiff. It was not easy for me to reach for the products. I could only see the red price tag but I wasn't able to read it. In the chiller cabinet I could identify a carton of milk but not make out whether it really was semi-skimmed. Very soon I started getting tired and the weight was squeezing my stomach, I felt like I needed to go to the toilet all the time. The next problem turned up at the checkout. My fingers were too clumsy to take the money out of my purse and I couldn't see how much I already had in my hand. The people behind me got impatient. Today I feel ashamed at my own impatience with my grandmother. I will never again tell her, "Hurry up, grandma, we haven't got all day!"

Marvin: "I already broke into a sweat when I tried to put on my shoes. Bending took so much effort! Unsteady on my feet, I nearly toppled over. I felt dizzy. Stepping out of the door, the first problem arose. I could hardly see the lock and find the right key. My hand and fingers weren't flexible. It took ages to close the door. Going down the stairs without falling was a great challenge. I only managed it by moving one foot at a time. Out in the street people looked like shadowy figures suddenly coming up half a meter in front of me. I felt isolated and totally disoriented in the crowd."

Working with the text

A Answer the following questions on the text.

1. What is the age suit and how does it work?
2. Why does Matilda Freemaker want her new students to wear the age suit?
3. What typical age-related problems did Sandra have at the supermarket?
4. Explain why she feels ashamed after her own experience with the age suit.
5. What were Marvin's problems when getting ready to go out?
6. Why was it difficult to close the door?
7. Looking at Marvin's experience out in the street, what problems could elderly people have in a crowd?

Interaction

B After the students' experience with the age suit, Matilda Freemaker presents the poster below to sum up the typical issues of advancing age. Most of the entries are missing. Work in pairs, go through the text once again and complete the poster.

less skin elasticity
– …(?)

blurred vision
– problems with …(?)
– need for …(?)
– …(?)

hardness of hearing
– need for hearing aid
– …(?)

skeletal problems
– brittle bones
– osteoporosis
– …(?)

muscle wastage
– less power
– …(?)

reduced organ capacity
– slower circulation
– slower healing, bruises and pressure sores
– …(?)

weak immune system
– poor health
– …(?)

lower sensory perception
– decrease of taste and thirst
– less sensitivity in finger tips
– …(?)

mental problems
– …(?)

other signs of old age
– …(?)

C Sit in small groups and think of typical everyday situations which could be a problem for elderly people. Interaction

1. List them and …
2. say why you believe them to be difficult.
3. think of what help elderly people need to master these problems

D Here are the pictures of some gadgets which help older people master their daily life alone.

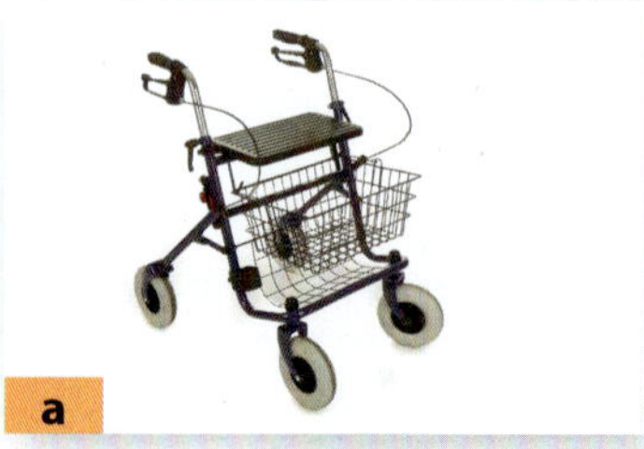
a

b

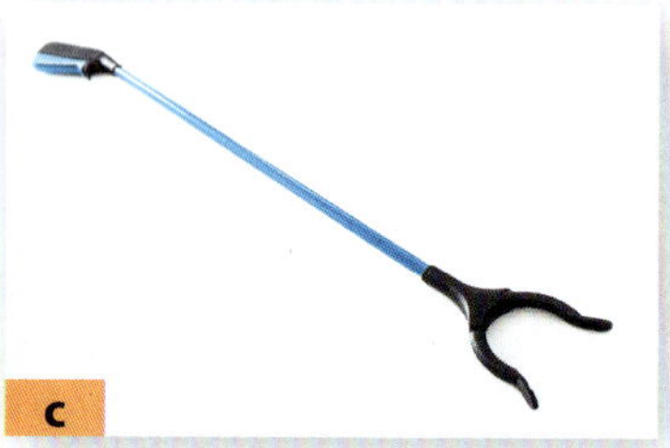
c

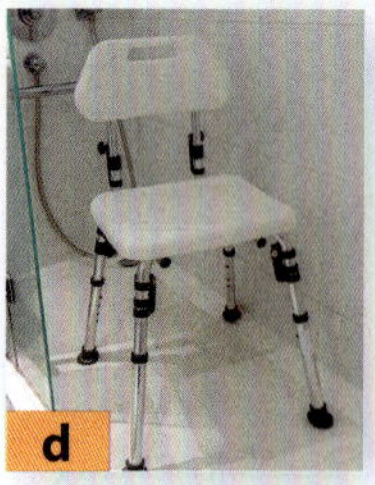
d

e

f

1. Say what gadget you can see in each picture.

large button phone – reacher – walker – stair lift – magnifying glasses – shower chair

2. Explain in what situations and how older people can use these gadgets.
   Look at the vocabulary box for help.

reach for objects	avoid falling over	stay mobile
have support	still do hobbies like …	overcome distances / obstacles like
use without reading glasses	transport sth.	be able to do sth. while so. is sitting / lying in bed …
store sth.	keep sitting	
contact so. for help / in emergencies	take a rest	

be a help for those who cannot … remember sth. / walk freely / bend down / carry loads

Listening Reception

7 **Listen to Joanna, Ronny, Sybil and Brian.**
Say what problem they have and what gadget they could make use of to overcome these problems.

Grammar box: **Simple Past** – Einfache Vergangenheit

- Das Simple Past beschreibt Vorgänge oder Handlungen, die in der Vergangenheit angefangen und ebenso in der Vergangenheit abgeschlossen wurden. Aus diesem Grund wird das Simple Past in Berichten von vergangenen Ereignissen, Arbeitsberichten, Biografien, sowie Pflegebiografien eingesetzt.
- Signalwörter: *yesterday, (one year) ago, in 2002, the other day, the day before yesterday, last (week), in those days, in the past*

Aussagen

Regelmäßige Verben: 1. Verbform (Infinitiv) *+ed*

like → liked

Ausnahmen

Bei Verben, die nach einem Konsonanten auf –y enden, ändert sich die Endung zu -i

copy → copied

Bei Verben, die auf einem betonten -er, -ir oder -ur enden, wird das -r verdoppelt

prefer → preferred

Nach kurzem, betontem Vokal (bei a, e, i, o, u) wird der Endkonsonant verdoppelt

stop → stopped

Unregelmäßige Verben: 2. Verbform (Past Tense)

go → went

fall → fell

break → broke

Ausnahme

"To be" hat zwei Vergangenheitsformen: *was* und *were*

I	***was***	*We*	***were***
You	***were***	*You*	***were***
He, she, it	***was***	*They*	***were***

Verneinungen

Hilfsverben werden direkt verneint

was	→	*wasn't*
were	→	*weren't*
could	→	*couldn't*
did	→	*didn't*
had	→	*didn't have*

Vollverben werden mit *didn't/did not* verneint

liked	→	*didn't like*
copied	→	*didn't copy*
preferred	→	*didn't prefer*
went	→	*didn't go*
fell	→	*didn't fall*
broke	→	*didn't break*

Practising Grammar

A Fill in the Simple Past of the auxiliary verbs be, have, and can.

Kathleen **1.** (be) 81 years old when her husband died. She **2.** (not be) able to care for herself alone and all of her children **3.** (be) far away from her. Going into an old people's home **4.** (be) the only way for her to manage her daily life. Kathleen **5.** (have) sad feelings giving up her flat and she **6.** (not be) happy about leaving her old home.

The first days in her new home **7.** (not be) pleasant for her because she **8.** (not can) forget about her old home and husband. But in St Raphael's nursing home all the residents **9.** (be) very friendly. Their lives and care stories **10.** (be) much the same and they all **11.** (have) the same problems. Kathleen's room **12.** (not be) too small and she **13.** (can) bring her favourite furniture with her and all those things which **14.** (be) very dear to her.

At first, it **15.** (not be) easy for Kathleen to get used to her new situation. But now she has been in St Raphael's for four years and she says, "After my first year I already **16.** (have) very dear friends like a family. My decision to come here **17.** (be) right."

B This is Kathleen's biography and health care story.
Fill in the Simple Past.
There is a list of irregular verbs on page 142.

Kathleen **1.** (grow) up with two younger brothers and one elder sister on a farm near Southampton. After school Kathleen **2.** (do) job training as a shop assistant in a grocery shop but she only **3.** (work) in that job for two years. At the age of 19 she **4.** (return) to her parents' farm and she **5.** (live) there until she **6.** (get) married.

She **7.** (marry) her husband John when she **8.** (be) 22 years old. One year later her daughter Ada **9.** (be) born. Kathleen **10.** (give) birth to a son, Malcom, two years later. Her husband Henry **11.** (work) as an electrician and Kathleen **12.** (stay) at home to look after the children and household. They **13.** (buy) a large flat in the city centre. Here Kathleen **14.** (live) with her children and husband and later alone until she **15.** (move) into St Raphael's nursing home.

Shortly after Kathleen's 80th birthday doctors **16.** (tell) her husband that he **17.** (have) lung cancer. Kathleen **18.** (care) for her husband until his death. First she **19.** (keep) up her own household. But one morning she **20.** (fall) in her bathroom and **21.** (fracture) her thigh bone. She **22.** (be) in hospital for four weeks but **23.** (not recover) fully. When she **24.** (leave) hospital she **25.** (sit) in a wheelchair and **26.** (go) into St Raphael's home for short-term care. After eight weeks she **27.** (return) home only being able to walk for short distances with a walker.

Back home she soon **28.** (see) that she **29.** (not be) able to care for herself. She **30.** (be) too weak to do household work. She **31.** (have) balance problems, very often she even **32.** (cannot manage) her personal hygiene. She **33.** (forget) to take her medicine and her health **34.** (become) worse.

Although she **35.** (feel) sad about giving up her flat she **36.** (go) into St Raphael's nursing home for long-term care aged 82.

Writing a nursing care plan for Michael Miller, aged 85

After a stroke which made independent living impossible, Michael Miller moved into an assisted living apartment at St Mary's Senior Residences. Michael, his daughter Sarah and care worker Ronda are discussing what care Michael needs and how it will be provided.

Ronda Good morning Mr Miller. How do you like your new apartment?

Michael (Michael searches for his words. He mumbles.) Fine, fine, just fine!

Sarah Well, I guess he still misses his old surroundings.

Ronda Of course, everyone does that at first. (Turning to Michael) Mr Miller, the apartment is barrier-free and we are going to ensure that you receive the help you need. I'm here to create your nursing plan.

Michael Okay, can you speak a bit slower, please?

Ronda Yes, certainly. Mr Miller have you already used a care service?

Saran (Michael looks at his daughter. She answers for him.) Yes, there was a care service who took over the medication management because he forgot to take his medicine. He also had meals on wheels.

Ronda Okay. We already have his medication plan and his medicine. Mr Miller, do you want to join us all meal times?

Michael Oh, no, can't you bring me my dinner?

Ronda Well, yes we can do that. But maybe you should try to come into our dining room and eat with the others? It's a great opportunity to make new friends and it keeps you active.

Michael I'd rather stay here in my apartment.

Sarah Well, after the stroke his left arm feels numb. Sometimes he has some coordination problems or he doesn't speak clearly and understand others. I think this is why he is asking to have his dinner here.

Ronda Mr Miller, I can fetch you for the first dinners. Later, you can go with one of your neighbours. What do you think?

Michael Okay, but I would like to make my own breakfast and supper.

Sarah He likes to sleep in, and in the evening sit in front of the TV and eat.

Ronda Okay. But I first have to make sure you're ok. Very often, stroke patients have problems swallowing food. What about getting ready for the day and night?

Michael That's no problem.

Sarah The stroke weakened his muscles but he manages to get dressed. I think taking a shower and washing his hair on his own will be difficult.

Ronda Okay, we can help with that. What about three times a week?

Sarah Yes, that's perfect. There is one more thing I'm worried about. Last month he fell and I found him lying on the floor. He was dehydrated and had some memory loss.

Ronda Don't worry. We have monitoring 24 hours a day. Mr Miller, there is an alarm button on your telephone and this pendant is connected to the wireless emergency system. You should always wear it around your wrist or neck. Press this button to send us a signal whenever you need help. (Hands it over to him). Remember, you're safe here because we're always at your side.

Michael: We will be good friends, won't we?

Ronda: Sure, we will. Mr Miller. What about cleaning your apartment?

Michael: I can still do that.

Sarah: Yes, he dusts every morning and I help him keep the flat tidy. I also do the shopping for him.

Ronda: What about doctor's appointments? As a stroke patient he should see a neurologist regularly.

Sarah: That's a problem because I'm working full-time.

Ronda: Oh, I can arrange transportation to doctor's appointments for him and we have a doctor who visits our residents at least once a month. Ok, finally I have our activities calendar for you. (Hands it over). I would love to see you at one of our activities.

Michael: What kind of activities?

Ronda: Well, you can take part in all kinds of daily social events like singing, doing handcrafts, painting or chair exercises. There are outings and yearly events like a New Year's party. Our residents often meet to talk or play games. There are also activities like our language and memory exercises which I advise you to take part in.

Working with language

A Find words in the text which fit the following definitions.

1. A plan which organizes the care and help someone needs.
2. Not having any obstacles, e.g. senior apartments are … which means that everything is at ground level.
3. Dinners which are brought into your house or apartment from a dinner service.
4. Not able to feel
5. Lack of liquid. Sometimes older people are … because they forget to drink.
6. Sometimes people, especially older people with dementia, forget about things and suffer from this.

Working with the text

B Complete the following sentences.

1. Michael's daughter thinks that her father is not really feeling at home in his new apartment because …
2. Michael has already used a care service for medication management because …
3. Sarah thinks her father wants to have his dinner in his apartment because …
4. Michael wants to make his own breakfast and supper because …
5. Ronda wants to watch Michael eating because …
6. Sarah is worried about her father being alone because …
7. With the wireless emergency system Michael will be safe because …
8. Ronda wants Michael to take part in the language and memory exercises because …

C It's always difficult to say whether an elderly person can still live alone or should go into long-term care in a nursing home. Do you think Michael Miller's health is still good enough to live alone in an assisted living apartment?

1. Make a list of reasons for and against living alone.
2. Compare this list with your partner and make a decision. Tell your class about it.

D Look at the nursing plan Ronda wrote for Michael. Some of the crosses and individual entries are missing. Read through the text again and fill them in.

Nursing Care Plan			
patient:	*Mr Michael Miller*	**day of birth:**	*April, 4th, 19…*
assessed by:	*Ronda Jennings*	**date:**	*August, 19th, 20…*

Medical Condition

Patient shows
( ) medical symptoms of aging, such as … (?) ____________
(x) other: *stroke patient*
(x) symptoms: *language problems, short memory loss, numb feeling in …* **(?)** ____________

Care Plan Outline

Tick those that apply.	***Fill in individual nursing interventions.***
Medication Plan Patient ( ) organises medicine intake alone ( ) needs medical management ( ) needs regular transport to doctor's appointments	*– medicine supply in the morning and evening according to doctor's medication,* *– regular transport to … (?)*
Personal Hygiene Plan Patient ( ) can perform personal hygiene ( ) shows self-care deficits because of ( ) loss of mobility, ( ) lack of motivation Help will be provides with ( ) bodily hygiene, ( ) oral hygiene, ( ) washing hair, ( ) brushing hair, ( ) dressing / undressing, ( ) bathing / showering	*– at first contact no signs of untidiness* *– Mr M. wants help with … (?), (?) times a week* *– Mr M's bodily hygiene should be monitored to make sure what help he really needs* *– possible application of body lotion to prevent dry skin after showering*
Eating Plan Patient ( ) takes dinner service ( ) can eat alone ( ) needs to be fed	*– Mr Miller is going to take part in … (?) but … (?)*
Housing Plan Patient needs cleaning service / home service like shopping etc. ( ) Yes ( ) No	*– Mr Miller … (?), his daughter … (?)*
Exercise Plan Patient takes part in activities offered ( ) Yes ( ) No	*– as a stroke patient Mr M. should … (?)*

E In the next staff meeting, Ronda reports to her colleagues about Mr Miller and the nursing plan she has written for him. Look at page 135 for help on how to summarise and write up a nursing history. Take down Mr Miller's nursing history. Production

Hands-on task

F Work in small groups and discuss Kathleen's biography (page 62). Write down a nursing plan for her. Present it in class. Interaction

Look at the cartoon first …	
physical strength	körperliche Stärke
unsteady	unsicher (körperlich)
the elderly	alte Menschen
How does being old feel?	
age suit	Anzug, der das Alter simuliert
splint	Schiene
(to) restrict	begrenzen
joints	Gelenke
torso	Oberkörper
(to) simulate	nachahmen, simulieren
simulation	Nachahmung, Simulation
loss (of)	Verlust
blur	Unschärfe
vision	hier: Sehvermögen
ear muffs	Ohrenschützer
wearer	Träger, die tragende Person
deaf	taub (Hörvermögen)
restriction	Begrenzung
advancing	fortschreitend
wrinkles	Falten
hardness of hearing	Schwerhörigkeit
reading glasses	Lesebrille
painful	schmerzhaft
unbearable	unerträglich
stiff	steif
(to) reach for	greifen nach
chiller cabinet	Kühlregal
(to) identify	hier: erkennen
(to) squeeze	hier: drücken
stomach	Magen
clumsy	ungeschickt
(to) feel ashamed	sich schämen
(to) break into a sweat	in Schweiß ausbrechen
(to) bend	bücken, vorbeugen
(to) topple over	umfallen
dizzy	schwindelig
isolated	isoliert, ausgeschlossen
disoriented	desorientiert
elasticity	Spannkraft
hearing aid	Hörgerät
organ capacity	Organleistung
bruise	blauer Fleck
pressure sore	Druckgeschwür
sensory perception	Sinneswahrnehmung

decrease	Abnahme
sensitivity	Sensibilität, Feingefühl
reacher	Greifstock
walker	Rollator
stairlift	Treppenlift
magnifying glass	Vergrößerungsglas
shower chair	Duschstuhl
store	speichern, verstauen
(to) overcome obstacles	Hindernisse überwinden
barrier- free	barrierefrei
(to) fracture the thigh bone	den Oberschenkelhals brechen
short-term care	Kurzzeitpflege
long-term care	Voll- / Langezeitpflege
Writing a nursing care plan …	**Pflegeplanung**
independent living	alleine leben / wohnen
assisted living	Betreutes Wohnen
(to) provide so. with	jmd. versorgen mit
(to) mumble	murmeln, nuscheln
surroundings	Umgebung
(to) ensure	sicherstellen
medication management	Medikamentenversorgung
medication plan	Medikamentenverschreibung
numb	taub (im Gefühl)
stroke patient	Schlaganfallpatient
(to) swallow	schlucken
(to) weaken	schwächen
dehydration	Austrocknung
memory loss	Gedächtnisverlust
(to) monitor	überwachen
monitoring	Überwachung
pendant	Anhänger
wireless emergency system	drahtloses Notrufsystem
(to) dust	staubwischen
transport	hier: Krankentransport
language exercise	Sprachtraining
memory exercise	Gedächtnistraining
assessed by	hier: festgestellt von
(to) tick	ankreuzen, abhaken
nursing intervention	Pflegemaßnahme
medicine intake	Medikamentenaufnahme
supply	Versorgung
(to) perform	hier: ausführen
self-care deficits	Mängel in der persönlichen Pflege / Körperpflege

Die Aussprache der blauen Vokabeln finden Sie in den Audio-Dateien DA0901055

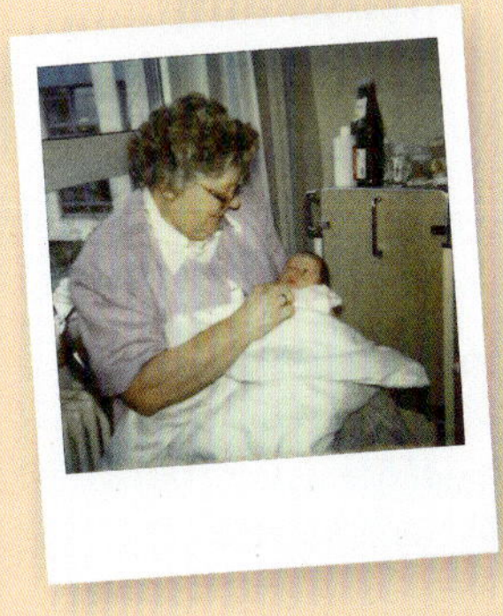

Looking at a life story

A Look at the photos.

1. Describe what you can see. What events might they have been taken at?
2. Do you have a family album? What family events do those photos show?
3. Do you like taking photos? When and why?

B Work in pairs and discuss the questions below. Then present your results to the class.

1. What kind of important events does a person have in his / her life?
2. Why is it important for care assistants and nurses to know about a person's life? Give examples.

Betty Brown's life story

Reception

A Listen to Betty Brown's life story and decide which of the following sentence endings fits to her story.
Before you start listening have a look at the vocabulary list to make sure you understand her story.

1. Betty Brown was born … *o before the Second World War* *o after the Second World War* *o during the Second World War*	***2. Talking about her family, she says that …*** *o she was an only child* *o she had three brothers and two sisters* *o she had three sisters and two brothers*
3. Talking about her brothers, you learn that … *o her brothers were younger than her* *o two of them were younger than her and one older* *o two of them were older and one was younger than her*	***4. Betty's sisters …*** *o are younger than her and they are still living* *o are older than her and they are still living* *o were older than her and they are dead*
5. Her parents had … *o a grocer's shop* *o a restaurant* *o a farm*	***6. All the males of her family had to go to war and Betty lost …*** *o her father and brothers in the war* *o her elder brothers; only her favourite brother Michael survived* *o all her brothers. However, her father survived.*
7. After the war … *o her father was a successful farmer* *o her parents had a grocer's shop* *o her father became a drinker and lost the farm*	***8. Betty then …*** *o did vocational training as a grocer* *o worked in a grocer's shop* *o stayed at home and helped her mother with the household*
9. When she married her husband, Joseph … *o her mother and sisters were at the wedding* *o only her sisters were at the wedding* *o none of her family were present*	***10. Betty and her husband had …*** *o just a daughter – Sybil* *o two daughters Kathy and Linda* *o three daughters Sybil, Kathy and Linda*

B Answer the following questions on Betty's life story.

1. Look back at Betty's photos and try to say who and what event in Betty's life they show.
2. Every life has its ups and downs. Looking at Betty's life story, can you say what her ups and downs have been?
3. What role did her younger brother Michael play in her life?
4. How did her father change after he came back from the war? What were the consequences for Betty, her mother and her sisters?
5. Describe how Betty's and her family's living standard changed.
6. How does Betty live and spend her time today?

Why do we need to do biographical work?

Every week, there is a long staff meeting at St Mary's Senior Residences. Every member of staff is present to discuss their cases. Today, they are talking about their new resident Michael Miller. This is the first staff meeting for Tom, who is a trainee.

Ronda Okay, we have a new resident Mr Miller. I have already prepared his care plan.

Barbara What do we know about his background?

Ronda Not much so far. He is 85 years old. His wife died of cancer three years ago and he has a daughter.

Barbara That's not enough. We need to do some biographical work with him.

Tom Biographical work? I thought we were only responsible for his medical care.

Ronda Good medical care also means knowing about your patient's life, significant life events, where they worked, their family, their interests, hobbies, likes and dislikes. Some of our patients are from the war generation. They were young children when war broke out and had to cope with dramatic situations which have had an influence on their lives. It's also useful to know where a person worked and what as. Mr Harris, for example, worked as a baker and he still gets up at four in the morning. Knowing our residents' backgrounds really helps us to understand the people we care for.

Tom How do we find out this stuff?

Barbara Well, mainly it involves listening to your patient and understanding how their background has shaped the person they are today.

Tom Okay, so it's just showing them that someone is listening to them.

Ronda Oh, no, it's much more, we not only listen but also record main aspects of their life and work with the information we get. We work with a special questionnaire and develop an individual biography for each patient.

Tom But what about those who have dementia and can't remember?

Barbara We also work with their family and talk to them. This is a task involving not only the care worker, but also the patient and their family.

Ronda We have a lovely activity we start with. We sit down with the patient and go through their family album. They love looking at their old photos and remembering special events and family parties. Even those with dementia can recall some aspects of their life. It makes their biography real and present.

Barbara And it is also a good opportunity to build up a close relationship.

Tom So, it's mostly something you do with elderly and forgetful people.

Ronda Actually, it's useful for anyone you need to care for. If you work with addicts, for example, doing biographical work with them helps you to understand when and why the person started taking drugs.

Barbara Elderly people at the end of their lives can also be helped through biographical work. It can reinforce the positive aspects of their life. Talking about their life helps them understand that it has had meaning and value and they can accept death more peacefully.

Tom That sounds really interesting.

Barbara Maybe you would like to do some biographical work with Mr Miller? You could work with Ronda and start looking at his family album.

Tom Yes, that sounds great.

Working with the text

A Find words in the text which fit these definitions.
You can follow the order of the text to find them.

1. noun: collecting information about a person's life
2. noun: getting together at work to talk things over
3. noun: someone doing vocational training
4. verb: deal with something difficult
5. verb: form, give someone or something a special kind of form or appearance
6. verb: remember

B True or false. Correct the false statements

1. Tom is doing vocational training at St Mary's.
2. He has already attended some of the long staff meetings.
3. Mr Miller has been at St Mary's for some years.
4. Ronda can already present a lot of important information about his life.
5. Looking at the family album is one of the last activities in biographical work.
6. Tom wants to do biographical work with Mr Miller.

C Before Tom took part in the long staff meeting, he had some wrong opinions about biographical work.
Take over Ronda's and Barbara's role and give him respond to his opinions.

1. *"Care work only involves medical care".*
2. *"Elderly people behave much the same".*
3. *"When you're old, your childhood, teenagerhood and career are no longer important".*
4. *"The patients are the people you talk to because only they can give you the information you need".*
5. *"Biographical work is only something you do with elderly people".*
6. *"You can't do biographical work with people with dementia".*

D Explain why biographical work …

1. … is a good opportunity to build up a close relationship to your patient.
2. … is a shared activity between the patients, their family and the care workers.
3. … is very important when you care for demented people.
4. … should also be done with someone who is addicted.
5. … should also be done with someone who is going to die.

E Try to think of why and how living at war times can have an influence on a person's later life.

Working with language

Mediation

Translate the following sentences into German.

l. 4 – 5: What do we know about his background?
l. 20 – 21: (They) had to cope with dramatic situations which have had an influence on their lives.
l. 30 – 33: (…) mainly it involves listening to your patient and understanding how their background has shaped the person they are today.

Grammar box: Questions in Simple Past → Fragen in der Vergangenheit

Questions with "did" / "was" / "were": Beispiele

Aussagen	Fragen	Antworten
Betty lived on a farm during her childhood.	***Did** Betty **live** on a farm during her childhood?* → **Bei der Frage mit "did" steht das Vollverb (hier: live) im Infinitiv**	*Yes, she did.* *No, she didn't*

siehe auch Beispiele für Fragen mit den Hilfsverben "was" / "were" / "could":
***Were** two of her brothers older? Yes, they were / No, they weren't; **Was** Michael Betty's favourite brother? Yes, he was / No, he wasn't; **Could** Betty and her husband buy a car? Yes, they could / No they couldn't.*

Wh-Questions mit dem Hilfsverb "did"

What	***did***	*Betty*	***buy***	*for her daughter on Christmas?*	**Was?**
Where	***did***	*Betty*	***live***	*in her childhood?*	**Wo?**
When	***did***	*Betty*	***meet***	*her husband for the first time?*	**Wann?**
Why	***did***	*Betty*	***sell***	*her house?*	**Warum?**
How	***did***	*Betty and her husband*	***feel***	*about her first car?*	**Wie?**
Who	***did***	*Betty*	***meet***	*at the grocer's shop?*	**Wen?**

siehe auch Beispiele für Fragen mit Fragewort und den Hilfsverben "was" / "were" / "could":
*What **were** Betty and her husband able to buy? Where **was** her parents' farm? When **could** her husband and Betty afford a car? Why **could** Betty not keep her own house?*

Ausnahme Frage ohne Hilfsverb:

Who	***asked***	*Betty to come with him to a fun fair?*	**Wer?**

Practising grammar

A Form questions in the simple past without a question word.

1. Betty / meet / her friends Emily and Emma / yesterday?
2. they / play / cards?
3. you / see / our family album?
4. John / like / to talk about his family and past?
5. you / can / reconstruct / his life story?
6. he / be a small child / at the beginning of the war?
7. many people / be / poor after the war?

B Use the question word and transform the statements into questions.

1. Betty lived on a farm during her childhood. → Where?
2. She felt happy to live among all the animals on the farm. → How?
3. Her husband worked as a bricklayer. → What?
4. Later Betty and her husband Joseph could afford a house and garden. → What?
5. Betty's life changed because the Second World War broke out. → Why?
6. Her brother Michael was her dearest friend. → Who?
7. Betty met her new friends Emily and Emma at the senior residence for assisted living. → Who?
8. Aged 85 Betty went into assisted living. → When?

C **This is part of St Mary's life story questionnaire about a person's past. First form the questions in the past tense.**

Biography questionnaire – questions about your past

your childhood

1. *Who / be / your best friends and classmates?*
2. *What / be / your best lessons?*
3. *What / you / struggle with?*

...?

your working life

4. What / you / do / as your first job?
5. You / have / different jobs?
6. How / be / your workplace?
...?

your relationships

7. Who / be / important people in your life?
8. You / get married?
...?

your home / the place you lived the longest

9. What happy times / you / spend / at home?
10. What / your home / look like?
...?

social activities and interests

11. What / you / like to do / in your spare time?
...?

significant life events

12. What event / have / a significant impact on your life?
13. What / be / highs and lows in your life?
...?

picture

Life story questionnaires

This is one part of a life story work questionnaire. There should also be a second part which deals with a person's present life.
With questions like: What is important now? Who are important people now? What clothes, hairstyle etc. do you like? What are your interests and hobbies? What are your wishes for your future / future care?
You can also add photos of the patients, present people they contact, their flat, clothes etc. These photos are especially important for those who have dementia.

D **Now sit in pairs and think of further questions which could be interesting and important to know about a person's past.**
Present your questions in class.
Decide which questions you want to add to the questionnaire.

Interaction

Writing a person's biography

Production

E **Work with your questionnaire and gather some information about your grandfather, grandmother, or an elderly person you know, maybe from your placement in an old people's home. Write this person's biography.**
Look at page 136, here you will find some help on how to write a biography.

Working with a family album

A Here is one of the photos taken from Mr Miller's family album. Mr Miller loved talking about the day it was taken. To document the most important information and to keep up the dialogue Tom asked some questions. Here are Mr Miller's answers. Can you think of the questions Tom asked?

1. This was my wife Gertrude right on the day my daughter was born.

2. The girl was from our neighbourhood.

3. She brought some flowers and wanted to have a look at the baby.

4. She did not buy the flowers but picked them from a meadow nearby.

5. We lived in a small flat at that time. Later we had our own house with a garden.

6. My daughter Sarah is lying in the cradle.

7. I took the photo.

8. I was really nervous and of course very proud on that day.

B Here are two more photos Mr Miller talked about. Work in pairs and think of a story behind the photo. Then work out a dialogue between Tom and Mr Miller. Interaction

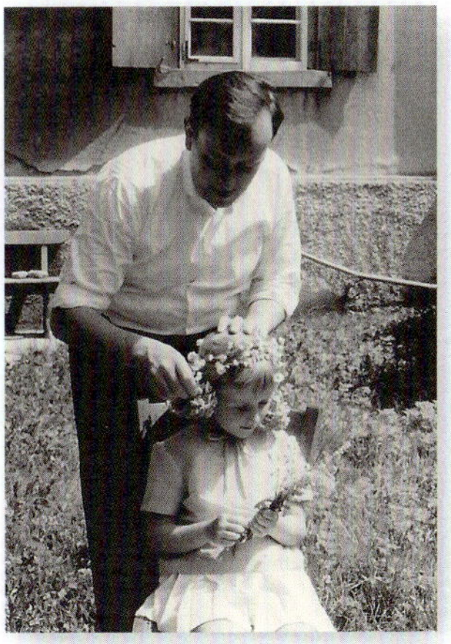

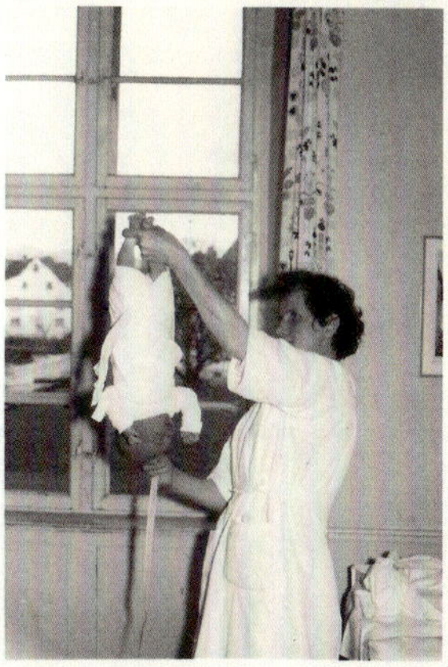

C Have a look at your family photos. Choose one and present it in class.

Looking at a life story

life story	Lebensgeschichte
family album	(Familien-)Fotoalbum
event	Ereignis, Anlass

Betty Brown's life story

adventure	Abenteuer
cattle	Vieh
chore	Haushaltsaufgaben
hardship	Entbehrung, hier: harte Zeit
(to) starve	verhungern
fun fair	Kirmes
bride	Braut
bridesmaid	Brautjungfer
bricklayer	Maurer
average	durchschnittlich

Why do we need to do biographical work?

staff meeting	Mitarbeiter- besprechung
case	Fall (eines Patienten)
trainee	Auszubildende(r)
be responsible for	verantwortlich sein für
significant	bedeutend, sehr wichtig
(to) cope with	umgehen mit, auch: ertragen
influence on	Einfluss auf
(to) shape	formen, hier auch: prägen
(to) record	aufzeichnen, dokumentieren
questionnaire	Fragebogen
(to) develop	entwickeln
biography	Biografie, Lebensgeschichte
dementia	Demenz
(to) recall	sich erinnern
addict	Süchtige(r)
(to) reinforce	bestätigen
(to) have meaning	Bedeutung haben
value	Wert
(to) give s.o. response	jmd. eine Antwort geben auf …
(to) accept	akzeptieren

Working with the text

(to) deal with	sich befassen mit
appearance	Aussehen
(to) behave	sich verhalten

Biography questionnaire

the past	hier: das vergangene Leben
(to) struggle	mit etwas kämpfen, sich abmühen
the present life	das gegenwärtige Leben
highs and lows	das Auf und Ab (des Lebens)
(to) add	hinzufügen

Working with a family album

meadow	Wiese
cradle	Wiege

Die Aussprache der blauen Vokabeln finden Sie in den Audio-Dateien DA0901055

Unit 9 Dementia

Is it just forgetfulness or dementia?

A Think about your own situation.

1. Have you forgotten anything during the last week or month?
2. What did you forget?
3. Do you know why you forgot?
4. Think of more reasons why we are sometimes forgetful.

B Now look at the cartoon pictures above.

1. Describe the situations they show.
2. Which of these pictures show people who are just forgetful? Which show people who have dementia? Give reasons.

Melissa Sandrino talks about her mother's dementia

Isn't it normal when an old woman of 85 forgets names, loses her handbag, or asks the same questions again and again? At first I thought she was forgetful because she had not drunk enough water. However, there were already clear signs of dementia.

Firstly, she was losing her short-term memory. Once, I phoned her to remind her of a doctor's appointment. When I went to collect her only half an hour later, I found her sitting in front of the TV. She was puzzled why I had come to fetch her. Her personality changed, she was once a cheerful person, but suddenly showed signs of depression.

She had always been very neat, but at my cousin's birthday party she turned up not only with uncombed hair, but also with a dirty dress and wearing a summer blouse over her winter dress. Later, she did not want to leave her flat any more. I thought it was because she was getting weak but then her neighbour told me that she had found her in front of the bins and she didn't know how to get back to her flat. I really became worried about her mental health.

Only the next day my mother phoned me very early in the morning and angrily told me her coffee maker had disappeared. I told her to calm down and have a good look for it. One minute later she called me again. She was outraged and told me that "the woman living upstairs" had stolen it.

I set off to her flat but when I arrived, she was sitting quietly at the kitchen table. When I told her that the coffee maker was still in its usual place, she only answered, "Why not?"

I called her GP and described the situation. They performed several tests on her which confirmed my worries.

My mother had Alzheimer's. I arranged a home care service to help, but I also had a lot of responsibility for her. I always worried about her when I wasn't with her. My mother had become my child. Sometimes, she phoned me up to 40 times a day, always asking the same questions. Very often she told me that I "let her starve" because I "didn't buy any bread". She changed, becoming insulting and saying hurtful things. In her war time stories she had always told us that sometimes she had only had a small piece of dry bread to eat.

This may have been on her mind because she tried to build up reserves of bread. I found mouldy bread in the microwave, oven, wardrobe, even in her handbag. Again and again she told me stories about "the woman" coming into her flat during the night and taking things away. She was always searching for something.

Once, her hairdresser called me to come quickly. I found her really upset, because "the hairdresser had dyed her hair grey". She couldn't remember what she looked like and thought she was younger with brown hair.

Since last year, my mother has needed permanent care. These days, when I visit her in her nursing home she doesn't recognize me. She has lost her long-term memory and is less able to communicate verbally. She hardly keeps eye-contact. But sometimes, when I yawn, she looks at me and starts laughing.

Working with the text

A All these statements are false. Correct them and give examples from the text.

1. Right from the beginning Melissa was sure her mother had dementia.
2. Despite her Alzheimer's, Melissa's mother's personality never changed.
3. Melissa's mother could not leave her flat, because she had got too weak.
4. She has always been friendly towards Melissa.
5. Only family members noticed her Alzheimer's.

B Now have a closer look at Melissa's story again and answer the following questions.

1. When did Melissa really become worried about her mother's mental health?
2. Can you imagine why Melissa started worrying about leaving her mother alone in her flat?
3. Why does Melissa say that her mother has become "her child"?
4. Why does her mother always ask for bread? What is Melissa's explanation?

Production

C What are typical examples which show that Melissa's mother lost her short-term and parts of her long-term memory? Create a table with your partner and present your results in class.

Interaction

D Maybe you have already had some experience with Alzheimer's patients from your placement. Share your experiences with your class.

Working with Language

A Make sure you understand the words in the word box below and put them into the text.

understand	eat	struggle	twice
suspicious	inappropriate	key	mood swings
telephone numbers	neighbourhood	personal hygiene	new
apathetic	smartly	entirely	basic
exactly	recent	reason	distracted

Diagnosing dementia – What are the early warning signs?

A. Memory loss

Everyone forgets meetings, names, or **(1)** … but a person with dementia forgets them a lot more frequently. Most people remember when they are reminded but people with dementia forget **(2)** … . They can't remember **(3)** … events or conversations. People who are very busy may be **(4)** … from time to time and leave their cup of coffee behind in the kitchen but people with dementia might prepare a meal and forget they made it or even forget to **(5)** … it.

B. Repetition

Maybe you repeat a question once or even **(6)** …, but a person with dementia may keep on asking the same question even if it has already been answered. They also tell the same stories again and again using **(7)** … the same words. Some repeat a sentence or a word without being able to stop.

C. Language problems

Sometimes we also **(8)** … to find words but a person with dementia may have problems using **(9)** … words. People with dementia often use wrong words which makes it hard to follow and **(10)** … them.

D. Disorientation of time and place
It's normal to forget a date but people with dementia forget about their children's and their own birthdays. Some have no idea if it is day or night. Getting lost in **(11)** … places is something which happens to everyone but people with dementia get lost in places they know like their own **(12)** … .

E. Lack of hygiene
People who have dressed very **(13)** … may start wearing dirty clothes and forget about their **(14)** … . They stop brushing their teeth, combing, or bathing and can't remember how to dress correctly.

F. Personality changes
People's personalities can change a bit with age but a person with dementia shows extreme changes in character. They become passive, **(15)** … or uncommunicative. They also have sudden **(16)** … from calm to tears to anger without a **(17)** … . For example they may become fearful and **(18)** … of people, even of family members or they are suddenly rude to the people around them.

G. Odd behaviour
Everyone searches for a lost **(19)** … sometimes but those who suffer from dementia place objects in wholly **(20)** … places like a comb in the fridge, or shoes in the dishwasher.

B Work in pairs and read Melissa's story again.
With the help of the list of warning signs, explain which symptoms of dementia her mother showed before she had to go into a nursing home.

Hands-on task

Interaction / Production

The fist step to diagnose dementia is to use a questionnaire. This investigates what typical symptoms the patient is showing. This is the beginning of a questionnaire which Melissa was asked to fill in. Work in small groups and create a complete questionnaire. Decide whether you want to design one for the patient or the relative. Compare your results in class.

Diagnosing questionnaire dementia: Observed Behaviour Checklist

Your name: *Melissa Sandrino*
Name of family member: *Eva Mays*
Family member's date of birth: *2/11/…*
Your relationship to family member: *daughter*
Does this person live with you? **Yes ( ) No (** *X* **)**

Behaviour	Not at all	Sometimes	Frequently	Does not apply
Does he/she repeat stories/sentences/the same questions again and again?				

Look at the method card "How to design a questionnaire" on page 138.

Grammar box: Past Continuous Tense – Die Verlaufsform der Vergangenheit

Aussagen

My mother ***was sitting*** *in front of the TV.*
The residents ***were playing*** *cards.*

und Verneinung

My mother ***wasn't sitting*** *in front of the TV.*
The residents ***weren't playing*** *cards.*

Fragen

Was *my mother* ***sitting*** *at the kitchen table?*
Were *the elderly people* ***painting*** *pictures?*

Kurzantworten

Yes, she **was.** */ No, she* **wasn't.**
Yes, they **were.** */ No they* **weren't.**

Bildung

Aussagen

I / he / she / it ***was*** + **ing-Form** des Verbs
We / you / they ***were*** + **ing-Form** des Verbs

Fragen

Was *I / he / she / it* + **ing-Form** des Verbs
Were *we / you / they* + **ing-Form** des Verbs

Zu den Rechtschreibbesonderheiten der ing-Form siehe Seite 24.

Past Continuous Tense wird verwendet

→ um eine Handlung zu beschreiben, die zu einem bestimmten Zeitpunkt schon im Verlauf war.
Yesterday at 9 o' clock I ***was serving*** *breakfast.* (= Zeitpunkt in der Vergangenheit)
Um die Dauer einer Handlung während eines Zeitraums zu betonen.
Yesterday between 10 and 11 o'clock we ***were having*** *our morning meeting.* (= Zeitraum in der Vergangenheit)

Grammar box: Past Simple Tense and Past Continuous Tense – Einfache Vergangenheit und die Verlaufsform der Vergangenheit

Past Simple Tense

→ Wenn mehrere Vorgänge in der Vergangenheit in kurzer Abfolge stattfanden.
Beispiel:
The doctor ***looked*** *at Mr Miller,* ***examined*** *his blood pressure and* ***took*** *his temperature.*

Past Continuous Tense und Past Simple Tense

→ Beide Zeiten werden in einem Satzgefüge genutzt, um die zeitliche Abfolge von zwei Handlungen in der Vergangenheit zu unterscheiden.
Past Continuous Tense wird benutzt für eine Handlung, die schon im Verlauf war, als eine zweite Handlung dazu kam.
Diese zweite wird mit der **Past Simple Tense** beschrieben.
Beispiel:

I ***was writing*** *some nursing plans*	*when the telephone* ***rang.***
= schon im Verlauf	**= neu einsetzende Handlung**
Past Continuous Tense	**Past Simple Tense**

Practising grammar

A Form sentences in the Past Continuous Tense.

1. From 7 till 8 o'clock – Sandra and John – prepare breakfast – and Susan – write the shopping list.
2. Tom – give the residents their medicine when the ambulance arrived.
3. our kitchen staff – prepare yesterday's dinner when they noticed they had no butter.
4. When the doctor arrived at 9 a.m., we – run around.
5. Between 10 and 12 o'clock – I - write nursing plans.
6. Mrs Miller and Mrs Taylor – not sit - with the others when we served coffee.
7. Yesterday afternoon, Mrs Taylor – watch TV in her room. Mrs Miller - not watch TV with her. She – read a magazine.

B Fill in the missing Past Simple or Continuous.

1. We – discuss our weekly nursing plans, when suddenly someone knocked at the door.
2. Mr Johnson – have tea, when his daughter came to visit him.
3. We were laying the table for dinner when Mrs Hendriks – sit down to have her dinner.
4. All the residents were sitting outside, but suddenly it – begin to rain.
5. John went into Mrs Miller's room in the evening to bring her some medicine but she – sleep.

C Fill in the missing Past Simple or Continuous form.

1. In the afternoon I (see) Mrs Taylor, she (sit) in her armchair asleep.
2. Mrs Miller (look) out of the window and I (ask) her what she (look) at.
3. She (tell) me that she (watch) the birds in the bird house.
4. All residents of the workshop (paint) pictures when Mr Miller (come) in late.
5. When I (go) into the recreation room in the evening, all the newspapers and magazines (lie) around.
6. In the late evening I (fill) in the medical documents when suddenly Mr Johnson (appear) telling me he had to go to the office.

A fake bus stop as a method to deal with Alzheimer's patients

More and more nursing homes are installing fake bus stops on their grounds. No bus will ever stop there. These bus stops are a good way to deal with Alzheimer's patients. Whenever they get confused and ask to go somewhere, like to go home, they can sit there safely. Their long-term memory tells them that it is correct to sit and wait at a bus stop. Soon, their restlessness and their current wish to go away are quickly forgotten. They will probably spend about five to ten minutes waiting for the bus before forgetting that they wanted to go somewhere. Then, a staff member will tell them the bus is running late and bring them back to the nursing home. People with dementia live in their own world and using rational arguments when they feel disoriented, holding them back, or even worse scolding them, is absolutely wrong. This will only upset them or make them aggressive. Their confusion will become worse and they will repeat their wish again and again. It's much better to listen and show them that they are respected. They need positive feedback. This is how the fake bus stop works.

If an Alzheimer's patient tells you, "I have to go to work now", it's much better to say, "Yes, of course, I understand!" and tell him or her to sit at the bus stop. This will create a feeling of support and will have a calming effect.

Working with the text

A Complete the following sentences.

1. A fake bus stop is a safe method to deal with Alzheimer's patients because …
2. It helps to calm down restless patients because …
3. Alzheimer's patients need positive feedback because …

Production

B Some people criticise the concept of the fake bus stop and say that it "makes fun of ill people".
What is your personal opinion?
Write down your statement.

Hands-on task

Interaction

C Work in small groups and read these short episodes.
How would you react?
How can you give these people with dementia positive feedback and help them out of their confusion?
Pick two examples and prepare role plays.
Perform and discuss them in class.

1. You're doing the night shift and you see Mr Thompson dressed in a coat and walking shoes walking up and down the corridor, repeating: "It's nice weather, I'm going for a walk outside".
2. For some time, Mrs Robertson has been carrying a doll with her, telling everyone, "Look, this is my son Paul!" Now you come to her room and hear her crying, "My baby. My baby!" Her son took her doll away, telling her that it is not a baby, just a doll.
3. Mr Meyer asks you to call the doctor because his "stomach is aching". He is really becoming angry, repeating "Call a doctor. Call a doctor!" On the table you see his dinner untouched. He very often forgets to eat and cannot tell the difference between feeling hungry and being ill.
4. Every morning when you wake up Mrs Hollander and want to help her get dressed she tells you that she cannot get up because she has no clothes, "during the night, a woman came in and took everything away".
5. Mrs Smith is walking up and down the corridor. She is very nervous and tells you, "I have to get home quickly. My husband is coming back from work soon and I haven't cooked his dinner".
6. Almost every morning after breakfast, Mr Taylor gets up from the table saying, "Good bye, I'll be back late in the afternoon. We're very busy at the office." Soon he enters the dining room again asking, "Where's my car?"

dementia	Demenz
forgetfulness	Vergesslichkeit
forgetful	vergesslich

Melissa Sandrino talks about …

sign	Zeichen, Anzeichen
short-term memory	Kurzzeitgedächtnis
doctor's appointment	Arzttermin
(to) collect	abholen, (ein-)sammeln
puzzled	verwirrt sein
cheerful	fröhlich
neat	ordentlich, adrett
bin	Mülleimer
mental health	geistige Gesundheit
coffee maker	Kaffeemaschine
(to) disappear	verschwinden
(to) calm down	sich beruhigen
outraged	aufgebracht
GP (general practitioner)	Allgemeinarzt / Allgemeinärztin
(to) perform tests on s. o.	jmd. Tests unterziehen
(to) confirm	versichern, bestätigen
responsibility	Verantwortung
(to) starve	hungern
(to) insult	beleidigen
hurtful	verletzend
(to) build up reserves	Vorräte anlegen
mouldy	schimmelig
oven	Backofen
upset	traurig
(to) dye	färben
(to) remember	sich erinnern
(to) recognize	erkennen
long-term memory	Langzeitgedächtnis
(to) yawn	gähnen

Die Aussprache der blauen Vokabeln finden Sie in den Audio-Dateien DA0901055

Diagnosing dementia – …

suspicious	verdächtig, argwöhnisch
apathetic	apathisch, regungslos
inappropriate	unangemessen
smartly	adrett
recent	kürzlich, neulich
(to) struggle	kämpfen (um)
entirely	völlig, gänzlich
mood swings	Stimmungsschwankungen
distracted	abgelenkt
memory loss	Gedächtnisverlust
(to) be reminded	erinnert werden
repetition	Wiederholung
(to) repeat	wiederholen
disorientation	Orientierungslosigkeit
lack of	Mangel an
anger	Wut, Zorn
fearful	ängstlich
rude	beleidigend
diagnosing	das Diagnostizieren
(to) diagnose	diagnostizieren
questionnaire	Fragebogen
(to) investigate	prüfen, ermitteln
observed behaviour	beobachtetes Verhalten

A fake bus stop …

(to) deal with	umgehen mit
fake	Attrappe
confusion	Verwirrung, hier: Verwirrtheit
safely (adv.)	sicher
restlessness	Unruhe, Ruhelosigkeit
rational arguments	rationale / begründete Argumente
(to) scold s. o.	mit jmd. schimpfen, jmd. beschimpfen
positive feedback	positive Rückmeldung
(to) criticise	kritisieren

The eatwell plate

What are healthy eating habits?

Hands-on task

Inter Interaction

Sit in five groups and choose one of the food groups you see on the "eatwell plate". Design a poster with different types of food which belong to that food group. Make sure you tell your classmates the English words for the food on your poster.

A **Why do you think is this plate called an "eatwell" plate?**

B **Talk about your eating habits.**

1. What food do you like to eat?
2. What do you never eat at all?
3. How many meals do you eat in one day?
4. Is the food you eat healthy?
5. Do you think you should change some of your eating habits?

Some basic rules on healthy nourishment

A Fill in the gaps in the text below using the words in the box.

vitamins	two	sugar	dairy products	fruit
small	wholegrain	five	potatoes	energy

Eating healthy food can help a lot to stay fit. Whatever your age, it's always important to eat a healthy and balanced diet. This means that you should eat …

- → plenty of **1.** … and vegetables, at least **2.** … portions of a variety of fruit and veg a day. They give you the **3.** … your body needs.
- → plenty of bread, rice, **4.** …, pasta and other starchy food, the best **5.** … products. These products are full of **6.** …
- → some milk and **7.** …
- → some meat, fish, eggs, beans and other non-dairy products which have a lot of protein, at least **8.** … portions of fish a week.
- → only a very **9.** … portion of foods that are high in fat or **10.** … .

B Everyone has got a favourite meal or snack. Here are some examples. Are these favourites healthy or not? Give your reasons.

Justin, 17
He loves eating cheeseburgers or chicken nuggets from fast food restaurants. He eats lots of ketchup on his French fries and drinks coke or milk shakes.

Madeline, 32
After work she often orders a pizza from a takeaway, usually pizza with salami or extra cheese. Then, she drinks some red wine, at least two glasses.

John, 81
He loves sitting in front of the TV in the evening and drinking two or three glasses of beer and eating cheese on white bread. Later in the evening, he eats some peanuts or crisps.

Some phrases on talking about healthy and unhealthy eating habits

It is very healthy / unhealthy to eat (food) …

You should always choose lower-fat products like (food).

(Food) contain(s) too much salt / sugar / fat …

You shouldn't eat too much salt / sugar / fat like in (food)

(Food) contain(s) a lot of healthy / unhealthy ingredients like …

It's better to avoid eating too much …

If you need more energy / vitamins / protein you should eat (food).

You should always go for fresh / organic food because it's healthier / full of vitamins / fibre.

It's better to eat (food) because (food) only contain(s) a little salt / sugar / fat.

(Food) gives you a lot of vitamins / protein.

You should eat (food) every day because …

It's a good / bad idea to eat (food) because …

It's better to eat only small portions of (food) because …

(Food) gives your body a lot of energy / vitamins / protein which you need to stay fit.

A healthy and balanced diet for the over 60s

The body changes when you get older and a balanced diet can help you to stay healthy. Here are the foods you should eat when you get older.

Fibre-rich foods like wholegrain bread, cereals, potatoes, oats, beans, peas, lentils, fresh fruit and vegetables. Digestion problems increase when people get older, therefore the body needs fibre.

Iron-rich foods
A lack of iron makes you feel tired. The best source of iron is lean red meat but don't eat more than 70 to 90 g cooked meat a day. Iron can also be found in pulses, oily fish, eggs, bread, green vegetables and cereals.

Calcium-rich foods
Osteoporosis is a real problem for older people. The bones lose their density and the risk of fractures becomes higher. Eating calcium-rich dairy products like milk, cheese, and yoghurt should be part of your diet. Soya beans and tofu also contain a lot of calcium.

Less salt
You should only have a little salt a day. Eating too much salt can raise your blood pressure.

Enough vitamin D
Foods like eggs or fish supply the body with vitamin D which is important for the bones.

Some more health tips
Older people should not only eat enough of the right foods but keep their weight at a healthy level. It's not good to be either overweight or underweight. Elderly people very often lose their appetite. It is normal to eat less because you're not as active any more but the body should still get the nutrients and energy it needs. Therefore, older people should eat five small healthy meals a day instead of three large meals. It's very important that you drink enough, at least 1.5, but preferably 2 litres a day because you may find you don't feel that thirsty anymore and can become dehydrated. You should go for healthy drinks like water or diluted juice, and not drink too much coffee or strong tea. Both of these contain caffeine which makes your body produce more urine and has a dehydrating effect.

Working with the text

A Follow the text again and find words that mean …

1. adjective: A good diet with a lot of different food is a … diet.
2. adjective: Just the opposite of white bread, bread with a lot of fibre is called … bread.
3. noun: Missing something, not having something
4. adjective: Meat without fat or with only little fat is very … meat.
5. noun: When you partially break a bone in your body, you have a …
6. noun: Fish and eggs have a high amount of ….
7. adjective: The opposite of being overweight. Someone who is too low in weight is …

B **You are doing a placement in a day care for elderly people.**
You and your colleagues are responsible for preparing the meals every day.
You always try to ensure the over 60s have a healthy, balanced diet.
Some of your patients tell you their opinion about food.
How can you answer?

Benjamin 82 years	*I have always been a good eater and like to eat large portions. I never put on weight as a young man. And I don't know why I should change my eating habits. I'm old, and don't care about my weight. Three large portions a day, that's how I like it.*
Maria 76 years	*I have a sweet tooth. I can't resist eating sweet puddings instead of a proper dinner. When I want to eat some fruit I open tinned peaches or pears. Tinned food is very easy to prepare and I also eat tinned vegetables and soups. In the afternoon I like to have a cup of coffee with some cake. When my friend comes around we also drink a couple of small glasses of Advocat with the cake. I'm old and I want to enjoy the rest of my life.*
Michael 80 years	*I don't want to eat whole-grain bread. It's too thick and I have to chew it for a long time. It makes you feel too full. I only want to have white bread.*
Charlotte 84 years	*I drink enough. I drink two cups of coffee in the morning and I put the rest of the coffee aside and drink the cold coffee in the early evening when I'm back home. I don't like drinking water all the time. Sometimes I drink a cup of tea or some lemonade.*

C **Looking at the main nutrients the text tells you about, say what these different dishes mainly contain.**
<u>Example:</u> A vegetable soup mainly contains vitamins. It also has some …

- lentil soup
- sweet, warm rice pudding with raspberry syrup
- pork chops with fried potatoes and carrots
- steak with herbal butter, green beans and potatoes
- toasted whole-grain bread sandwich with bacon and cheese
- omelette with bacon and tomatoes
- sweet pancake with fruit salad, ice cream and whipped cream
- warm vegetable salad with cottage cheese and boiled egg
- salad and tofu with a topping of basil pesto

D **Now sit in pairs and discuss which of these dinners are healthy for people over 60.**
Choose two dinners and tell your class your reasons for your choices.

10

E **Listen to Zara 19, Sandra 39 and James 78.**
Which of the above dinners is their favourite and least favourite dinner?

Reception

F **Choose one of the statements and write a comment on it.**
Look at page 139 for some help on comment writing.

Production

1. Healthy eating is the "best medicine" to keep fit and young.
2. Today a lot of people are ill because of bad eating habits

Hands-on task

Interaction

G You've been asked to plan the dinner for a week in the day care for older people. Work in small groups and work out a weekly dinner plan from Monday to Friday.
Present and discuss your dinner plans in class.

How to feed someone.

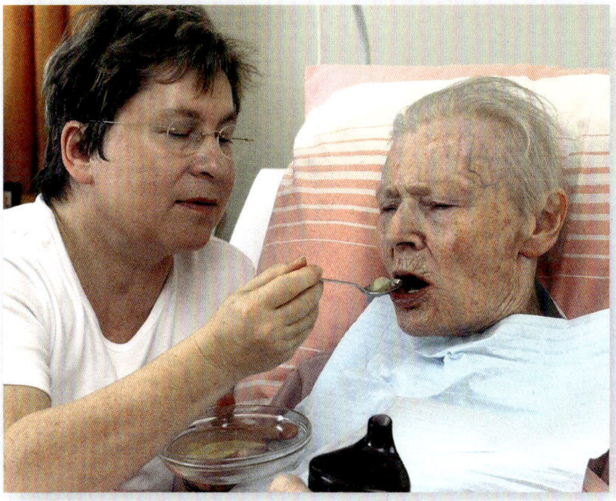

Someone may need to be fed or have help during mealtimes because of an operation, injury on an arm or hand, blindness, disability, or a stroke. There is one basic rule which you have to keep in mind: **Never** feed someone when they are lying down or in a sleeping position. This is **very dangerous.** Feeding them in this position can increase the risk of food going the wrong way.

Here are some strategies how to feed someone. The words of the word box below are missing. Can you fill them in?

sit	help	feed
stop	tell	allow
place	put	add
watch	ask	clean

Strategies to help you feed someone a meal:

1. … the person's face and hands.
2. … them to sit upright as much as possible, for example by putting pillows behind their back for support.
3. … everything you need for feeding before you start such as an over-bed table, meal tray, towels, straws, special spoons etc.
4. … in a chair next to the person to be fed. Make sure that you sit at the best side of the body. For example someone who has had a stroke can have weakness or numbness on one side of the body. Then sit on the side which is not numb or weak and put the spoon on the side of the mouth that can still experience sensations.
5. … the person what food is on the plate and describe how it has been prepared if the person has vision problems.
6. … the person what food they want to eat first.
7. … a small amount of food on the tip of the spoon.
8. If the person tends to choke, … a little water or another liquid on the spoon which will help them to swallow the food.
9. … the person to eat at their own pace. Give them time to completely chew the food.
10. … the throat to make sure the person has swallowed all the food.
11. Ask if the person is ready for more food before you … them more.
12. … feeding if the person shows you that they have had enough.

Working with the text

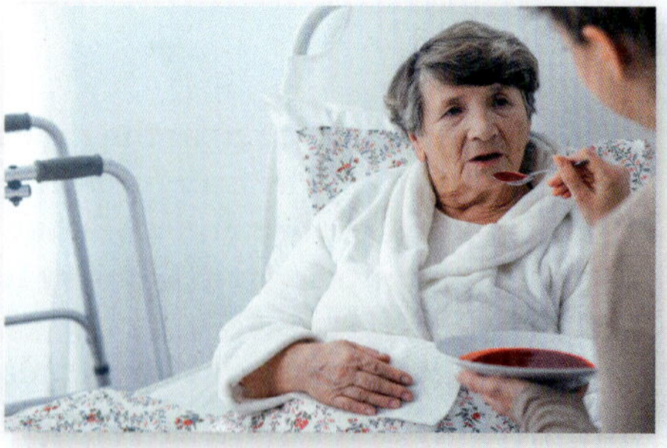

A Finish the following sentences.

1. Some people need to be fed …
2. People lying down or in a sleeping position …
3. You can help the patients to sit upright and …
4. If someone has vision problems …
5. While feeding someone you should always …
6. You should stop feeding …

B Helen feeds Mrs Brian who has had a car accident. Both of her arms are fractured. This is the beginning of their dialogue. The rest is mixed up.

Helen Hi, Mrs Brian, here's today's dinner. It's vegetable soup with some bread and butter.
Mrs Brian That's great, I like vegetable soup.

With a partner reconstruct the dialogue and read it out in class.

1.	Helen	(Goes on feeding. Then after some time:) *Mrs Brian, tell me when you are full, please.*
2.	Mrs Brian	*No, thanks. I'd like to eat the soup first and drink a glass of water afterwards.*
3.	Helen	*I'll wait a bit longer then.* (Stirs soup again) *Can you swallow this amount of soup ok?*
4.	Mrs Brian	*I'd like some bread, please.*
5.	Helen	*Okay, then. I'll help you to get out of bed. Do you need a pillow to rest your arms?*
6.	Mrs Brian	*Okay, that's enough now. I'd like something to drink, please.*
7.	Helen	*Before we start, do you want to sit in bed or at the table?*
8.	Mrs Brian	*Yes, please. That will be more comfortable.*
9.	Helen	*Are you sitting comfortably? Here's your bowl of soup, spoon and napkin. I would also like to put a cloth around your neck just to make sure you don't spoil your clothes by getting food on them. And I'd just like to clean your face beforehand, so we're ready to start. May I do that?*
10.	Mrs Brian	*I can get up and sit at the table. That's much better than sitting in bed.*
11.	Helen	*Here you are* (Lets her take a bite from a slice of bread). *Do you want to drink some water now?*
12.	Mrs Brian	(Opens mouth and swallows the first spoonful) *Oh, it's still a bit hot but very tasty.*
13.	Helen	*No problem* (lifts glass to her mouth and helps her to drink).
14.	Mrs Brian	*Yes, that was fine.*
15.	Helen	*Okay, I'll make sure the next spoonful isn't as hot. Do you want some bread, or to drink some water next?*
16.	Mrs Brian	*No problem, go ahead.*
17.	Helen	(Sits down at the table next to Mrs Brian) *Okay, the soup is hot, I'm going to stir it, just a second.* (Does so.) *I'll only put a bit onto the spoon because I don't want you to get a burnt mouth.* (After a short time:) *Here you are.*

Hands-on task

Interaction / Production

C Sit in small groups and choose one of the feeding situations below and think of how the dialogue could look like.
Write down your dialogue and read it out in class.

Situation 1
Mr Hank needs to be fed. He is almost blind and struggles with Parkinson's. He finds it difficult to hold cutlery and can't cut with a knife. As his home worker you bring his dinner: two slices of roast pork with brown sauce, peas and mashed potatoes. Mr Hank likes to drink a glass of diluted apple juice with his dinner. He does not want to eat the chocolate pudding for dessert but tells you to put it in the fridge. Mr Hank always sits at his kitchen table for his dinners.

Situation 2
Mrs Spring has had a stroke. She is in hospital and can't leave her bed. She is numb on the left hand side of her body and has problems swallowing. She is still too weak to eat alone. She often doesn't want to eat all of her dinner and soon says that she is full, sometimes after just two or three spoonfuls. She also doesn't like drinking anything. Her dinner today is chicken curry with rice with a strawberry yoghurt for dessert.

Grammar box: **Plurals** – Mehrzahl

Regelmäßige Bildung

→ **+"s" an den Singular / die Einzahl anhängen**
bone – bones

→ **+„es" nach Zischlaut**
peach – peaches
glass – glasses (=Gläser)

→ **+„ies" für Konsontant+y am Ende**
cherry – cherries

→ **+„oes" nach Nomen mit Endung auf „o"**
tomato – tomatoes
(Ausnahme Fremdwörter: kilos, pianos, radios, photos, studios)

→ **+„ves" nach Nomen mit Endung auf „fe", „f"**
knife – knives, leaf – leaves
(Ausnahmen: roofs, proofs, handkerchiefs, beliefs)

Unregelmäßige Pluralformen
child – children, foot – feet, tooth – teeth, man – men, woman – women, foot – feet

Nur im Plural
trousers – Hose, *scissors* – Schere, *glasses* – Brille, *earphones* – Kopfhörer,
Plural z. B.: *two pairs of glasses / trousers*

Gleicher Singular und Plural – nicht zählbare Subsantiven

→ **Warenbezeichnungen** wie
fish, water, butter, oil, salt, iron, food = Essen, Nahrung (*foods* = Lebensmittel)
fruit = Obst (*fruits* = Früchte)

→ **Abstrakte Begriffe / Oberbegriffe:**
advice, information, knowledge, damage, strength, progress, work, homework, furniture

Formung des Plurals durch z. B.
a piece of information – eine Information
two pieces of furniture – zwei Möbelstücke
some good advice – ein guter Ratschlag / gute Ratschläge

Practising Grammar

A Put the nouns into the plural.

1. child
2. foot
3. potato
4. lentil
5. life
6. woman
7. spoon
8. salt
9. loaf of bread
10. photo
11. tooth
12. half
13. man
14. roof
15. glasses
16. city

B Translate the following sentences into English.
(You could look back at page 47 to revise the usage of much / many / a lot of.)

Mediation

1. Das ist ein guter Ratschlag.
2. Man kann nie zu viel Wissen über gesunde Ernährung haben.
3. Hast du viele Hausaufgaben?
4. Es ist gesund, viel Obst zu essen.
5. Zu viel Salz ist ungesund.
6. Putze deine Zähne nach jeder Mahlzeit.
7. Wo ist meine Brille?
8. Soll ich deine Hose waschen?

Grammar box: The Formation of Adverbs – Die Bildung der Adverbien (Umstandsworte)

Bildung der Adverbien

Adverbien beschreiben Verben.
Viele Adverbien werden gebildet, indem man an das Adjektiv **„-ly“** anhängt.

nice – *nicely*
slow – *slowly*
quick – *quickly*

Sonderregeln:

Bei mehrsilbigen Adjektiven wird das „y“ zu i:
easy – *easily*

Nach Konsonant entfällt „le“:
simple – *simply*

Stummes „e“ entfällt:
true – *truly*
whole – *wholly*

Endet das Adjektiv bereits auf “ly”, fügt man “in a way” an:
friendly – *in a friendly way*

Endet das Adjektiv auf “-ic”, bildet man das Adverb mit “-ally”:
fantastic – *fantastically*

Adjektive auf „-ll“ bilden das Adverb mit „y“:
full – *fully*

Das Adjektiv *„good“* heißt als Adverb *„well“*.

Einige Adjektive und Adverbien haben die gleiche Form:
Beispiel: *daily, hourly, weekly, monthly, yearly, early, fast, long, far, straight, low*

Grammar box: Einige Adjektive haben zwei Adverbformen mit ganz unterschiedlicher Bedeutung:

Adjektiv	Adverb	Adverb
right (richtig)	right (richtig)	rightly (zurecht)
hard (hart)	hard (hart)	hardly (kaum)
fair (fair)	fair (fair)	fairly (ziemlich)
pretty (hübsch)	pretty (ziemlich)	prettily (hübsch)
high (hoch)	high (hoch)	highly (höchst)
late (spät)	late (spät)	lately (in letzter Zeit)
most (am meisten)	most (am meisten)	mostly (meistens)
just (gerecht)	just (nur)	justly (gerecht)
ready (fertig)	ready (fertig)	readily (bereitwillig)
short (kurz)	short (kurz)	shortly (in Kürze)

Practising Grammar

A Write down the adverb.

1. quick
2. basic
3. angry
4. nervous
5. silly
6. healthy
7. hopeful
8. good
9. hard
10. sensible
11. quiet
12. correct
13. careful
14. honest
15. true
16. weekly
17. excited
18. friendly
19. simple
20. easy

Grammar box: Adverbien – weitere Ausnahmen

Bei Verben, die einen Zustand beschreiben, steht kein Adverb, sondern ein Adjektiv.

Verbbeispiele: *be, become, get, grow, turn* (= werden), *remain, stay, keep* (bleiben), *seem* (scheinen)

She seems to be healthy. *This food is healthy.* *You will stay healthy with a balanced diet.*

Bei Verben der Sinneswahrnehmung steht kein Adverb.

Verbbeispiele: *look* (aussehen), *feel, smell, sound, taste*

The cheese smells bad. *This sounds good.* *The pudding tastes sweet.*

B Adjective or adverb? Fill in the correct form of the word in brackets.

How to maintain your weight

Being overweight is **1.** … *(unhealthy)*. To keep your weight normal, you should choose your food **2.** … *(careful)* and stick to a healthy diet **3.** … *(daily)*. Today a lot of people become **4.** … *(overweight)* because they **5.** … *(regular)* eat fast food and unhealthy snacks like chocolate or crisps. But this food is too **6.** … *(sugary)*, **7.** … *(fat)* and **8.** … (salty). Sometimes it is **9.** … *(hard)* to avoid eating fast food and some people **10.** … *(consequent)* point out that if you feel **11.** … *(nervous)* or **12.** … *(exhausted)* you should **13.** … *(just)* eat a bit of this food. You should always eat **14.** … *(good)* balanced. Elderly people very often lose their appetite and their weight **15.** … *(quick)* reduces. Some become **16.** … *(underweight)*. Therefore older people should watch their weight **17.** … *(attentive)* and make sure they eat and drink **18.** … *(sensible)*.

What are healthy eating habits?

eating habits	Essgewohnheiten
food	Essen, Nahrung
foods	Nahrungsmittel

Some basic rules

nourishment	Ernährung
wholegrain	Vollkorn-…
dairy products	Milchprodukte
fruit	Obst
balanced	ausgewogen
diet	Ernährung, auch: Diät
vegetables	Gemüse
starchy	stärkehaltig
French Fries / chips	Pommes Frittes
peanuts	Erdnüsse
crisps	Chips
(to) contain	beinhalten
ingredient	Inhaltsstoff, Zutat
(to) avoid + ing-Form	vermeiden
fresh	frisch
organic	biologisch

A healthy and balanced diet …

fibre-rich	balaststoffreich
oats	Haferflocken
peas	Erbsen
lentils	Linsen
digestion	Verdauung
fibre	Balaststoff
iron-rich	eisenhaltig
lean	mager
meat	Fleisch
pulses	Hülsenfrüchte
oily	ölig, ölhaltig
calcium-rich	kalziumreich
bones	Knochen
density	(Knochen-)Dichte
fracture	Knochenbruch
soya beans	Sojabohnen
(to) raise	heben, steigern
overweight	übergewichtig
underweight	untergewichtig
(to) lose appetite	den Appetit verlieren
nutrient	Nährstoff
preferably	möglichst
thirsty	durstig
(to) dehydrate	austrocknen
diluted juice	mit Wasser verdünnter Saft
caffeine	Koffein
(to) ensure	sicherstellen
proper	richtig, angemessen
Advocat	Eierlikör-Marke
(to) chew	kauen
herbal butter	Kräuterbutter
pancake	Pfannkuchen
whipped cream	Schlagsahne
rice pudding	Milchreis
raspberry syrup	Himbeersirup
cottage cheese	Hüttenkäse
boiled egg	gekochtes Ei
fried potatoes	Bratkartoffeln

How to feed …

(to) feed	Essen anreichen
mealtimes	Mahlzeiten
blindness	Blindheit
disability	Behinderung
stroke	Schlaganfall
lying down	liegend
sleeping position	Schlafposition
food going the wrong way	sich verschlucken
upright	aufrecht
meal tray	(Essens-)Tablett
towel	Handtuch
straw	Strohhalm
numbness	Taubheit, Gefühllosigkeit
numb	taub, gefühllos
(to) experience sensations	Empfindungen wahrnehmen
vision problems	Sehstörungen
amount	Menge
(to) choke	ersticken
(to) swallow	schlucken
on your own pace	im eigenen Rhythmus
(to) stir	(um)rühren
bowl	Schüssel
napkin	Serviette
(to) spoil	verderben
bite	Biss
slice of bread	Brotscheibe
cutlery	Besteck
roast pork	Schweinebraten
mashed potatoes	Kartoffelpüree
(to) reduce	reduzieren
attentive	aufmerksam
sensible	vernünftig

Die Aussprache der blauen Vokabeln finden Sie in den Audio-Dateien DA0901055

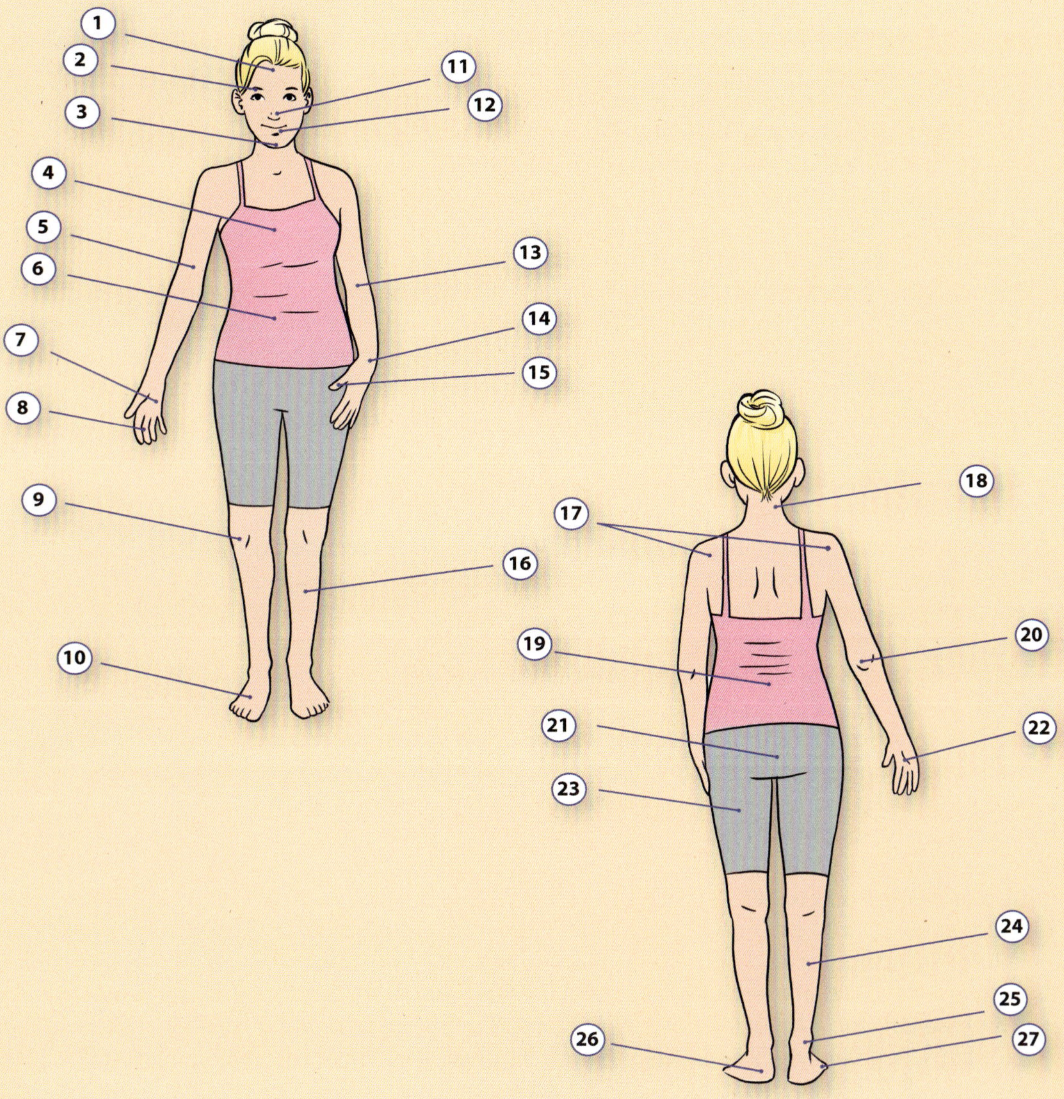

Parts of the body

A Match the body parts in the box below with the numbers 1 to 26.

knee – thumb – fingers – arm – foot – chin – bust / chest – eyebrows – wrist – forehead – hand – leg – hips – lips – palm – neck- ankle – shoulders – bottom – calf – elbow – waist – heel – thigh – sole of the foot – toes – nose

B Do you think you are an active person or are you rather lazy? What do you do to stay active? Tell the class.

Keep moving!

It's no secret. Everyone knows that being physically active and doing exercise regularly is one of the healthiest things you can do. Those who make physical exercise a regular part of their life can maintain and improve their health. Therefore everyone should try and be as active as possible. Being lazy and taking it easy is risky. There are a lot of health problems and diseases you can avoid by being active. Of course it's best to be active right from scratch but it's never too late to begin.

How much exercise do you need to improve your health?
Some activity is better than none but to get best health benefits, you should do at least two to three hours of physical exercise every week. Anything that gets your body moving is good. But those daily routines don't really help to become fitter. Daily chores such as shopping, cooking, or housework don't really count as a real physical exercise. The effort to do them isn't hard enough to raise your heart rate which you should to achieve physical fitness.

What are the health benefits of physical exercise?
The first thing which comes into people's minds is that overweight people can lose weight and improve their health when they start doing some kind of sport. But that's not the only example for the positive effect physical exercise has.
People with arthritis, heart disease or diabetes benefit from weekly exercises. People with a high blood pressure can reduce it by being active. Those who exercise are in a better mood than those who stay inactive because endorphins are produced by exercise which help to reduce feelings of sadness and depression. After a workout you fall asleep more easily and sleep more deeply. And everyone knows that a good night's sleep is also important for your overall health.

Should seniors exercise?
Older adults who are active are healthier and stay independent for longer. Strokes and heart failures are attributed to many elderly people's lifestyles. Very often they are reluctant to exercise or they are afraid that exercise will be too hard and harm them. But those who stay inactive have a high health risk. A lot of elderly people suffer from brittle bones and have balance or walking problems. Regular exercise can help them to improve their balance, which means they are less likely to fall. Exercising enables cells to be active and strengthens your bones. Being physically active also keeps your brain active, which slows down cognitive decline and dementia.

Working with the text

A Go through the text again and find the words which fit the following explanations.

1. verb: make something better
2. adjective: something which could be dangerous for you
3. expression: from the beginning, from the start of something
4. noun (plural): advantage, here: everything which helps you to become and stay healthy
5. noun: regular tasks like housework.
6. verb: become less, take or do less
7. noun: an illness in which it is difficult to feel positive emotions
8. adjective: not wanting to do something
9. adjective: weak, breaks easily

B These sentences have wrong facts in them. Correct them so they explain the benefits of physical exercise.

1. Irregularly exercising is good for your health.
2. Being active can support a lot of chronic diseases.
3. Weekly exercising has no health benefits.
4. Daily chores is a form of real physical exercises.
5. People with arthritis, heart disease or diabetes suffer from regular exercise.
6. The production of endorphins causes depression.
7. Physical exercise slows down your brain.

C Explain …

1. … why being lazy and taking it easy is a health risk.
2. … why doing your housework does not really help you become fit and healthy.
3. … why people who struggle with depression can benefit from exercising.
4. … the relationship between exercise, good sleep and overall health.
5. … why being active is very important for seniors.

Hands-on task

Interaction / Production

Work in small groups and give answers to try and convince these people to start exercising. Compare your answers in class.

Monica, 35:
I don't have any weight problems. I can eat anything I like without putting on weight. There is really no need for me to exercise. I'm a lazy person and I hate exercising.

Sam, 40:
I'm disabled. I use a wheelchair. I can't exercise sitting down.

Paul, 52:
I have diabetes which means I also have high blood pressure. It would be risky for me to do exercise. I could have a heart attack!

Maria 58:
Why should I do any exercise? I'm old, almost 60. I'm going to get older whether or not I do anything. It's just too late now.

Robert, 75:
Elderly people need to rest. They don't have enough energy to exercise! I don't, so I sit down and just watch sport on TV. I have some age-related health problems; I suffer from arthritis and I'm a bit overweight. Sitting is much better than walking or even exercising, that's all too exhausting for me.

Lorna, 80:
Physical exercise is too dangerous. I'm 80 and stiff. My bones are fragile. I can't exercise because I'm afraid of falling and breaking my bones.

Grammar box: Use of the Adjective and Adverb – Gebrauch des Adjektivs und Adverbs

Adjective

→ **Bezieht sich immer auf ein Nomen oder eine Person**
*Exercising should be a **regular** part of your life.*
*Melanie is a **resolute** person.*

Adverb

→ **Kann sich beziehen …**
- **auf ein Verb**
  *He exercises **regularly.***
- **auf ein Adjektiv**
  *Exercising is **extremely important.***
- **auf ein anderes Adverb**
  *She exercises **extremely resolutely.***
- **Auf einen ganzen Satz**
  ***Unfortunately,** he started exercising too late.*

Ausnahmen

→ **kein** Adverb, sondern Adjektiv, bei Verben, die einen Zustand beschreiben, z. B. bei:
to be, to become, to get, to grow, to turn (= werden),
to remain, to stay, to keep (= bleiben), *to seem* (=scheinen)

→ **kein** Adverb, sondern Adjektiv, bei Verben der Sinneswahrnehmung, z. B. bei:
to look (= aussehen), *to feel, to smell, to sound, to taste*

Practising Grammar

Do you have to change the adjective in brackets to an adverb or not?
Have a look at page 90 to revise forming of adverbs before you do this exercise.
1. *(regular)* 2. *(physical)* activity and exercise are very 3. *(important)* to stay 4. *(fit)* and 5. *(healthy).* Everyone knows that you should not be 6. *(lazy)* but it's 7. *(hard)* to be 8. *(strict)* with yourself. For seniors it is also very 9. *(important)* to be as 10. *(active)* as 11. *(possible).* Most elderly people don't 12. *(sudden)* lose their ability to do things on their own because of an illness or because they are old. It 13. *(usual)* happens because they're not 14. *(active)* enough. Taking it 15. *(easy)* is too 16. *(risky).* Seniors can start with 17. *(moderate)* exercises which are not that 18. *(exhausting).* Everyone should follow the 19. *(simple)* rule of doing some 20. *(physical)* activities twice a week to improve overall health. This also helps to manage stress more 21. *(easy)* and keep you in a 22. *(good)* mood. For example, going to a gym for two to three hours every week will keep you 23. *(strong)* and 24. *(fit)* enough to do your job 25. *(good)* and 26. *(effective)* manage your everyday life. But to be 27. *(physical)* 28. *(active)* you don't need to join a fitness club or to buy 29. *(special)* equipment. One of the best exercises is walking or jogging in the 30. *(fresh)* air. Always remember, 31. *(inactive)* people visit a doctor more 32. *(frequent)* because of 33. *(chronic)* diseases, they have to go to hospital more often than 34. *(active)* people and they also have to make more 35. *(frequent)* use of 36. *(various)* medicines.

How to get seniors moving?

Mrs Harris is a new resident at St Michael's nursing home. Amanda, Nadine and John work on her ward. They are talking about her in a staff meeting.

Amanda What do you think of Mrs Harris? I'm a bit worried because she seems to be quite depressed.

John Well, being depressed happens quite often when someone is new here. She has to get used to her new circumstances and she also has some signs of early dementia. I'm afraid that depression is common in that phase of dementia.

Nadine Yes, sure. But I think we have to do something because she just sits in her armchair not doing anything. Yesterday she did not want to accompany me to the dining room and asked me to bring the dinner to her room.

Amanda Yes, I also think we have to do something to strengthen her mobility. We should do some physical exercise with her and maybe motivate her to go to the weekly excercise course.

John That would be a great challenge, I think. But first we should have a close look at her medical file and check her condition before we start an exercise programme with her. I'm sure there are activities which we should avoid.

Amanda Yes, I already spoke to Dr. Miller. She is in the early stages of dementia and she suffers from arthritis, but her heart is fine.

Nadine Her daughter told me that she has not been active for quite some time, so we should start slowly and build up an exercise programme little by little. Maybe we could start with a 5 minute programme in the morning just after breakfast. Then she will have enough energy. And we should not let her stay inside her room for meal times. We should be firm with her and take her out to the dining room and for little walks.

John Yes, sure, What do you think of trying that for two weeks and doing some exercises once a day and then maybe twice a day. Later we can do more exercises for about 10 minutes.

Amanda Okay, we can try that. But what do you suggest to begin with?

Nadine We should start with chair exercises. She is not steady enough on her feet and these exercises will give her the chance to sit and build strength in her arm, shoulder and back muscles. And they will help her with her arthritis as well.

Amanda Yes, that's a good idea. There are a lot of chair exercises which can also help to improve Mrs Harris' hand to eye coordination. If she manages them well, she will notice her balance improving and will be steadier on her feet.

John Yes, that sounds good. Let us work out a little programme.

Working with the text

A All these statements about Mrs Harris are wrong. Correct them.

1. Mrs Harris has already lived at St Michael's nursing home for some years.
2. She doesn't have any relatives.
3. She takes part in the excercise course and often leaves her room for small walks.
4. She is a very cheerful person.
5. She was also very active before she came to St Michael's.
6. She has some heart problems.
7. She is still very steady on her feet.

B Answer the following questions.

1. Why is Amanda worried about Mrs Harris?
2. Why is John not surprised about Mrs Harris' depression?
3. Why does he suggest having a look at Mrs Harris' medical file?
4. How do Amanda, Nadine and John want to improve Mrs Harris' mobility?
5. What are the advantages of chair exercises?
6. When do they want to exercise with Mrs Harris? Why?

Working with language

Senior exercise programmes

Production

The pictures show some exercises seniors can do.
Pick out three and write down how to do the exercises.
Have a look at the vocabulary boxes below but also look at page 93 again to make sure you remember the body parts.

Example:
To do this exercise you need a Swiss ball.
Sit on a chair and … .
Take the ball in your both hands.
Lift it above your head. …
Repeat this exercise 4 times …

exercise activities	
move up and down / to and fro	jump
sit down	run on the spot
sit on	make a movement like you're (swimming)
lift	clench your fist
raise	swing your hips
bend	sit / keep straight
bend / lean forward	keep your balance
stretch	hold / take in your hands
tense your muscles	turn right / left
relax your muscles	bob up and down

exercise equipment	
chair	swing stick
ball	mat
Swiss ball	clubs
dumbbells	hoop
resistance band	bean bags
ribbon	juggling veils
skipping rope	juggling rings

Hands-on task

Interaction / Production

A Work in small groups and design two new exercises for Mrs Harris. Maybe take down your results on a transparency and present them in class.
B Imagine that you are asked to do a 10 minutes programme for the weekly excercise course in St Michael's nursing home. Work out this programme and instruct your class to do it.

Listening

Reception

1 **Here are three exercises called "the tightrope walk", "rock the boat" and "flamingo stand".**
Listen to them and do them with your class.

Parts of the body	Körperteile
knee	Knie
thumb	Daumen
chin	Kinn
bust / chest	Brust
wrist	Handgelenk
forehead	Stirn
cheek	Wange
hips	Hüften
palm	Handfläche
neck	Nacken
ankle	Knöchel
bottom	Po
calf	Wade
thigh	Oberschenkel
elbow	Ellbogen
waist	Taille
heel	Ferse
sole of the foot	Fußsohle
toes	Zehen
Keep moving!	**Bleib in Bewegung!**
physical	körperlich
physically active	körperlich aktiv
(to) do exercise / (to) exercise	(sportl.) Übungen machen
(to) maintain	erhalten
risky	risikoreich
from scratch	von Beginn an
benefit	Vorteil, Nutzen
chores	Haushaltspflichten
(to) count as	zählen / gelten als
effort	Anstrengung
arthritis	Arthritis, Gelenkentzündung
heart disease	Herzerkrankung
diabetes	Diabetes
(to) benefit	profitieren
blood pressure	Blutdruck
endorphins	Endorphine, „Glückshormone"
(to) stay independent	unabhängig bleiben
stroke	Schlaganfall
heart failure	Herzversagen
reluctant	widerwillig
(to) harm	hier: schaden
brittle	porös
balance	Gleichgewicht
(to) prevent	vermeiden
(to) enable	ermöglichen
cell	Körperzelle
cognitive decline	geistiger Verfall
dementia	Demenz
heart attack	Herzinfarkt
stiff	steif
fragile	zerbrechlich
resolute	entschlossen
moderate	gemäßigt
frequent	häufig
How to get seniors moving?	
resident	Bewohner
ward	Pflegestation
(to) accompany s. o.	jmd. begleiten
(to) strengthen	stärken, ausbauen
mobility	Bewegungsfähigkeit
(to) motivate	anspornen
challenge	Herausforderung
medical file	Krankenakte
condition	Zustand
(to) be firm with s. o.	gegenüber jmd. entschlossen / bestimmt bleiben
chair exercise	Stuhlübungen
(to) build strength	Kraft aufbauen
steady	sicher, ruhig
Senior exercise programmes	
Swiss ball	(großer) Gymnastikball
back and fro	hin und her
(to) lift / (to) raise	heben / hochheben
(to) bend	beugen
(to) bend / (to) lean forward	nach vorne beugen / lehnen
(to) stretch	strecken, dehnen
(to) tense	anspannen
(to) relax (muscles)	lockern
(to) clench fist	Faust ballen
(to) swing	kreisen lassen
straight up	aufrecht
(to) bob up and down	rauf und runter bewegen
dumbbell	Hantel
resistance band	Gummiband
ribbon	Band
skipping rope	Springseil
swing stick	Gymnastikstab
clubs	Gymnastikkegel
hoop	Gymnastikreifen
bean bags	Bohnensäckchen zum Jonglieren
juggling veils	Jonglier-Tücher
juggling rings	Jonglier-Ringe

Die Aussprache der blauen Vokabeln finden Sie in den Audio-Dateien DA0901055

Unit 12 Caring for people with disabilities

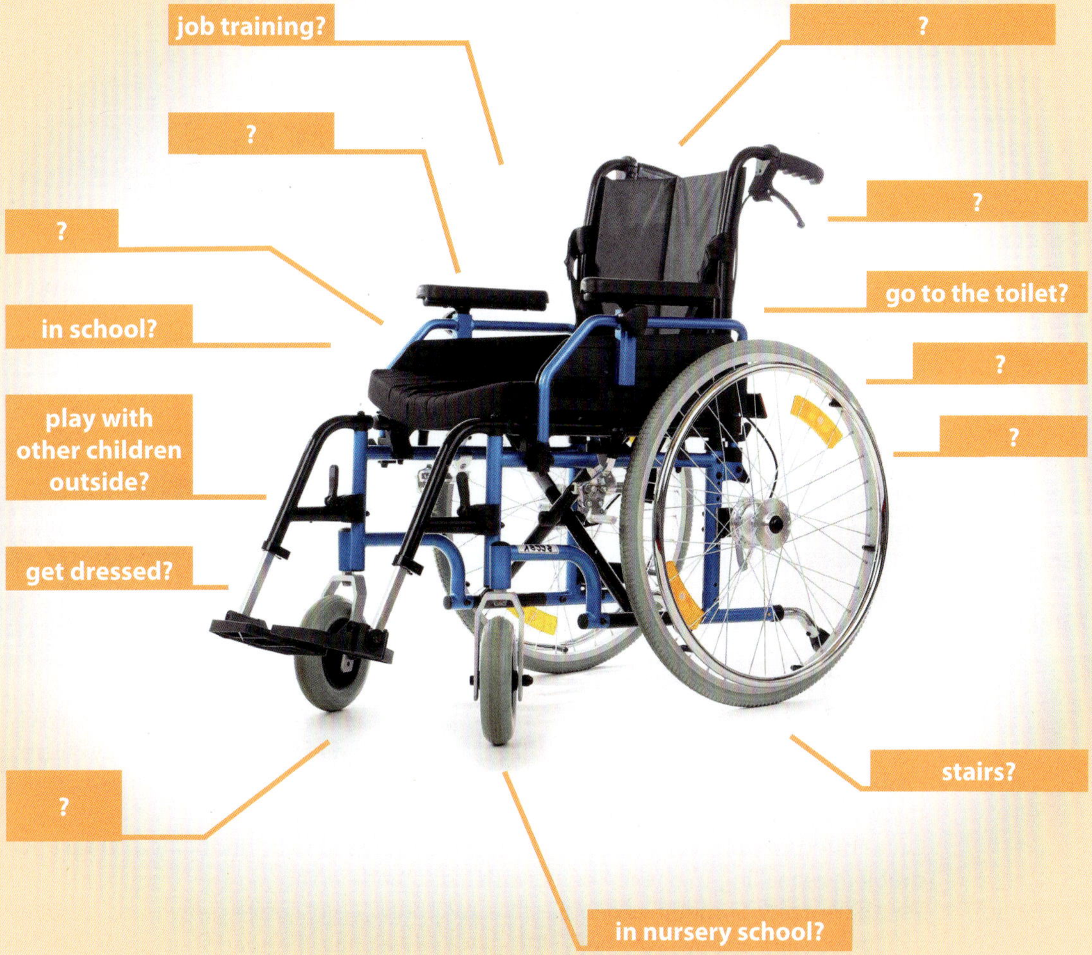

This is Andrew's wheelchair

Andrew is five years old and because of a birth defect he is a bit different.
He has from cerebral palsy and sits in a wheelchair.
Because of brain damage he has intellectual and language difficulties.
Andrew is a child with disability.
What could be a problem for him?

Andrew McArthur – a child with special needs

Katherine McArthur is Andrew's mother. Andrew, who has from a physical and mental disability, attends an integrated nursery school class at Windham Integrated Nursery School in Manchester. Katherine, who is the chairperson of the Manchester Needy Child Fund, helps other parents to cope with their child's disability. She recommends that parents send their children to integrated nursery school classes. She also wants to raise money for these classes. In an interview she explains why.

Reporter: Mrs McArthur, in the brochure of the Needy Child Fund you say that it's normal to be different and that you don't accept the word disability.

Katherine: Yes, I don't think of my child Andrew as disabled. He is just different. He has special needs but he's a normal person with his own personality. Everyone has got their own personality and this is his. He may sit in a wheelchair and perhaps his ability to take things in may be limited but he has a wonderful smile and a terrific sense of humour.

Reporter: But it's difficult to believe that you can lead a normal life with Andrew.

Katherine: I feel that we lead a very, very normal life. You get used to the situation. When you meet other people they often say, 'What a burden! How can you bear it?' But our life is as normal as any other life. Of course we had to adapt our household to Andrew's needs. The fact that he is sitting in a wheelchair is just one of many things which may cause a problem. But we have our daily routines. Andrew needs special care and attention but this has become very normal for us.

Reporter: Quite often people don't know how to treat someone with disability or they have problems speaking to or even being with a disabled person.

Katherine: Yes, that's a pity. Sometimes people stare at Andrew – most often grown-ups. Children just look at him and ask why he is sitting in a wheelchair. It's not disgust they feel, but real interest. I tell them openly about Andrew. When they know everything about his health condition they treat him like any other child. That's how I would like everyone to react. Openness is the best for all of us!

Reporter: Has Andrew got a sister or a brother? How do they cope with his cerebral palsy?

Katherine: Andrew's sister is two years older. Well, sometimes there were moments when she complained and said: "It's not fair! Why always Andrew first?" But it's wonderful to see her together with Andrew. She fully accepts him as her brother and she loves him dearly.

Reporter: Is this the reason why you support integrated nursery school classes?

Katherine: Yes, absolutely! Andrew attends an integrated class at Windham Integrated Nursery School. The experience there is positive and enriching. Such groups teach the children to accept other people as they are. It's always a real pleasure watching the children playing together. For this reason I want the Needy Child Fund to support integrated nursery schooling.

Working with the text

A Answer the following questions on the text.

1. Katherine says her son isn't disabled. How does she describe his situation?
2. Why does she feel that her family leads a very normal life?
3. How do people – grown-ups and children – react to Andrew?
4. How does Andrew's sister cope with his disability?
5. What is an integrated nursery school class?
6. Why does Katherine want to support this kind of schooling?

B Find phrases in the text which mean the same as the following phrases.

1. Andrew can't move and he has an intellectual deficit.
2. Andrew lives with a disability.
3. They had to change their household so that Andrew can live in it with all his disabilities.
4. Some people don't know how to behave towards someone who is disabled.

C Now it's your turn.
Explain in your own words what Katherine wanted to express with the following phrases.

1. Andrew is a normal person with his own personality. (line 17 / 18)
2. It isn't disgust they feel, but real interest. (line 35 / 36)
3. Openness is the best for all of us. (line 38)

Hands-on task

Interaction

Katherine talks about adapting their home to Andrew's special needs. What kind of adaptation could this be? How do you have to change a normal household so that Andrew can live in it? Sit in groups and work out your adaptation plan for his home. Present your suggestions in class.

Here are some keywords which might help:

(to) alter / design s.th. to fit the needs of the disabled	behindertengerecht umbauen / umgestalten
(to) equip with	ausstatten mit
adapted to the needs of the disabled	behindertengerecht
sanitary facilities	Sanitäranlagen
accessible for wheelchairs	rollstuhlgerecht
ramp, wheelchair ramp	Rollstuhlrampe
lift	Aufzug
hospital bed	Krankenbett
invalid chair	Krankenstuhl
invalid toilet seat (raised toilet seat)	Krankentoilettensitz
automatic opening / close	automatisches Öffnen / Schließen
(to) remove obstacles	Hindernisse aus dem Weg schaffen

Information on the topic

Die Aussprache der blauen Vokabeln finden Sie in den Audio-Dateien DA0901055

birth defect	Geburtsfehler
paralysis	Lähmung
(to) be paralysed	gelähmt sein
malfunction	Fehlbildung
malfunction, deformation	Missbildung
cerebral palsy	spastische Lähmung
brain damage	Gehirnschaden
Down Syndrome	Down-Syndrom
dyspraxia	Motorikstörung
hearing loss	Gehörverlust
hearing impairment	Gehörstörung
(to) be deaf	taub sein
visual loss	Sehverlust
visual impairment	Sehstörung
speech / language impairment	Sprachfehler
cleft palate	Gaumenspalte
autism	Autismus

Gardens of Life – a good example of an inclusion project

In the Gardens of Life project, disabled and non-disabled people work hand in hand. A group of 30 people grow organic vegetables and fruit. They also run their own grocery shop to sell their harvest and hand made products like jams and chutneys. Each month there is an open weekend and visitors can have a vegetarian meal, a salad, cakes, tea, coffee, or fruit juices which they offer in their own small bistro.
Mainly people with Down Syndrome, learning disabilities and emotional impairments take part in the project and learn everything about gardening. This includes sowing seeds, potting, planting and harvesting, weighing, and then selling their fruit and vegetables. Their highest earnings come from their "Veggy Boxes" with the fresh produce which they deliver to over 70 households each month. Over the last ten years, the project has helped a lot of people with disabilities to develop working skills and achieve real improvements in their lives. For example, Jim (aged 21) has Down Syndrome. When he joined the Gardens of Life project he was rather shy and had problems with his fine and gross motor skills. But with the help of the trained staff, care workers and gardeners he has managed to do a lot of different gardening tasks and also improve his motor and communication skills. Jim is very popular among the customers of the grocery shop because he is a very affectionate person and welcomes everyone with a brilliant smile. The positive feedback has made him a lot more self-assured. About the project he says, "Watering plants helps me to be myself". Sonja (aged 19) who has an emotional impairment says, "I like the peaceful work and that everyone is really friendly. It helps me to forget about my problems which are always there when I get home". Her favourite work is planting, harvesting and preparing the Veggy Boxes. All the project participants do gardening work as well as supporting one of the teams who work in the grocery shop, kitchen, bistro or on the Veggy Boxes delivery.
The project was set up by Harry Waters and Pamela Whittacker who are social workers. Their idea was to bring disabled and non-disabled people together and give them all the chance to both develop as individuals and learn to work independently. Pamela Whittacker says, "Gardening work not only helps people to improve their motor skills, but also to better feel and develop their emotions which is very important for those who have an emotional impairment". Harry Waters adds, "The project shows that if we all work together to break down barriers, we can educate and support each other to have an equal chance in the working world."

What is Down Syndrome?
In 1866, Dr. John Langdon Haydon Down worked in an English hospital for people with mental disabilities. He noticed that many of them showed the same physical features, those features that we today know as Down Syndrome or Trisomy 21. Dr. Down didn't know what caused these features but a French scientist in 1959 found out that the problem was genetic. There is an extra chromosome which causes delays in the child's development, both mentally and physically. DS children share certain physical features such as a flat facial profile, an upward slant to the eyes, small ears, and a protruding tongue, seizure disorders, or obesity.

The physical and mental problems Down Syndrome people have can vary from child to child. DS affects the children's ability to learn, but most have mild to moderate intellectual impairment. With special support, DS children can learn and develop skills which help them to lead a more independent life later.
Despite their problems they can go to regular schools, make friends, enjoy life and get jobs. They simply reach their goals at a slower pace than others.

Working with the text

A Here is a short summery of the Gardens of Life project. Look through the text again and fill in the missing words.

In the Gardens of Life project, people with and without 1) … work together. They grow organic 2) … and 3) …, which they then sell in their own 4) …. Here they also offer 5) … products. The project always needs money, therefore they run a small 6) … on open days and a delivery service for their 7) …. These boxes, which they 8) … to more than 70 9) …, are full of their fresh produce. The people with special needs who take part in the project are mainly people with 10) …, but also people with learning 11) … and emotional 12) …. The gardening work helps them to improve their 13) … skills. They develop good 14) … skills because they often come into contact with customers in their shop and bistro and with visitors on their open days. Some people in the project team say that the gardening work helps them to 15) … about their personal 16) …. The project shows that everyone can have an 17) … chance in the working world.

B Jim and Sonja take part in the Gardens of Life project. Answer the following questions about them.

1. What kinds of disability do Jim and Sonja have?
2. What are their favourite jobs?
3. What skills can they develop and improve during the Gardens of Life project?
4. Why is the work in the grocery shop important for Jim?
5. Why is it very important for Sonja to "feel her emotions" like Pamela Wittacker says?

C What does inclusion mean?

1. First read the info box on inclusion. Make sure you understand it. If you need to, translate it.
2. People say that the Gardens of Life project is a good example of inclusion. Explain why.

What is inclusion?

The principle of inclusion means that everyone can attend and benefit from the same educational system and take part as an equal partner in the working world. Schools for example and projects like the Gardens of Life make sure that no one is excluded because of their disability. The idea behind all this is friendship, non-discrimination and participation of all people. Inclusion means to establish an educational system without any kind of exclusion and a working world which offers equal chances to everyone. Diversity is seen as a chance for everyone to gain valuable experience.

Hands-on task

Production / Interaction

D **Work in small groups and gather some information about inclusion projects in your area. Do you know of any good examples? Why not surf the web and present a short summary of the project to your class?**

Interaction

E **Here are some questions which people who visited the Gardens of Life project on an open day asked Harry Waters. Play his role and answer them in a role play. To answer these questions read the text on Down Syndrome as well.**

Do all of your project teams work in the garden? Or do they do other tasks as well?

How does your project help people with disabilities to take part in the working world?

I have only seen people with Down Syndrome here. Does your project only focus on this condition?

How do you raise money for your project?

Do your project participants just develop their motor skills? Or is there anything else they can improve?

Can people with Down Syndrome really learn to do a job?

How do your project members like the work they do?

Listening

Reception

12

F **Mandy Short is a reporter for the local newspaper and she interviews some of the project participants on the open day. Listen to the interview and match the sentences.**

1. Sonja has difficulties with numbers	a. because it has stopped her depressive moods.
2. John joins the gardening team	b. because he likes picking the fruit and tasting it right away.
3. Emma feels good about attending the project	c. because the people he works with have become his best friends.
4. Robert loves the work	d. because he likes doing hard work.
5. Tom can't live without the project	e. but she manages and enjoys packing the Veggy Boxes.

Hands-on task

Interaction

G Here are some prejudices about people who have Down Syndrome. Answer them.

1. People with Down Syndrome have severe intellectual impairment and can't learn anything.
2. They will never be able to join the workforce / get a job.
3. People with Down Syndrome will always be dependent on others.

**H The Gardens of Life project always needs people who support it with their money. Therefore, the Veggy Boxes team is thinking of putting some advertising flyers into the neighbours' letterboxes to find more customers or donors.
Here are the basic rules on how to create advertising flyers.**

a. Make sure you understand them.

Some rules on how to create an advertising flyer

Rule 1: Write a snappy headline or slogan.
Write a few powerful words about your product to get attention. Popular slogans or headlines very often have one or more of the following words: easy …, top quality … Discover … now! Now you can …!, Buy … and feel / taste …!

Rule 2: Use an eye-catching design
Interesting colours, graphics and especially photos / pictures get attention and are easier to remember. They can create a positive impression and "draw the reader in".

Rule 3: Clearly say what your product can do for the reader.
Every reader asks the question, "What can the product do for me?" You should answer this question and use the word "you" and "your" instead of "I, we, us, our" to make clear that the product will be good for the reader. But keep your text short and use powerful / positive words like, "free", "new", "love", "wonderful", "healthy" …

Rule 4: Don't forget to include names, addresses, or maps.
No one likes to guess who is talking to him. Give your name, the project name, addresses and how to get there.

Rule 5: Offer discounts or a special offer.
Everyone likes special offers. They can arouse the interest of new customers but don't forget to limit the validity.

**b. Work in groups and design an advertising flyer.
Present your results in class.
For some further help look at page 134 where you can find some general information on how to design posters and fly posters.**

Grammar box: Conditional sentences (Type I) – Bedingungssätze (Typ I)

Simple Present im if-Satz	Will-Future im Hauptsatz
If *you* ***water*** *the plants regularly,*	*they* ***will*** *definitely* ***grow.***
If *they* ***have*** *a good harvest and sell all of their vegetables,*	*they* ***will earn*** *enough money to build up their own kitchen and restaurant.*

→ Bedingungssätze des Typs I drücken aus, dass die Bedingung **erfüllbar / wahrscheinlich** ist.
Im Nebensatz kann auch anstatt will „can" eingesetzt werden.
If we have enough money, we can run our own kitchen and restaurant.

Grammar box: Conditional sentences (Type II) – Bedingungssätze (Typ II)

Past Tense im if-Satz	Conditional I (would + Vollverb im Infinitiv) im Hauptsatz
If *we* ***had*** *more money left over,*	*we would build our own restaurant.*
If *we* ***sold*** *more Veggy Boxes,*	*we would earn more money.*

→ Bedingungssätze des Typs II drücken aus, dass die Bedingung **eher unwahrscheinlich,** damit nicht oder kaum erfüllbar sein wird. Vorsicht! Auch wenn die Past Tense eingesetzt wird, bezieht sich dieser Satz nicht auf die Vergangenheit.
Im Hauptsatz kann auch anstatt would „could" eingesetzt werden.
If we had enough money, we could run our own restaurant.

Practising Grammar

A If-clauses type I: Put the verbs in brackets into the correct tense.

1. People with disabilites should join the Garden Eden project. If they (do) gardening work regularly, they will improve their senses.
2. They will definitely strengthen their muscles, if they (try) doing gardening work like mowing the lawns, or planting.
3. If Jim (work) in our team, we will have a lot of fun.
4. If we sell all of our harvest, we (raise) enough money to keep up the project for the next two years.
5. If we maintain the quality of our products, we (find) enough customers for our Veggy Boxes.
6. If you buy a Veggy Box every month, you (receive) enough fresh food to stay fit and healthy.

B If-clauses type II. Put the verbs in brackets into the correct tense.

1. Money is always a great problem. If we had more money, we (offer) more places for people with disabilities.
2. If more people bought our products, we (build) a new house for our restaurant.
3. If the local newspaper reported on our project, maybe we (get) more attention and interest in our project.
4. If Harry (have) more money for new care workers, we could give our project members more one-on-one-time.
5. If we (have) another minibus, we (deliver) more boxes.
6. If I could spend some money on social projects, I … . ***Go on!***
7. If I had the chance to take part in the Gardens of Life project, I … . ***Go on!***

C This exercise has both types of if-clauses - I and II.
Put the verbs in brackets into the correct tense.

1. We really have to raise more money. If we (have) more money, we (start) a second Gardens of Life project.
2. Raising money is very difficult. If I (have) a real good idea how to find more people who support our project, I (put) it into practice. But right now, I can't think of what we could do.
3. Ken has already watered the plants. He (help) you delivering the Veggy Boxes, if you (be) short of time.
4. If there (be) more time, I (come) over to help you in the kitchen. But I'm too busy right now, sorry!
5. Next week we have our open day and I know that everything is well-organised. If this day (not be) the usual great success, I (feel) very disappointed.

Grammar box: Who and Which

Who → für Personen

*This is Harry **who** is in charge of the Gardens of Life project.*
*Jim is one of the project participants **who** supports the grocery shop team.*

Which → für Gegenstände

*The Veggy Boxes **which** they deliver to the households are full of fresh vegetables.*
*This is the Veggy Box **which** I ordered from the Gardens of Life project.*

Practising Grammar

Pamela Whittacker shows some of the visitors around on the day open.
Fill in who or which.

I'd like to welcome you to our Gardens of Life project **1 ...** we started ten years ago. On our tour you will see the various fruit and vegetable gardens but also our kitchen, bistro, grocery shop and delivery service **2 ...** we have run for five years. We have a Veggy Box delivery service and grocery shop to try and raise the money **3 ...** we need to keep the project going in the future. Our project participants and the staff consist of people **4 ...** are disabled and people **5 ...** aren't. Those **6 ...** have disabilities mainly have Down Syndrome, learning disabilities or an emotional impairment. With the help of a trained staff **7 ...** include care workers, gardeners and a chef, the project participants learn gardening and how to run a grocery shop, kitchen, bistro and delivery service. Let's first have a look at our Veggy Box service **8 ...** is right here next to our grocery shop. Every month we pack 70 Veggy Boxes **9 ...** we take right to our customers' front doors. The Veggy Boxes are cardboard boxes with a cool label **10 ...** was designed by our project participants. Now we are going into our grocery shop **11 ...** is full of fresh fruit and vegetables. Here we also sell jams and chutneys **12 ...** we have produced in our kitchen. Here is Jim **13 ...** is one of our best sellers. Hi, Jim, would you like to tell our visitors something about yourself and the tasks **14 ...** you do here at the Gardens of Life project.

wheelchair	Rollstuhl
child with special needs	Kind mit einem besonderen Bedürfnis, Kind mit Behinderung
intellectual difficulties	intellektuelle Schwierigkeiten
language difficulties	Sprachschwierigkeiten
cerebral palsy	spastische Lähmung
Andrew McArthur – a child with special needs	
integrated nursery school class	integrative Kindergartengruppe (Gruppe mit Kindern mit und ohne Behinderungen)
chairman	Vorsitzende, Vorsitzender
(to) bear s.th.	etwas ertragen
(to) recommend	empfehlen
(to) raise money	Geld aufbringen
(to) be disabled	eine Behinderung haben
disability	Behinderung, Unfähigkeit
ability	Fähigkeit
(to) be able to	fähig sein zu
personality	Persönlichkeit
(to) be limited	eingeschränkt sein
sense of humour	Sinn für Humor
What a burden!	Was für ein schweres Schicksal!
(to) withstand	standhalten, durchhalten
(to) adapt	anpassen
adaptation	Anpassung
special care	besondere Pflege, Fürsorge
(to) stare at s.o.	jmd. anstarren
disgust	Entsetzen, Ekel
(to) treat s.o.	jmd. behandeln
openness	Offenheit
(to) complain	sich beschweren
(to) support	unterstützen
enriching	bereichernd
intellectual deficit	intellektuelles (geistiges) Defizit, Mangel
physical disability	körperliche Behinderung
mental disability	geistige Behinderung
Gardens of Life…	
grocery shop	Lebensmittelgeschäft
(the) harvest	(die) Ernte
learning disabilities	Lernbehinderung
emotional impairment	emotionale Einschränkung
(to) sow	säen
seed	Saat
(to) pot	eintopfen
(to) plant	pflanzen
(to) harvest	ernten
(to) weigh	wiegen
produce	Erzeugnis, Produkt
fine motor skills	Feinmotorik
gross motor skills	Grobmotorik
communication skills	kommunikative Fähigkeiten
affectionate	(sehr) emotional
brilliant	strahlend
self-assured	selbstsicher
participant	Teilnehmer
work independently	selbstständig arbeiten
equal	gleichberechtigt
working world	Arbeitswelt
What is Down Syndrome?	
physical	körperlich
features	Merkmale
genetic	genetisch
chromosome	Chromosom
delay	Verzögerung
facial profile	Gesichtsprofil
upwards	nach oben gerichtet
slant	Neigung
protruding	hervorstehend, herausragend
seizure disorder	Krankheit, die Anfälle verursacht
obesity	Fettleibigkeit
affect	angreifen, negativ beeinflussen
moderate	mittelmäßig, moderat
at a slower pace	in langsamerem Tempo
inclusion	Aufnahme, hier: Inklusion
(to) benefit from	Nutzen ziehen von, profitieren von
(to) exclude from	jmd. ausschließen von
exclusion from	Ausschluss von
participation	Teilnahme, Beteiligung
diversity	Vielfalt
Some rules on how to create an advertising flyer	
snappy	treffend, flott
(to) discover	entdecken
eye-catching	Blickfang
impression	Eindruck, Wirkung
(to) draw s.o. in	jmd. an-/hereinziehen
discounts	Rabatte
(to) arouse interest	Interesse wecken
(to) limit	beschränken
validity	Gültigkeitsdauer
one-on-one-time	Zeit für den Einzelnen
(to) keep the project going	das Projekt in Gang halten

Die Aussprache der blauen Vokabeln finden Sie in den Audio-Dateien DA0901055

1

Why do people lose control of their lives?

2

3

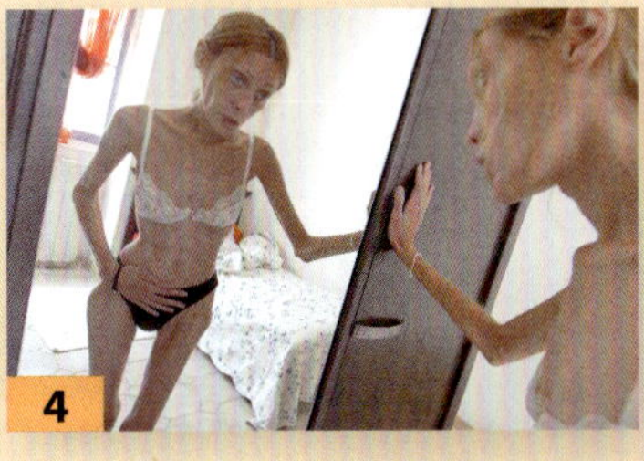
4

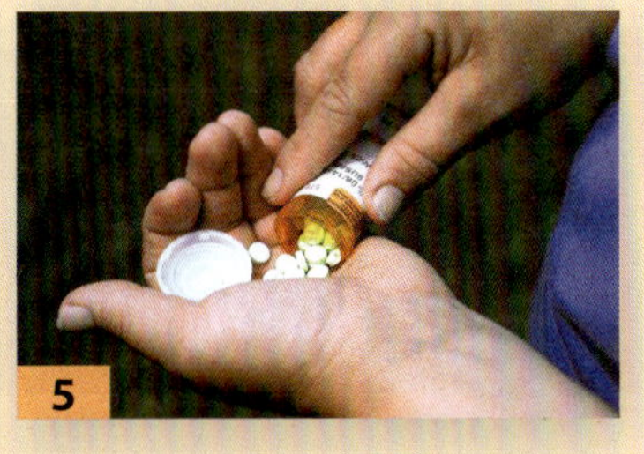
5

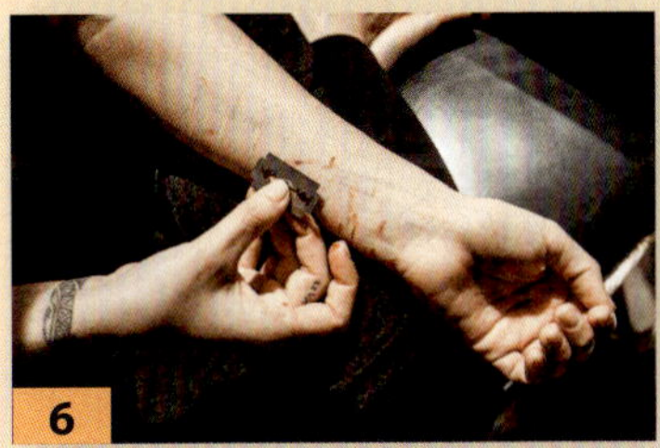
6

7

8

Losing control of your life

1. Look at the pictures and describe the situations they show. Use the words in the boxes for help.

nouns	verbs
habit – addiction – gambling / shopping addiction – addiction to pills / alcohol – self-harm – eating disorder – bulimia – anorexia – hoarding disorder	gamble – overeat – starve oneself – go on eating / drinking binges – harm oneself – lose control – shop until you drop – hoard things – overdose – cut arms / legs

2. What could be the consequences of these people's habits?
3. Can you think of reasons why people may fall into such extreme habits and / or addictions and live a life on the edge?

Living with borderline personality disorder

My name is Debbie, I'm only 22 years old but I have already experienced depression several times. I have overdosed on pills several times, have gone on lots of alcohol binges, have struggled with bulimia, have had lots of sexual relationships and have self-harmed countless times. As my mother has always told everyone, "She is mad and moody, better leave her alone!". Today I know that I have borderline personality disorder – BPD.

I have always been searching for someone who loves me. My dad went away when I was 3 and I never saw him again. At about age 10, I started telling myself that only my dad loves me. I searched for someone I could love instead. I had lots of teddy bears, later pets, and as a teenage girl of 14 I started sleeping with boys.

I have always had strange feelings of emptiness and tension deep inside me. At 15 I began self-harming. I cut deep into my arms and legs. Even today I still have rapid mood changes. I can feel very sad or extremely angry. When this happens there is a voice in my head repeating: "Hurt yourself" While I'm self-harming, I feel like I'm outside my body and watching someone else. It's like another person has taken over my body and I have no control of what is going to happen next. All this is scary but self-harm releases my tension, so I continue. This habit stops whenever I'm in a happy relationship but I fall back into it as soon as something goes wrong and I feel bad or under stress. Then it becomes a part of my routine at night. I wash my face, brush my teeth and self-harm. At 16 I felt that I couldn't stop this habit and I stole my mother's tranquilisers and tried to commit suicide for the first time. I was transferred to a psychiatric ward and started therapy for the first time. But I overdosed 6 more times before I was 19. Then suddenly, at 20, I started vomiting up everything I ate. I felt very ill for a number of weeks and my mother took me to a doctor. He gave me some medicine but the vomiting kept on. Several weeks passed and no physical reason was found. Doctors talked of bulimia. Again I went into a psychiatric ward, but this time I was diagnosed with BPD.

Up to now there hasn't been a clear answer why I have borderline personality disorder, but I think that my unfulfilled wish for real love plays a role. My mother has never understood my feelings. She abused me emotionally when I was a teenage girl, calling me "my lunatic girl". Now I'm in a special therapy programme for women with BPD. Meeting and talking to the other women was a real turning point. When I saw how much we have in common I could accept my bipolar personality. I try to live a normal life but life with borderline personality disorder will always be a life on the edge!

Working with the text

Read Debbie's story and answer the questions.

A Debbie's life story

1. Say what happened when she was 3 – 10 – 14 – 15 – 16 – 19 – 20 years old.
2. When did she experience a turning point in her life? How has her life changed since then?

B The diagnosis with borderline personality disorder.

Read the information box on borderline personality disorder and look at Debbie's story again. What typical symptoms did she show? What does she still show?

C Debbie's relationships

1. She couldn't build up a relationship with her father because …
2. She compensated for his missing love by …
3. She was already sexually active in her early teens because …
4. The relationship with her mother is rather complicated because …

D Causes for her personality disorder

Can you find possible reasons for her personality disorder? What are they?

E Her therapy

What has Debbie done to cope with her personality disorder? What kind of treatment does she still get today?

F Debbie says that her life with borderline personality disorder will always be "a life on the edge". Explain why.

What is borderline personality disorder – BPD?

Some facts

- BPD is a mental health problem which very often starts as a teenager.
- More females (about 75%) than males have BPD

Symptoms

- emotions go up and down very quickly
- strong feelings of emptiness, anger and stress
- problems maintaining relationships
- unstable identity, people think differently about themselves depending on who they are with
- take risks or do things without thinking about consequences
- harm themselves (e.g. cutting themselves or overdosing)
- fear of being left alone or rejected
- believe, hear and see things which are not real or true (hallucinations)
- go through phases of depression
- some struggle with eating disorders
- some misuse alcohol or drugs

Treatment

- long-term psychotherapy with a therapist who specialises in personality disorder
- Some symptoms respond to medication, like antidepressants

Causes

Causes are still unclear but patients have often had stressful and difficult life experiences such as loss of a parent, childhood neglect, (sexual, emotional, physical) abuse, break up of a relationship, loss of job.

Working with language

A Here is the beginning of a summary of Debbie's case. The following connectors are missing. Fill them in.

instead of – after – as a result – when – for example – that – although – without a doubt – in order to – whenever – because – despite – due to

Look at page 141. Here you will find a list of the most common connectors with their translation.

Debbie's story began 1. … she was only three years old. Her father left the family and 2. … he went away Debbie started to feel unloved. 3. … having her father's love Debbie had lots of teddy bears and pets. 4. … that lack of love she had her first sexual relationships at 14. At 15 she was filled with feelings of emptiness and tension and 5. … she started self-harming. 6. … she cut her arms and legs. 7. … she loses control of her body and mind 8. … she feels that something is wrong in her life. But her situation became so unbearable for her 9. … she tried to commit suicide 10. … she felt that she couldn't stop her habit. She was taken into a psychiatric ward 11. … start therapy for the first time. But 12. … she was in therapy she could not stop her habit. 13. … her therapy she overdosed 6 more times. (…)

Production

B Now use your notes to summarise the main aspects of Debbie's case (her further life story, the diagnosis, her relationships and causes for her mental illness). Don't forget to make use of connectors!

Losing control because of addiction

Reception

13 Listening

Listen to Bernard's and Kayla's stories of addiction.

1. What addictions did they struggle with?
2. Work in pairs and look at the keywords below. They are typical aspects in drug addiction. Choose either Bernard's or Kayla's story. Pick out the keywords which are in their story and give examples from their story.

- ignorance of problems
- fear of failure
- slovenly appearance
- multiple drug abuse / multiple addictions
- aggression
- therapy and reintegration
- loss of living standards (no money to pay flat, bills …)
- changes in personality
- problems staying awake and / or sleeping
- health problems (physical and mental problems)
- loss of job
- influence of wrong friends
- need to have more energy and 'pep'
- overdose and death
- stress
- wish to be accepted / admired
- fun and excitement
- drug related crimes (commit crimes to finance addiction)
- loss of social contacts (loss of family and friends)
- vicious circle

How a smartphone can help you in a crisis

What can people do if they experience distress or fall into crisis? Some talk with a friend or their parents. Those who are in therapy can contact their therapist. But how can you find a safe place if you don't have a safety net? You could make an emergency appointment with your doctor during the day, or call a doctor's out-of-hours-service at night. There are mental health crisis service teams in every city. And you can call the police emergency number. They will support you in finding help. Research shows that a lot of teenagers have suffered a crisis but only a few of them research or get professional help from counselling services. Very often they keep on struggling with their difficulties without telling anybody which may lead to mental health problems, addiction, or suicide. Young people prefer to get information and advice from the internet. Therefore the British "get connected" project has provided a free app to give teenagers in distress access to confidential help whenever they need it. It is a helpline for people under 25 who don't know where to turn. The service is available 365 days a year and young people can get in touch by smartphone, web-chat, email, or text message. Each time someone gets in touch with the helpline, one of its 100 volunteers offers emotional support and connects them to a specialist from a database of 10,000 trusted organisations. The app also uses geolocation technology to identify where the person is and where he or she can find a crisis service team nearby.
Currently, there are about 20 apps for smartphone users, for example a music app which plays music to calm down. The app designer believes that "emotional wellbeing music" can increase positive emotions to help overcome feelings of depression. There are also digital tools to prepare for a doctor's appointment or for counselling. The tools help you to ask the right questions and describe your symptoms.

(information taken from nominet trust, 2014)

Working with the text

A Read the text again and find words that mean …

1. noun: a time when you feel really bad because of a difficult life situation or a big problem
2. noun: a person who helps you by giving you psychological treatment.
3. noun phrase: medical help you can get outside the usual consultation and counselling times in an emergency.
4. adjective: help you get from a trained person is … help.
5. noun: taking your life, killing yourself.
6. adjective: something you must keep secret is … information.
7. noun: a person who helps without being paid for their work.
8. verb: to become less nervous or excited

B Where can people in a crisis find help? Complete the following sentences.

1. At first you can talk to people who are close to you like …
2. When you are in therapy you …
3. Depending on when you need emergency help from a doctor, you have two possibilities …
4. Every city has …
5. But if you don't have any plan in place, you can always …
6. Teenagers …

C Now answer the following questions about the British "get-connected" project.

1. Why do the designers believe that teenagers, especially, will make use of their helpline?
2. What do you need to make use of this help service?
3. What kind of help do teenagers who contact the helpline receive?
4. Why does the app use geolocation technology?

Hands-on tasks

Interaction

A Imagine you work in a crisis service team. At a staff meeting, you discuss whether you want to make use of the "get-connected" project and tell young people to use it or not. Here are two of the main opposing opinions.
Work in small groups and create a role play.

No app can be as effective as a real person sitting next to you in a crisis. This is the best way to give intensive, individual and personal help.

Young people are attached to their smartphones, so are very likely to use them to get help. The app can give them the first steps to get help. This is much better than not knowing what to do and maybe taking drugs or commiting suicide.

B Here are two people in crisis.
Choose one of them and give some advice. Look at the useful phrases.

I'm not sure whether I can manage to complete my training as a nursing assistant. Both my parents have that job. If I don't continue, I am going to disappoint them. I've tried to forget my problems by going on alcohol binges with my friends. Now I drink whenever I feel down. I often feel down. Once, I drank all night and my colleagues could smell the alcohol in the morning. My boss told me that I will get fired if that happens again. My life is a mess, what can I do? (Ron, 18)

I was reported to the police for shoplifting. I'm in a gang with two other girls; we go into shops stealing. I love the thrill. My parents will go mad and throw me out if they get to know about that. One of the girls once gave me some pills to cheer me up. Yesterday, when I stood in the bathroom where my parents keep all our pills, I thought maybe I should take an overdose and that would be it! (Linda, 17)

Some helpful phrases on giving advice

I advise you to …	Ich rate Ihnen …
Before you … (do something)	Bevor Sie …
That depends on …	Das kommt darauf an …
I don't think you should …	Ich denke, Sie sollten nicht …
You should discuss your problems / doubts with …	Sie sollten Ihre Probleme / Zweifel mit … diskutieren …
If you feel … you will have to …	Wenn Sie fühlen, dass …, dann müssen Sie …
This is for you to decide …	Das müssen Sie entscheiden …
It is obvious that …	Es ist offensichtlich, dass …
It might be better if you … (+ Simple Past)	Es könnte besser sein, wenn …
The right thing to do is …	Das Richtige zu tun, ist …
Don't hesitate to …	Zögern Sie nicht …
Take the first step and …	Machen Sie den ersten Schritt und …
It is always better to …	Es ist immer besser zu …
In any case, why don't you …	In jedem Fall, warum … Sie nicht …
What are you waiting for?	Worauf warten Sie?
Now the time has come to …	Jetzt ist die Zeit gekommen, um …

Grammar box: Present Perfect – Das Perfekt

Beispiele:

bejahter Satz	verneinter Satz	Fragesatz
*I **have talked** to Debbie.*	*I **haven't talked** to Debbie.*	***Have** I **talked** to Debbie?*
*I **have been** in therapy.*	*I **haven't been** in therapy.*	***Have** I **been** in therapy?*
*He/She **has talked** …*	*He/She **hasn't talked** …*	***Has** he/she **talked** …?*
*He/She **has gone** …*	*He/She **hasn't gone** …*	***Has** he/she **gone** …?*
*We/You/They **have talked** …*	*We/You/They **haven't talked** …*	***Have** we/you/they **talked** …?*
*We/You/They **have gone** …*	*We/You/They **haven't gone** …*	***Have** we/you/they **gone** …?*

Bildung: → have / has + 3. Verbform

Verwendung

Das Present Perfect Simple wird verwendet …

- für Handlungen, die in der Vergangenheit angefangen haben und bis in die Gegenwart andauern.
  I have known Debbie for more than six years now.
- für Handlungen, die gerade erst vollendet wurden.
  I have just talked to Debbie on the phone.
- für Handlungen, die zwar in der Vergangenheit abgeschlossen wurden, aber noch Auswirkungen auf die Gegenwart haben.
  The number of teenagers addicted to alcohol has risen in the last two years. (Seit zwei Jahren steigt die Zahl der alkoholsüchtigen Teenager.)

Zeitadverbien stehen dabei nach dem ersten Bestandteil des Verbs:

*John **has never tried** any drugs.*	John hat niemals Drogen probiert.
*My father **has always smoked.***	Mein Vater hat (schon) immer geraucht.
***Have** you **ever tried** any drugs?*	Hast du jemals Drogen probiert?

Practising Grammar

A Write sentences in the Present Perfect.

1. I / already smoke 40 cigarettes / today.
2. Debbie / not cut herself / for two months.
3. Paul / be in therapy / for three months.
4. The number of teenagers addicted to alcohol / go up / in recent years.
5. I / be drunk a several times / this month.
6. I / never / try drugs.
7. Chantelle / struggle with bulimia / for 2 years.

B Write questions in the Present Perfect.

1. You / ever drink alcohol?
2. How long / Paul / have problems with harder drugs?
3. How long / you / smoke?
4. Debbie / manage to cope with her depression / since her therapy?
5. The number of teenagers who drink too much alcohol / increase in the last two years?
6. You / finish / the medicine plan yet?

C David has had some problems with alcohol.
He visits a drug advice center and talks to Mrs Cary, a social worker who specialises in teenage drug addiction.
Fill in the Present Perfect.

1.	Mrs Cary	(you / ever / be) on alcohol binges?
2.	David	Yes, I (often / drink) large amounts of alcohol and my parent (always complain) about it!
3.	Mrs Cary	(your mother / tell) you that she called the drug advice center? She (be) extremely worried about you and your health for the last two months.
4.	David	I know, she told me this morning that she thinks my habit (become) worse in the last two months.
5.	Mrs Cary	(you / ever / feel) worried about your alcohol habit?
6.	David	No, never, I (have) a lot of binges since I was 14, but I (not suffer) from any severe health problems as a result.
7.	Mrs Cary	(you / ever / try) other drugs?
8.	David	No, not really, I (never / smoke) joints. And I (not take) any hard drugs either. But I (drink) alcohol regularly since I was ten.
9.	Mrs Cary	(you / ever / think) of going into therapy because of your alcohol problem?
10.	David	Well, I know my parents want me to start therapy, but I (manage) without therapy so far and I (always feel) sure that I have everything under control.
11.	Mrs Cary	I'm afraid I disagree. I think you have a real problem with alcohol and that you (have) a problem for some years!

D Fill in since or for.

since = „seit"	**for = „seit"**
I have not touched any alcohol again ***since*** *my 18th birthday.*	*I have not touched any alcohol* ***for*** *the last five years.*
→ **Zeitpunkt**	→ **Zeitspanne**

1. He hasn't done any schoolwork **...?** the last three months.
2. **...?** her childhood she has missed her father.
3. I have felt depressed **...?** my best friend died.
4. John hasn't been back to work **...?**Tuesday.
5. I don't think I have seen him **...?** at least four to five days now.
6. My son has managed not to touch any alcohol **...?** he was in therapy two years ago.
7. My parents haven't been on holiday **...?** the last three years.
8. Because of my health problems I haven't gone on any alcohol binges ... a year now.
9. Brian lives a healthy life. He hasn't eaten any unhealthy food or even drunk a drop of alcohol ... he stopped being a teenager.
10. I have never tried smoking a cigarette but my husband has been a smoker ... he started his job training.

Grammar box: Comparison of Past Tense and Present Perfect –
Vergleich der Vergangenheit und der vollendeten Gegenwart

Debbie's father ***left*** *his family many years ago.*	*Debbie* ***has*** *never* ***seen*** *her father again.*
→ in der Vergangenheit abgeschlossene Handlung	**→ bis in die Gegenwärt andauernde Handlung**
Signalwörter yesterday (gestern), one year ago (vor einem Jahr), in 2002, the other day (an jenem / dem Tag), the day before yesterday (vorgestern), last week (letzte Woche), in those days (in jenen Tagen / damals), in the past (in der Vergangenheit / damals)	**Signalwörter** just (gerade erst vorbei) – already (schon), since / for (seit) – till now / up till now (bis jetzt), so far (bisher), not … yet (noch nicht), ever (jemals), never (noch nie), this morning / week / year … (heute Morgen, diese Woche, dieses Jahr)

Why don't you look back at page 61 to revise the past simple tense?

Practising Grammar

Fill in the Past Simple Tense or Present Perfect Simple.

1. Pauline (not see) her mother since she (go) into therapy three weeks ago.
2. Mrs Martin (ask) for some help at the drug advice service yesterday morning because her son (have) an alcohol problem for six months.
3. I (never / touch) any hard drugs but I (have) my first alcoholic drinks at my 18th birthday party. At that party I (have) too many cocktails and (feel) really sick the next morning.
4. (you / go) on a binge with your friends last weekend?
5. Mr Bart (start) work in our crisis house 10 years ago and he (never think) of giving up his job although he (experience) a lot of difficult situations since his first day here.
6. When they first (visit) their daughter at therapy clinic last month, they (be) very nervous about seeing her again. But they like to see the progress she (make) since the last visit.
7. I (always / hate) parties with lots of alcohol. Last week I (be) at a party with lots of drunk people and later on that evening I also (see) that some of the people were taking harder drugs.
8. Last year I (take) part in a therapy programme for women with BPD. Hearing about the other women's problems in the therapy sessions (help) me to accept my problems and since then I (become) less depressed.

Losing control of your life	
habit	Gewohnheit, Sucht
addiction (to)	Sucht / Abhängigkeit von
gambling addiction	Spielsucht
shopping addiction	Kaufsucht
self-harm	Selbstverletzung
eating disorder	Essstörung
bulimia	Bulimie, Ess-Brechsucht
anorexia	Magersucht
(to) gamble	Spielen (um Geld)
(to) overeat	(sich) überessen
(to) starve oneself	hungern, (sich) aushungern
(to) go on binges	auf ein (Sauf- / Fress-)Gelage gehen
(to) harm oneself	sich selbst verletzen
(to) lose control of	Kontrolle verlieren
(to) shop until you drop	kaufen bis zum Umfallen
(to) hoard	sammeln, horten
(to) overdose	Überdosis, (sich) überdosieren

Living with borderline personality disorder	
borderline personality disorder (BPD)	Borderline-Persönlichkeitsstörung
countless	zahllos
moody	launig
emptiness	Leere
tension	Anspannung
rapid	schnell, rapid
(to) self-harm	sich selbst verletzen
(to) release	abbauen, (frei) / (heraus) lassen
tranquiliser	Beruhigungsmittel
(to) commit suicide	Selbstmord begehen
(to) be transferred to	(über-), eingewiesen werden
psychiatric ward	psychiatrische Station
(to) vomit (up)	erbrechen
(to) diagnose with	diagnostizieren
unfulfilled	unerfüllt
lunatic	verrückt
turning point	Wendepunkt
(to) have in common	gemeinsam haben
bipolar	manisch-depressiv

Die Aussprache der blauen Vokabeln finden Sie in den Audio-Dateien DA0901055

What is borderline personality disorder?	
mental health	geistige / mentale Gesundheit
anger	Wut
(to) maintain	aufrechterhalten
unstable	instabil
(to) depend on	abhängen von
(to) reject	ablehnen
(to) misuse	missbrauchen
long-term	Langzeit...
psychotherapy	Psychotherapie
antidepressants	Antidepressiva
loss	Verlust
neglect	Vernachlässigung
sexual / emotional / physical abuse	sexueller/ emotionaler / körperlicher Missbrauch

Listening	
(to) admire	bewundern
fear of failure	Versagensangst
drug related crimes	Drogenbeschaffungskriminalität
multiple	mehrfach
slovenly	heruntergekommen
appearance	Erscheinungsbild
reintegration	Reintegration, Wiedereingliederung
pep	Pepp, Schwung
vicious circle	Teufelskreis

How a smartphone can help you in a crisis	
distress	Verzweiflung
safety net	Sicherheitsnetz
crisis service team	Krisenberatungsteam
emergency number	Notfallnummer
counselling service	Beratungsdienst
"get connected"	Anschluss finden, Kontakt aufnehmen
(to) provide	zur Verfügung stellen
confidential	vertraulich
available	verfügbar
volunteer	Freiwillige(r)
(to) connect to	vermitteln, zusammenführen
database	Datenbank
trusted	bewährt
currently	derzeit
(to) calm down	(sich) beruhigen
(to) be attached to	an etwas hängen
effective	wirksam
gang	Bande
drug advice center	Drogenberatung

Dear residents,

We are deeply saddened to inform you that our resident Betty Harris passed away Thursday night surrounded by her loving daughters and our care assistants.

Betty Harris was a mother of two daughters and grandmother to five grandchildren. She lived here in St Michael's Nursing Home for three years. As many of you know, she suffered from heart problems. We are relieved that her passing was peaceful and painless.

Her family invites you to her funeral which will be held on Monday in St Raphael's church at 11:30 a.m.

We will remember her as a very cheerful person and her wonderful voice will be greatly missed in our home's choir!

In memory of

Betty Harris

April 4th, 1928 – August 19th 2015

When someone dies …

Above you can see a typical obituary British nursing homes very often use to inform their residents about someone's death. Some also give their residents the opportunity to write down their feelings about a resident's death in a book of condolence which is then handed over to the grieving family.

A **Look at the obituary and list what type of information there is about Betty Harris (e.g. her age)**

B **What does the obituary tell you about her death?**

C **Do German obituaries look the same? What is similar, what is different?**

D **Did you experience the death of a resident or patient during your placement at an old people's home, nursing home, or hospital? How did the home / hospital deal with the death of a resident / patient?**

Death as a part of care work

You can't do a nursing job without being confronted by death and grieving. Tana, Matthew and Sophie talk about their experience with dying patients.

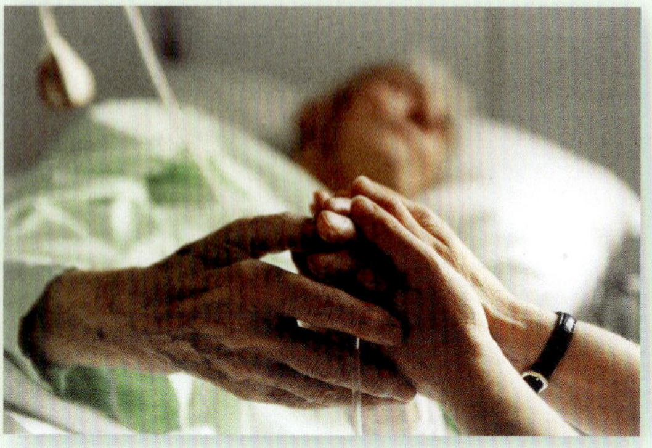

Tana Matasu: I work in an intensive care unit and very often I have to see people die. Sure, there is some kind of a routine in the last care we give to a dying person. But you should not forget that nurses are also human and death affects everyone. The worst day in my career was the death of a 5-year-old boy who was run over by a car. I will never forget his mother's crying and holding his hand as he died. Somehow I got through that day, but even today this picture still haunts me. After some years in that job you learn to push your emotions aside because there are all the other patients waiting for you. You know how to care for a dying person and how to speak to grieving relatives, but no one can tell you how to deal with your own feelings of sadness. For me it helps to talk about my patient's death with one of my colleagues. I feel much better if I am able to arrange a "good death" for our patients, if their family is at their side and they can gently pass away without pain.

Matthew Barns: I'm a nursing assistant in an old people's home. My patients range from 80 to 102 years. I know that I will see all of them die. Most of my patients are ready to die. Our residents speak about their death openly. This is very helpful for all of us because both resident and care assistant have the opportunity to say goodbye. During their last days, most of our residents like to talk about their life. In their opinion, they have lived a full and long life. We do everything we can for them to make it easier. All they want is to die with dignity. Although people dying happens regularly in my job, I always shed tears for those in my care that pass away. They have become dear to you and you really feel a loss.

Sophie Young: My workplace is a hospice. I mostly deal with patients who are in the final stages of terminal illnesses, very often cancer. Our patients come here with a prognosis of 3 months or less. We give care to patients when they are at their weakest. But compared to hospitals we are able to spend a lot of time with the patients and their grieving relatives. This allows me to care for and speak to them more intensively. For our patients, death is a release and should be seen as positive for the dying person. My role is to keep the patient comfortable, for example by reducing pain or nausea. I try to minimise discomfort for the patient and family however I can. To begin with, we monitor our patient's symptoms. When the patient becomes less alert and responsive, we help the family to cope with the passing. We create a warm and loving atmosphere for our patients. Gently speaking to and lightly stroking the dying person go a long way. It is vital to establish trust with all involved in the dying process because you are really sharing a very intimate moment in these people's lives.

Working with the text

A Look at the sentences describing Tana's, Matthew's and Sophie's work and workplace. The information in them is wrong. Can you correct them?

1. Tana works in a nursing home.
2. Her patients are mostly old people in the last phase of their lives.
3. Tana is able to quickly forget about a patient's death.
4. Matthew is a nursing assistant and he works with people of all ages.
5. He doesn't really feel sad when elderly people die.
6. He never speaks to the residents he cares for about the fact they are going to die.
7. Sophie's work at the hospice is much the same as in a hospital.
8. Her patients stay in the hospice for a year or more.
9. Sophie only cares for the patients, not their relatives.

B How do they feel about their patients' deaths? Answer the following questions.

1. How does Tana manage to cope with her patients' deaths?
2. What was the worst day in her life? How does she feel about that day many years later, and why?
3. How does Matthew feel about his residents' deaths?
4. How does Sophie act when her patients are dying?

C What is important for them when they are caring for a dying person? Complete the sentences.

1. For Tina, a "good death" means …
2. Matthew thinks it's very helpful to talk openly about death because …
3. When caring for a dying patient, Sophie tries …
4. Sophie also cares for the relatives by …
5. She thinks that death can be considered positive for her patients because …

Working with language

Mediation

A Go through the text again and find translations for the following German words.

1. sterben (2 words)
2. das Sterben (2 words)
3. Sterbender
4. Tod
5. Sterbeprozess
6. sich verabschieden
7. trauernde Angehörige
8. weinen (2 words)

B Translate the following German sentences into English. Again, you can find the English words you need in the texts.

1. Der Tod meiner Mutter war ein großer Verlust.
2. Mein Großvater war 95 Jahre alt, als er starb.
3. Er hatte ein erfülltes und langes Leben.
4. Im Hospiz kümmert man sich häufig um Patienten mit einer tödlichen Erkrankung.
5. Für viele Patienten im Endstadium Krebs ist der Tod eine Erlösung.

How to talk to someone who is grieving

Sophie Young speaks about her hospice work with a class of nursing assistants. After having talked about end-of-life care, they are interested in her experience with grieving relatives.

Sam Some people say they wouldn't have been able to talk to a grieving relative if they hadn't experienced the loss of someone close to them themselves. Is that true?

Sophie Well, yes and no. Experiencing my father's death has allowed me to speak to grieving relatives with more empathy. But grief is a very individual process. You never exactly know how someone feels.

Mary How do people react to a relative's death?

Sophie Again, there is no typical reaction. In my work at the hospice I have experienced a wide range of emotions. First of all, the death of someone close to you is a shock. Most people find it very hard to understand what has just happened, what it really means that a life has come to an end. The shock can make them feel numb and they aren't able to speak at all.

Toni How do you make them speak then?

Sophie Speaking is not always the best way. First of all, you should be a good listener. Saying too much may hinder the griever from speaking about their feelings. A hug or touch can help to reduce the mental and physical pain they are suffering from and encourage them to release their emotions. Afterwards, there is enough time to talk.

Kim How do you start such a conversation?

Sophie After saying some consoling words, you should give the person time to sit at the dead relative's side for as long as they need to. But before you leave them alone, tell them that you are available if they need you. Offer them a room where they can be alone and give them a warm drink. In this relaxing atmosphere, the person is free to react how he needs to. Here they can cry, talk, or even be angry. Some feel that their relative's death was cruel and unfair, particularly if they had to go before their time.

Edda What do you do if someone doesn't want to talk?

Sophie You have to accept that some don't want to talk at all. Never push them or tell them how they should feel, like "I know just how you feel". You don't know because everyone experiences grief differently. It's better start the conversation with, "I know that talking about these things is never easy …" Or simply ask "How can I help?" That is a door-opening question.

Sabine So are there some no-go sentences?

Sophie Sure. Don't use clichés like "Time is a great healer", "You should be grateful for the time you had together". Even worse, "Life goes on!".

Sam I work in an old people's home and some residents don't see their relatives at all, or very rarely. Do they really need them when their time has come?

Sophie Yes, of course! Always try to inform their relatives in time. On the one hand, your residents need to say goodbye to die in peace and on the other hand the relatives should have the chance to say things they feel they should tell the dying person. If I hadn't had the opportunity to tell my father about my feelings, I would have felt sad and guilty for the rest of my life.

Working with the text

A When Sam returns back from nursing school, he tells his colleagues about what he has learnt from Sophie.
Here is what he said at their staff meeting.
Fill in the missing words.

First of all, I think I was interested to hear that there really is no **1. …** reaction you can expect from **2. …** relatives. Sophie told us that in her work at the **3. …** she has been confronted with a wide range of **4. … .** The way people show their **5. …** can be different from person to person. Some are very **6. …** because they think life is unfair and **7. …** to take away a beloved person. But generally the first reaction is **8. …** because it's hard to understand that the person's life has come to an end. Sophie also told us not to speak too much at first but to be a good **9. …** and give the griever a **10. …** or gently touch them to encourage them to **11. …** their emotions. Later there is enough time to talk but only if the person really wants to talk. You should never **12. …** someone. At the hospice, first of all they give people the opportunity to sit at the dead **13. …** side as long as they want to. They offer to talk in a separate room. Here they try to create a **14. …** for the griever so they feel **15. …** to talk. And there are some things you should never do. For example, you should never tell the grieving relatives how they should feel or use **16. …** like, "Time is a good **17. …**".

B Try to explain why …

1. … you can talk with more empathy to a grieving relative when you have already experienced a loved person's death yourself.
2. … death is seen as unfair and cruel when a young person dies.
3. … some people find it hard to talk immediately after a loved person's death.

C In their staff meeting, they talk about how Betty Harris is dying.
Here are some questions about how to cope with the situation.
Take Sam's role and answer them from what Sophie told the students.

We already have a separate room for dying residents and we can talk to the relatives in there. So, do we really need an extra room to talk to grieving relatives?

Why shouldn't I say, "I know how you feel"? And if I shouldn't say that, what should I say instead?

Mrs Harris' daughters haven't been here for the last two years. Should we really tell them that she is dying?

Listening

Reception

14

Amanda Miller calls Christina Gray, one of Mrs Harris' daughters, to tell her about her mother's soon coming death.
The telephone dialogue below is mixed up.
Listen to it and reconstruct it.

1. Well, Mrs Gray, I'm sorry to tell you that your mother's health has become very bad during the last few days.
2. Goodbye Mrs Gray.
3. She was examined by Dr. Bonham again this morning and I'm sorry to tell you that her heart has become very weak.
4. Thank you for calling and goodbye.
5. Hello, is that Christina Gray? My name is Amanda Miller and I'm your mother's nurse at St Mary's Home.
6. Yes, sure, I'll come with my sister, as soon as possible.
7. I'm afraid so, yes. I'm sorry to have to tell you that your mother is dying. We have already transferred her into a separate room and have started end-of-life care.
8. Oh, ok. How bad is her health then?
9. Oh. That's a real shock. I'm shaking. I don't know what to do.
10. Oh, my God, what do you mean? "Very weak"? Is she going to die?
11. Hello?
12. Mrs Gray, calm down, your mother is comfortable and ok at the moment. Would you be able to tell your sister about your mother, and both come here to be with your mother in her last days?
13. What's happened? Is something the matter with my mother?
14. That's great. We look forward to seeing you.

Hands-on task

Interaction

Work in small groups.
Choose one of the situations below.
Write a telephone call and read it out in class.

Situation 1:
Mr Terence Woods (87) is a resident in your nursing home. He had suffered from a heart condition and passed away in his sleep during the night. You call his son to tell him about his death.

Situation 2:
Mrs Jane Doe (82) has been in hospital for a week now because of kidney problems and general poor health. Her kidneys have begun to fail, treatments aren't working anymore and the doctors are sure she will pass away soon. You call her husband.

Grammar box: Past Perfect – Vollendete Vergangenheit

*After I **had phoned** the dying person's relatives, they came to sit at his side.*
*Didn't her death surprise you or **had** she **told** you about her terminal illness?*
*No, she **hadn't told** me, I was shocked to hear about her death.*

Bildung

→ **had + 3. Verbform**

Verwendung

→ Um deutlich zu machen, dass eine bestimmte Handlung schon vorher passiert ist.
*I **had done** a placement at an old people's home, before I started my job training as a nursing assistant.*

Practising Grammar

A Fill in the Past Perfect

1. After the students (listen) to Sophie's lecture, they could deal with grieving relatives much better.
2. She was sent to hospital after the doctor (find) a tumour on her x-ray.
3. They (not visit) her father in the nursing home before they heard about his bad health condition.
4. Before the accident happened, he (be) a very sporty person.

B Fill in the Past Simple Tense and Past Perfect

1. After the students (take) part at Sophie's lecture, they (know) much better how to speak to a dying person.
2. Sophie (spend) some time on preparing her lecture before she (speak) to the students.
3. Before his wife (die), Mr Scott (not leave) her bedside for six hours.
4. After her death, Mr Scott (sit) at his dead wife's bedside in complete silence for over two hours, before he (be) able to talk about his wife's death.
5. Yesterday morning Mr Harris (come) to sit at this wife's bedside after being phoned by the nurse on the ward and he (stay) with her until her death in the late evening.
6. I (not be) surprised about Mrs Harris' death because I (got) to know about her terminal cancer some months before.
7. John (tell) me about Mr Summer's death on Thursday when I (meet) him, he (see) his obituary in Monday's newspaper already.

When someone dies …	
obituary	Traueranzeige
book of condolence	Kondulenzbuch
grieving	trauernd, in Trauer
Death as a part of care work	
intensive care unit	Intensivstation
human	menschlich
(to) affect	hier: angreifen, beeinflussen
(to) haunt s. o.	jmd. verfolgen
(to) push aside	hier: verdrängen
pain	Schmerz
(to) range from … to	reichen von … bis
(to) live a full life	ein erfülltes Leben leben
(to) shed tears	Tränen vergießen
(to) pass away	sterben
loss	Verlust
hospice	Hospiz
final stage / s	Endstadium
terminal illness	tödliche Krankheit
cancer	Krebs (Krankheit)
(life) prognosis	Lebenserwartung
at their weakest	im schwächsten Zustand
release	Erlösung, Befreiung
(to) maintain	erhalten
(to) keep sb. comfortable	dafür sorgen, dass sich jmd. wohl fühlt
discomfort	Unbehagen
nausea	Übelkeit
responsive	ansprechbar
alert	aufmerksam, wach
(to) cope	mit etwas fertig werden, etw. verarbeiten
passing	das Ableben
(to) stroke	streicheln
trust	Vertrauen
(people) involved	Beteiligte
dying process	Sterbeprozess

How to talk to someone who is grieving	
end-of-life care	sterbebegleitende Pflege
wide range	große Bandbreite
numb	stumpf, abgestumpft
(to) hinder from	hindern an
hug	Umarmung
(to) encourage	ermutigen
(to) release emotions	Gefühlen freien Lauf lassen
consoling words	tröstende Worte
available	verfügbar, hier auch: ansprechbar
relaxing atmosphere	entspannte Atmosphäre
cruel	grausam
(to) push s. o.	jmd. (zu etwas) drängen
cliché	Klischee, Floskel
healer	Heiler
grateful	dankbar
guilty	schuldig

Die Aussprache der blauen Vokabeln finden Sie in den Audio-Dateien DA0901055

Introducing yourself and writing a personal profile

Steckbrief und persönliche Vorstellung

Steckbriefe geben Angehörigen, Besuchern und Patienten eine kurze Information darüber, wer in einer Einrichtung arbeitet. In vielen Einrichtungen gibt es Tafeln mit Fotos und Namen der Mitarbeiter, aber auch Steckbriefe von zeitlich befristeten Mitarbeitern und Praktikanten, die an das schwarze Brett des Eingangsbereichs gehängt werden und so eine erste Auskunft darüber geben, wer neu zum Arbeitsteam hinzugekommen ist. All diese Möglichkeiten stellen eine Vertrautheit für den Besucher her und sollen einen „Wiedererkennungseffekt" haben. Daher ist das Foto ein tragendes Element des Steckbriefes. Persönliche Vorstellungen haben den Zweck, wichtige Informationen zur eigenen Person an eine andere Person, insbesondere an ein Arbeitsteam, weiterzugeben. Kommt man in ein neues Arbeitsteam, so ist es bei der ersten Vorstellungsrunde nicht nur wichtig, Informationen zu bekommen, mit wem man künftig zusammenarbeitet, sondern auch, die Kollegen darüber zu informieren, was man selbst als neu hinzukommendes Mitglied in die Gruppe einbringen kann. Erzählen Sie dem Team, welche besonderen Qualifikationen Sie besitzen und warum Sie im Team mitarbeiten möchten.

Aufbau der "personal introduction" – "personal description" Zeitstufe: Present Simple Tense!

1. Schritt: Personalien (Name, Alter, Wohnort, Herkunftsland, Familie, Beruf)	Hello, my name is … and I'm … years old. I live in … (Wohnort). I come from / My family comes from … (Herkunftsland). I live with my family in **a** flat (Wohnung) / house … (Bei erster Nennung: "**a / an**", bei weiterer Nennung: "**the**", z. B. dann: **The** flat / house has … rooms / a garden / a balcony …). I'm married (verheiratet). / I live with my partner. / I'm single. I have … sisters and … brothers. I'm an only child (Einzelkind). / I have got … children. I work as … / I'm a … (Beruf). I'm training to be a … (Berufsausbildung).
2. Schritt: Hobbys, Vorlieben, auch Abneigungen, Fähigkeiten, die ich in das Team einbringen kann.	I like / love / enjoy + *Verb in ing-Fom* für die Angabe von Hobbys (I like playing football, I love reading books, I enjoy eating ice-cream). I'm fond of + *Verb in ing-Fom* (I'm fond of swimming). I dislike + *Verb in ing-Fom* (Ich mag nicht … / I dislike swimming). I hate + *Verb in ing-Fom* (Ich hasse … / I hate watching football). I'm good at + *Verb in ing-Fom* (I'm good at listening to people). I know a lot about … I have some experience as a … (Ich habe Erfahrungen im Beruf des / der …). I speak … languages, which are … I'm a trained (Berufsbezeichnung) … (Ich bin ausgebildet in …).
3. Schritt: Warum bin ich im Team?, Zukunftspläne	I'm here in this class / team because … I'm interested in *(Verb in ing-Form)* … I want to gain more work experience in … (Ich möchte mehr Berufserfahrung mit … sammeln). I look forward to + *Verb in ing-Fom* (sich freuen auf). In the future, I want to …

Talking to patients and new residents

Mit Patienten und neuen Bewohnern sprechen

• Persönliche Begrüßung und Eröffnung eines Gesprächs

Begrüßen Sie den neuen Patienten / neuen Bewohner mit einem Händedruck und stellen Sie sich persönlich vor. Nennen Sie dabei nicht nur Ihren Namen, sondern auch Ihre „Funktion" (Beruf, Zuständigkeitsbereich).
Die non-verbale Körpersprache spielt dabei eine wichtige Rolle, denn mit einem Lächeln, Blickkontakt und einer offenen Körperhaltung vermitteln Sie dem Patienten / Heimbewohner, dass Sie sich um ihn / sie kümmern.

Hallo Mr / Mrs (name). My name is (name) and I'm the new trainee. My name is (name) and I'm training to be a (job).	Nice to meet you, my name is (name). My name is (name) and I'm in charge of (zuständig sein für …). Welcome to our home Mr / Mrs (name).

• Mitteilen, warum man mit dem Patienten / dem Heimbewohner Kontakt aufnimmt.

I'm here to check your pulse. Mr / Mrs (name) I'd like to help you with your dinner. I'm your nurse / nursing assistant and I want to make sure everything is fine / okay.	I need to check your blood pressure. I'm going to take some blood. Mr / Mrs (name), we haven't met yet. I'm (name) and I'm here to bring you your medicine.

• Offene Fragen stellen, die den Patienten / den Heimbewohner dazu „einladen", mehr von sich / dem Gesundheitszustand / den eigenen Gefühlen zu erzählen.

Stellen Sie Fragen möglichst **nicht** so, dass der Patient / der Bewohner nur noch ja oder nein antworten kann oder so suggestiv, dass die Antwort vorgegeben wird. ("Don't you think I should open the window?") Fragen können geschlossen sein, wenn man nach einem konkreten Sachverhalt fragen möchte, „Do you take a sleeping pill every night?". Bei jeder Frage sollte der Patient / Heimbewohner genügend Zeit haben, in Ruhe zu antworten. Nutzen Sie immer auch Höflichkeitsfloskeln.

Can you tell me what medication you take?	Können Sie mir bitte sagen, welche Medikamente Sie nehmen?
Could you please answer some questions about your health for me?	Würden Sie mir bitte einige Fragen zu Ihrem Gesundheitszustand beantworten?
Where does it hurt?	Wo tut es weh?
How do you feel?	Wie fühlen Sie sich?
How bad is the pain?	Wie schlimm ist Ihr Schmerz?
How can I help you?	Wie kann ich Ihnen helfen?
Can you describe your symptoms / pain, please?	Können Sie bitte Ihre Symptome / Ihren Schmerz beschreiben?
Don't hesitate to tell me what I can do for you.	Zögern Sie nicht, mir zu sagen, was ich für Sie tun kann.
Is there anything else you need / you want me to do?	Brauchen Sie noch etwas? / Kann ich noch etwas für sie tun?

• Informationen über die geplante Pflege geben und Pflegetätigkeiten mit Worten begleiten, sodass der Patient immer weiß, was geschieht.

Überfordern Sie dabei jedoch den Patienten / den Bewohner nicht mit zu vielen Informationen und Fachbegriffe, die er / sie nicht versteht. Ebenso wichtig ist es, dem Patienten auch Ergebnisse, z. B. von einer Blutdruckmessung, mitzuteilen, damit keine Zweifel entstehen.

Roll up your sleeve please. I'd like to take your blood pressure. Okay, it's … That's good / okay.	Machen Sie bitte den Arm frei. Ich möchte Ihren Blutdruck messen. Dieser ist … Das ist gut / ziemlich in Ordnung.
Well, it seems your blood pressure is a little too high.	Nun, ich muss Ihnen sagen, dass Ihr Blutdruck etwa zu hoch ist.
Don't worry, I'll tell the doctor and we'll see what we can do next.	Machen Sie sich keine Sorgen, ich sage dies unserem Arzt und wir schauen, was wir als nächstes tun können.
Next, I need to check your pulse. Okay, it's …	Dann / als nächstes werde ich Ihren Puls messen.
Step onto the scales please, I need your weight. Your weight is …	Stellen Sie sich bitte auf die Waage. Ich brauche Ihr Gewicht. Ihr Gewicht ist …
Now, I'm going to take your temperature.	Jetzt werde ich Ihre Temperatur messen.

• Gespräch abschließen

Fassen Sie hier noch einmal die wichtigsten Ergebnisse zusammen. Informieren Sie den Patienten / Bewohner über das weitere Vorgehen und vergewissern Sie sich, dass er oder sie alles verstanden hat und akzeptiert.
Beruhigen Sie den Patient / Bewohner, um ihm oder ihr die Angst vor weiteren Behandlungen zu nehmen.
Bedanken Sie sich am Ende für die Mitarbeit / Aufmerksamkeit, die der Patient / Bewohner Ihnen entgegengebracht hat und verabschieden Sie sich.

Let me sum up what we are going to do next.	Lassen Sie mich zusammenfassen, was wir als nächstes tun werden.
We need to x-ray your leg / arm …	Wir brauchen eine Röntgenaufnahme von Ihrem Bein / Arm …
I'd like to take you with me for an x-ray.	Ich möchte Sie zu einer Röntgenaufnahme bringen / mitnehmen.
Please sit down in the wheelchair. I'd like to take you to some further treatment / tests.	Setzen Sie sich bitte in den Rollstuhl. Ich werde Sie zu weiteren Untersuchungen / Tests bringen.
Hello Mr / Mrs (name) I'd like to take you for a visit to …. Shall I hold your arm and give you some support?	Hallo Herr / Frau (Name), ich würde Sie gerne zu einem Besuch bei … abholen. Soll ich Ihren Arm festhalten, um Ihnen Halt zu geben?
Don't worry, we can help you.	Machen Sie sich keine Sorgen, wir können Ihnen helfen.
Relax, I'm going to bring you something to drink / eat.	Entspannen Sie sich, ich bringe Ihnen etwas zu trinken / essen.
Lie down in bed and make yourself comfortable.	Legen Sie sich ins Bett und machen Sie es sich bequem.
I'm sure you will feel at home here soon.	Sie werden sich hier sicher bald zuhause fühlen.
Our hospital / home will give you all the care you need.	In unserem Krankenhaus / unserer Einrichtung bekommen Sie jegliche Pflege, die Sie brauchen.
I'm sure you can go home soon.	Sie gehen bestimmt bald nach Hause.
I'm sure you will be better soon.	Sie werden bald gesund sein.
Thank you very much!	Vielen Dank!
Thanks for your support.	Danke für Ihre Mithilfe.

Die Mindmap

Wozu?

Die Mindmap (auch Netzbild genannt) eignet sich überall da, wo Gedanken gesammelt und dargestellt werden sollen, z. B.

- zur Visualisierung eines Themas, eines geplanten Projektes;
- zum Einstieg in ein Thema oder ein Projekt. Hier können mit der Mindmap zunächst Gedanken gesammelt werden;
- zur Vertiefung eines Themas, da in der Mindmap Gedanken nicht nur gesammelt werden, sondern gleichzeitig Strukturen sichtbar gemacht und Beziehungen hervorgehoben werden.

Nachteil

Bei vielen Gedanken kann die Mindmap unübersichtlich werden.

Wie?

Vorbereitung:

Man benötigt

- eine größere Schreibfläche, z. B. Tapete, ein Plakat oder Papierbogen einer Flipchart
- verschiedenfarbige Stifte und Stärken

Durchführung

- Der Ausgangspunkt ist immer ein in der Mitte des Plakats aufgemalter Kreis, in dem das Thema, zu dem gesammelt werden soll, in einem Schlagwort, in Stichworten oder in einem Fragesatz (= Problemstellung) angegeben wird. Beispiel: Eine Mindmap erstellen oder Wie erstellt man eine Mindmap?
- Jetzt kann man Ideen zum Oberthema sammeln und anfügen. Dabei ist wichtig, dass man
  - ☞ Hauptpunkte sucht und anschreibt,
  - ☞ Unterpunkte an diese Hauptpunkte anhängt, sodass das Bild von innen nach außen wächst,
  - ☞ Beziehungen durch Pfeile und Verästelungen darstellt, sodass eine Art „Ideenbaum" entsteht,
  - ☞ mit unterschiedlichen Farben / Symbolen arbeitet, die Beziehungen hervorheben.

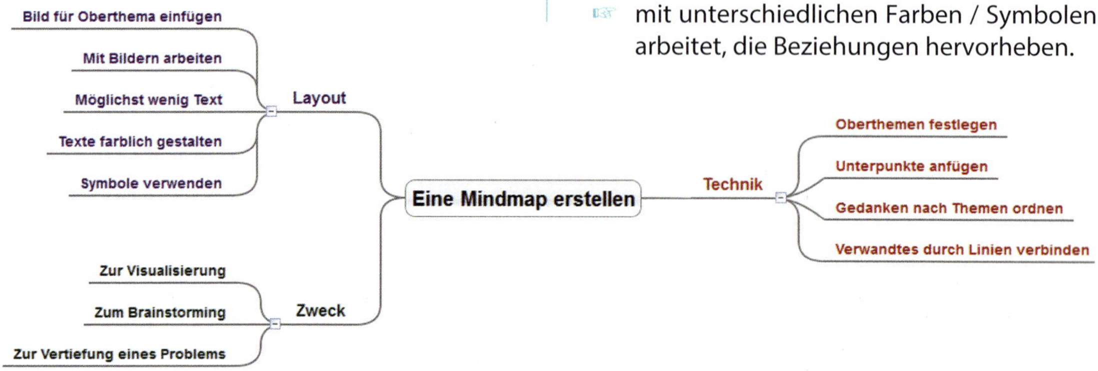

Vokabelhilfen für die Präsentation

The main subject / topic of this mind map is …	Das übergeordnete Thema der Mindmap ist …
There are (number) branches connected to the main topic …, they are …	Mit dem Hauptthema sind (Zahl) Verzweigungen verknüpft, diese sind …
There are (number) subdivisions to this topic: …	Es gibt (Zahl) Unterteilungen zu diesem Thema …
The mind-map consists of (number) branches which are (names).	Die Mindmap besteht aus (Zahl) Zweigen, diese sind (Namen).
The keywords for this branch / aspect are …	Die Stichpunkte, die zu diesem Zweig / Aspekt gehören, sind …

Explaining words and expressions in English

Worte und Ausdrücke in Englisch erklären

Manchmal fehlt uns in einem Gespräch das passende englische Wort oder ein englischer Ausdruck. Man muss diese dann seinem Gesprächspartner verständlich machen. Oft hilft dabei die „Show and tell"-Methode. Das heißt, man zeigt einfach auf den realen Gegenstand, auf den man sich beziehen möchte, oder man stellt den Begriff pantomimisch dar, macht sozusagen vor, was man meint. Aber dies ist nicht immer möglich. Eine alternative Methode ist, das Wort oder den Begriff im Englischen zu umschreiben:

1. Möglichkeit: Ein Wort mit gleicher Bedeutung / ein Synonym nutzen.

To communicate means the same as to talk.

To talk is the same as to communicate.

You can use another word for communicate, which is talk.

Another word with a similar meaning is to talk.

2. Möglichkeit: Ein Wort mit gegensätzlicher Bedeutung / ein Antonym nutzen.

Being ill is the opposite of being healthy.

Ill has the opposite meaning to healthy.

3. Möglichkeit: Die Funktion des Wortes beschreiben.

A walker is medical equipment / a thing / an object (which) you use for walking. But you can also sit on it, for example when you need to take a rest.

People who have walking problems can use a walker as a support.

4. Möglichkeit: Besondere Merkmale des Wortes beschreiben.

A walker has four wheels and two handles. You can use it as a support for walking.

A walker consists of four wheels and two handles.

5. Möglichkeit: Das Wort einem Oberbegriff zuordnen oder Unterbegriffe zum Wort nennen.

A nursing home is a home for people who suffer from health problems and cannot live alone, ….
→ **Zuordnung zu einem Oberbegriff**

A nursing home usually consists of a number of rooms such as …. In a nursing home care workers like a nurse, nursing assistant … care for their residents who can be elderly people or people who suffer from … → **Benennen von Unterbegriffen zum Wort**

6. Möglichkeit: Das Wort mit einem anderen Wort vergleichen.

A nursing home can be compared to a hospital because people who suffer from health problems live there. Just like in a hospital, people receive medical care such as …

7. Möglichkeit: Ein Beispiel nennen.

As a healthcare worker you care for people who need medical help. For example: nurses, nursing assistants, doctors, physiotherapist etc. are healthcare workers because they take care for people who have some kind of health problem.

8. Möglichkeit: Ähnlichkeiten mit dem Deutschen hervorheben.

The English word diabetes is very similar to the German equivalent / translation which is Diabetes. Only the pronunciation is different.

9. Möglichkeit: Eine Definition des Wortes geben.

A walker is medical equipment which you use to stabilise the walk of people with balance or mobility problems ….

10. Möglichkeit: Mehrere Methoden miteinander kombinieren.

A walker is medical equipment which people with walking problems use. It looks a bit like a shopping trolley because it has four wheels and ….

Creating a poster or a transparency

Ein Plakat oder eine Folie gestalten

Folie und Plakat sollen Informationen visualisieren und damit einen Themenvortrag unterstützen oder ein Thema in seinen wesentlichen Punkten verdeutlichen. Mit dieser Art der Visualisierung können folgende Ziele verfolgt werden:

- den Zuhörer zu motivieren oder einen visuellen Anreiz zu bieten
- das Behalten von vorgetragene / wichtigen Informationen zu erleichtern
- ein besseres Verständnis für ein bestimmten Thema herzustellen
- wichtige Informationen zu betonen

Bei Folien, die durch Fernmedien (Overheadprojektor, Beamer) präsentiert werden, gelten die gleichen Gestaltungsregeln wie für das Plakat:

Eine Folie bzw. ein Plakat muss
→ deutlich erkennbar,
→ kontrastreich und
→ auf ein Thema begrenzt sein.

Farben

- Farbig ist ansprechender als nur Schwarz-Weiß
- Aber: **keine** grellen Farben
- Wichtige Informationen farblich hervorheben
- Nicht zu „bunt", höchstens drei Farben, sonst entsteht zu viel Unruhe
- Grundsätzliche Informationen in einer neutralen Farbe festhalten (z. B. Schwarz)
- Texte können durch Farbunterlegung hervorgehoben werden.

Vorsicht: Keine zu grellen Farben oder dunkle Farben wählen, die den Kontrast zur Schrift verschwinden und den Text undeutlich werden lassen.

Schrift

- Weitgehend einheitliche Schriftart und Schriftgröße wählen, keine Unruhe erzeugen
- Buchstabengröße so wählen, dass diese auch in einigem Abstand erkannt werden können (Folie: Hand Schriftgrad 18 – 24 Pt, Computer 14 / 16 / 18 Pt – 1 Pt entspricht 0,375 mm)
- Titel und wichtige Informationen können durchaus größere Schriftgrade als 24 Pt haben
- Wichtige Informationen können durch Fettdruck und Unterstreichung hervorgehoben werden
- Sperrung und durchgehende Großbuchstabenverwendung eignen sich eher für die Hervorhebung einzelner Worte

Bilder und Skizzen

- Nicht zu viele Bilder, damit der Überblick nicht verloren geht
- Bilder mit ausreichender Erklärung versehen
- Bilder müssen zum Text passen
- Bildunterschriften / Erklärungen zum Bild in kleinerer Schrift gestalten
- Nur aussagekräftige Bilder verwenden, Bilder nicht als bloße Ausschmückung nutzen
- Bilder müssen in angemessener Größe zum Text erscheinen
- Besser farbige Bilder einsetzen

Aufbau und Gestaltung

- Klare Gliederung der Aussagen, die direkt mit dem Auge erfasst werden kann
- Folie / Plakat nicht überladen. Faustregel: Niemals mehr als 6 – 8 Zeilen mit 6 Wörtern
- Stichwörter, **keine** ganzen Sätze
- Wenn Sätze, dann kurze Merksätze
- Mit Titel und Untertitel arbeiten, d. h. Unterpunkte zu Überschriften einrichten, insbesondere komplizierte Sachverhalte in Teilaspekte und Unterpunkte auflösen
- Kernaussagen markieren (Farbe, Schrift oder Rahmen setzen)
- Gestaltungselemente (Symbole, Grafiken) zur Hervorhebung und Verdeutlichung von Informationen und als Gliederungshilfen (z. B. Pfeilsymbole) nutzen

Nursing Documentation Pflegedokumentation

Der Pflegebericht

Je nach Pflegeeinrichtung gibt es unterschiedliche Dokumentationsformen. Zumeist ist dies eine Tabelle (nursing chart), die die pflegende Person ausfüllt, um einen Überblick über die stattgefundene Pflege und den Zustand des Patienten zu geben. Die Eintragungen sollen bei einem Wechsel des Pflegepersonals schnell einen Überblick über die stattgefundene Pflege ermöglichen, z. B.

- Patient, Geburtsdatum etc.
- Datum und Uhrzeit der Pflegemaßnahme
- Beschreibung der Pflegemaßnahme
- Wirkung der Pflegemaßnahme
- Beschreibung des (körperlichen und seelischen) Zustands des Patienten
- Vermerk über Besuche eines Arztes, eines Therapeuten, etc.
- Besondere Vorkommnisse
- Kürzel / Unterschrift der pflegenden Person

Medical Record			**Patient:** *Mrs Miller*	
date	**hour** a.m.	p.m.	**nursing notes**	**staff**
8/15	*7:30*		*Mrs Miller was already awake when I arrived, helped her with her personal hygiene and getting dressed. Mrs Miller told me that she had had a restless night once again and asked for a sleeping pill, she was tired but focused. Her mood is rather low because of her sleep problems, I prepared breakfast for her and could convince her to eat a bit and drink, I'm going to ask Dr. Bonham to prescribe something for her sleeplessness*	*H. Brian*
8/15	*10:30*		*Dr. Bonham came to see patient, new medication, see medication chart*	*M. Sons*

Ein ausführlicher Pflegebericht (nursing report) / eine Pflegegeschichte (nursing story)

Ein ausführlicher Bericht kann nötig sein, um einen neuen Patienten auf einer Teambesprechungvorzustellen oder an eine andere pflegende Einrichtung zu übergeben und über die Pflegegeschichte, seinen Erkrankungen, Lebensweisen und Gemütszustand zu berichten.

Darin sollten enthalten sein:

- Informationen zum Patienten
- Vorerkrankungen, Diagnosen
- Momentaner Gesundheits- und Gemütszustand
- Besonderheiten der Person
- Medikation, ärztliche Verordnungen, Behandlungsplan

Mrs Jennings is 85 years old and she has been living in assisted living for three years now. Mrs Jennings has a son and a daughter who see her regularly.
When she came into our home she suffered from slight memory loss because of a stroke she had had three years ago. But she was well-oriented, her language production was okay. She had some problems moving her left leg and we organised regular physiotherapy and walker training for her. At that time her medication was …
She joined some of our home activities. She was a very friendly, cheerful person but now she seems depressed and prefers to stay alone.
In the last six months her health has deteriorated (der Gesundheitszustand hat sich verschlechtert). *She has some kidney problems* (Nierenprobleme) *and we have twice transferred her to the hospital. She does not drink regularly and we watch her liquid intake. But she still has memory and orientation problems and we will take her for some neurological tests and a dementia test. We also have to watch her food and liquid intake more intensively and think of taking her into our nursing home for full-time care. Now she has problems with her bladder* (Blase), *which does not empty fully. Therefore she needs a catheter, but has problems getting used to it. After talking to her attending physician* (behandelnder Arzt) *Dr. Bonham we want to contact her daughter and son to talk about full-time care. With regard to her medication she now ….*

How to write a biography Wie schreibt man eine Biografie?

Um eine individuelle Pflege zu gewährleisten, die sich an den Bedürfnissen des zu Pflegenden orientiert, sollte man sich intensiv mit dessen Lebensgeschichte befassen.
Sammeln Sie zu Beginn gezielt Informationen mithilfe eines **Fragebogens.** Dieser Fragebogen sollte mit dem Patienten, aber auch mit den Angehörigen besprochen werden, um ein möglichst vollständiges Bild zu erhalten. Lassen Sie auch **eigene Beobachtungen** dabei einfließen. Anders als der Lebenslauf in Bewerbungen geht es in der Biografie eines zu Pflegenden nicht nur um **reine Fakten** und **persönliche Daten,** sondern auch um die **Bewertung** dieser. Stellen Sie beim Verfassen der Biografie immer auch die Frage, welche Bedeutung bestimmte Ereignisse auf die Entwicklung des zu Pflegenden hatten.

Die Biografie sollte folgende Bereiche beinhalten:

> persönliche Daten / Personalien,
> der familiäre Hintergrund,
> schulische Bildung,
> Berufsausbildung und Arbeitsleben,
> einschneidende Ereignisse und Erlebnisse,
> Beziehungen und Freundschaften,
> Lebensumstände,
> die frühere und heutige Lebenssituation,
> besondere Fähigkeiten,
> Interessen und Hobbys,
> gesundheitlicher Zustand

Guided biography

birth and origin (Geburt und Herkunft)	(name) was born in (place) on (date of birth) He / She lived in (place) from … until … He / She comes from …
parents and siblings (Eltern und Geschwister)	His / Her father / mother worked as … His / Her mother was a housewife and stayed at home. His / Her father / mother raised the children alone. His / Her father / mother died early at just (number) years. His / Her father / mother was killed in the Second World War. He / She was the eldest / youngest child. He / She had (number) brothers and (number) sisters. He / She was an only child. His / Her brother /sister was younger / older than him / her. (number) brothers / sisters were younger / older than him / her.
school and further education (Schule und Weiterbildung)	He / She started school when he / she was (number) years old. He / She ***enrolled*** at university and studied. He / She ***graduated from*** school / university when he / he was (number) years old. He / She finished school at the age of (number)
profession (Beruf)	He / She trained as a (job) He / She worked in (place) / as (job) He / She was the main ***breadwinner.*** At (age) he / she had / owned his / her own business. He / She ran a shop / his / her own business. He / She stayed at home and took care of the children. He / She retired aged (number). He / She retired at (number).

Vocabulary help

(to) enroll	einschreiben
(to) graduate from	absolvieren / einen Abschluss machen an (z. B der Universität)
breadwinner	Hauptverdiener
(to) retire	in den Ruhestand gehen
retirement	Ruhestand
(to) propose to	sich verloben mit

marriage (Heirat)	He / She fell in love with (name) He / She met (name) / went out with (name) He / She ***proposed to*** (name) aged (number) He / She married (name) in (year). He / She lived together with (name) as an unmarried couple.
children (Kinder)	She got ***pregnant*** with her first child when she was (age). She gave birth to (number) children. He / She had (number) children. He / She ***raised*** (number) children.
relationships (Beziehungen)	He / She had a very close relationship to (name). One of his / her dearest friends was (name). Together with (name) he / she (activities). He / She spent a lot of time with (name). (name) had a strong influence on him / her because …
past and present living circum-stances (vergangene und heutige Lebensumstände)	He / She earned a good ***salary*** / only a low salary as … At (age) he / she could buy his / her own house / could afford his / her own house. He / She travelled a lot and could afford holidays in (place / country). He / She went into assisted living aged (number). He / She needs care and lives in a nursing home. Because of health problems he / she moved into a nursing home. He / She is still ***independent*** and lives alone in his / her own flat / house. He / She can still manage alone / on her own. He / She can't manage alone / on her own.
significant events / changes (bedeutende Ereignisse und Veränderungen)	He / She moved to another town. He joined the army. He / She learned to drive. One significant event in his / her life was when … He / She lived during the Second World War and had to experience … He / She suffered from … during the war. His wife / her husband / one of his / her children died when he / she was (age) He / She had a good time / bad time when … His / Her life changed when … From that time on … He / She ***immigrated*** from (country) and lived in (country) since (date) He / She became a grandfather / grandmother at (age) and helped to look after the grandchildren.
special skills (besondere Fähigkeiten)	He / She is good at … He / She can speak another language / other languages. He / She was a good (job). He / She is still ***able to*** …
hobbies and interests (Hobbys und Interessen)	He / She is interested in … He / She loved / still loves travelling / doing sports / watching TV … He / She still takes part in political life. He / She still reads the daily newspapers / listens to the news / still knows about …
death (Tod)	He / She died at the age of (number). He / She died on (date).

pregnant	schwanger	independent	selbständig, unabhängig
(to) raise	aufziehen	(to) immigrate	auswandern
salary	Gehalt	(to) be able to	fähig sein zu

Designing a questionaire Einen Fragebogen gestalten

Allgemeines

Bevor Sie Fragen für einen Fragebogen sammeln, sollte Ihnen klar sein, welche Informationen Sie mit dem Fagebogen gewinnen möchten: Welche übergeordnete Fragestellung steht über dem Fragebogen? Außerdem sollten Sie wissen, welche Zielgruppe Sie ansprechen möchten. Diese bestimmt zum Beispiel auch den Fragestil. Ein guter Fragebogen hat ein breites Spektrum an Frageformen, sodass eine möglichst umfassende Erhebung von Daten / Ergebnissen möglich wird. Die Fragen sollten dabei immer so konkret wie möglich gestellt werden. Formulieren Sie die Fragen kurz und verständlich, damit sie schnell gelesen und verstanden werden können. Auch sollte der Fragebogen nicht zu viele Fragen beinhalten, damit die befragte Person den Fragebogen ohne Probleme in kurzer Zeit bewältigen kann. Achten Sie dabei immer darauf, dass Sie keine Doppelfragen stellen. Wichtig noch: Suggerieren Sie bei einer Frage nie schon eine Antworten, damit ein „ehrliches", „nicht manipuliertes" Ergebnis erreicht werden kann. Beispiel, wie man es nicht macht: *Don't you think that our home service is one of the best?*

Fragenbeispiele

- **Alternativfragen:** Fragen mit zwei Antwortmöglichkeiten, häufig ja oder nein
  Beispiele:

Do you smoke?	o yes	o no
Are you	o female	o male

- **Auswahlfragen:** Aus einer Auswahl an Antwortmöglichkeiten soll die befragte Person jene Antwort auswählen, die am ehesten auf sie / ihn zutrifft.
  Beispiele:

What are your current living arrangements?			
o with wife / husband / partner	o with family	o alone	o with friends
o in assisted living	o in nursing home	o day care and living alone	o other

- **Fragen mit Schätzskalen:** Die befragte Person gibt dabei eine Einschätzung über einen Sachverhalt ab, indem auf einer Skala eine für sie / ihn zutreffende Aussage angekreuzt werden kann.
  Beispiele:

Please answer by marking (x) in the most relevant space.	never	seldom	sometimes	always
Do you need lists to remember things?				
Do you find it difficult to remember names?				
Do you often have to search for items?				
Is it difficult for you to follow a conversation?				

	1	2	3	4	5	6
How would you rate our overall home service on a scale of 1 to 6, where 1 is "not at all satisfying" and 6 is "completely satisfying"?						

- **Offene Fragen:** Ein Fragebogen kann auch offene Fragen beinhalten. Offene Fragen dienen der Erhebung der Meinung der befragten Person. Einerseits ermöglicht die offene Frage eine individuelle und weitergehende Antwort, andererseits ist diese daher auch aufwändiger auszuwerten.
  Beispiele: What do you like / dislike about our home care service?
  What should we do to improve our home care service?

Expressing your own opinion – Writing a comment

Die eigene Meinung darlegen – Einen Kommentar schreiben

In einer Diskussion möchten Sie Ihre eigene Meinung darlegen können. Ihre Meinung bekommt dann Aussagekraft, wenn Sie diese gut begründen können.
Auch in schriftlichen Kommentaren ist es wichtig, die eigene Meinung zu begründen. Einen schriftlichen Kommentar verfassen Sie in der Regel auf der Grundlage eines Textes (z. B. eines argumentativen Zeitungstextes) oder auf der Grundlage eines Ausgangsstatements.
Mit der **Pro-Argumentation** werden Sie die Aussage des Ausgangstextes stützen, mit einer **Kontra-Argumentation** hingegen entkräften Sie die im Ausgangstext dargelegte Position. Mit Beispielen und Statistiken untermauern Sie dabei Ihre eigene Meinung.
Bevor Sie mit dem Schreiben des Kommentars beginnen, überlegen Sie sich möglichst viele Argumente, die sowohl für als auch gegen eine bestimmte Meinung sprechen. Danach entscheiden Sie sich, welche Argumentation Sie führen möchten: Pro oder Kontra.

Aufbau

Einleitung

- → Ausgehend von einer **Textvorlage oder einem Ausgangsstatement:** Fassen Sie zunächst die vorgegebene Postion kurz mit Ihren eigenen Worten zusammen, stellen Sie hier klar, wie Sie selbst zur vorgegebenen Aussage stehen.
- → Ausgehend von einem **bestimmten Thema:** Führen Sie mit der Einleitung an das Thema heran, wecken Sie Interesse für das Thema!

Eine Möglichkeit ist hier zum Beispiel, rhetorische Fragen zu stellen. Diese erzeugen Aufmerksamkeit und machen gleichzeitig Ihre eigene Position deutlich, denn rhetorische Fragen geben die Antwort bereits vor:
„Don't we all know, that fast food can only be bad for our health?",

Vocabulary help

I think this statement wants to express that …	Ich denke, diese Aussage will ausdrücken, dass
With this statement the author wants to say that …	Mit der Aussage möchte der Autor sagen, dass …
As far as I understand it / know …	So viel wie ich verstehe / weiß …
The text deals with …	Der Text handelt von …
The main argument of this text is that …	Das Hauptargument des Textes ist, dass …
The writer argues that …	Der Autor argumentiert, dass …

Hauptteil

Im Hauptteil begründen Sie Ihre Argumente.
Variante 1: Wechseln Sie jeweils ab:
Pro-Argument – Kontra-Argument,
Pro-Argument – Kontra-Argument usw.
Dabei kann z. B. das Pro-Argument das Kontra-Argument entkräften. Stützen Sie Ihre Argumente durch Beispiele! Bedenken Sie: Das Schlussargument ist das wichtigste Argument. Dieses bleibt dem Leser im Gedächtnis.
Variante 2: Sie zählen z.B. erst alle Kontra-Argumente auf. Dabei fangen Sie mit dem stärksten Kontra-Argument an bis Sie beim schwächsten Kontra-Argument angelangt sind. Nach dem Wendepunkt wenden Sie sich nun den Pro-Argumenten zu: Nun beginnen Sie mit dem schwächsten Argument und steigern sich zum Ende hin zum stärksten Pro-Argument. Denn, das stärkste Argument am Ende bleibt dem Leser im Gedächtnis!
Natürlich können Sie auch erst mit den Pro-Argumenten anfangen und mit den Kontra-Argumenten enden. Je nachdem, wie Ihre Meinung zum Thema ist.

Vocabulary help

In my opinion …	Meiner Meinung nach …
From my point of view / To my mind …	Von meinem Standpunkt / meiner Meinung aus …
I'm of the opinion that …	Ich bin der Meinung, dass …
I think / believe / suppose …	Ich denke / glaube / nehme an …
I can imagine that …	Ich kann mir vorstellen, dass …
Firstly (secondly …), I would like to say / mention that …	Zuerst / Erstens (zweitens …) möchte ich sagen, dass …
I'm / I'm not sure / certain / convinced that …	Ich bin / bin nicht sicher / überzeugt, dass …
The point / main argument is that …	Der Punkt / das Hauptargument ist, dass …
It is obvious that …	Es ist offensichtlich, dass …
There are several reasons for this …	Da gibt es verschiedenen Gründe dafür …
On the one hand …, on the other hand …	Einerseits …, andererseits …
I'm of mixed opinion about / on …	Ich bin geteilter Meinung über …
The reason is that …	Der Grund ist, dass …
Let me give you an example …	Lassen Sie mich ein Beispiel geben …
One could also argue that …	Man könnte ebenso argumentieren, dass …
I think the author is wrong when he says that …	Ich denke der Autor hat unrecht, wenn er sagt, dass …
I don't agree with …	Ich stimme nicht zu, dass …
I reject the opinion / idea that …	Ich stimme der Meinung / Vorstellung, dass …, nicht zu.
I have to contradict the author because …	Ich muss dem Autor widersprechen, weil …
There are a lot of arguments against the author's opinion, like for example …	Es gibt eine Menge Argumente gegen die Meinung des Autors wie zum Beispiel …
… is a striking example of …	… ist ein gutes Beispiel für …
It is completely / totally wrong to argue that …	Es ist völlig falsch zu argumentieren, dass …
My example proves that …	Mein Beispiel beweist,

Schluss

Zum Schluss fassen Sie das Wichtigste kurz zusammen. Hier sollten keine neuen Gedanken mehr ausgeführt werden, sondern das Hauptargument noch einmal als Schlusspunkt bestärkt werden. Hier können Sie auch die Frage, die Sie in der Einleitung formuliert haben, beantworten:

„Yes, all of my arguments clearly show that fast food is dangerous for our health!",
oder Sie geben einen Ausblick auf die Zukunft:
„If we go on eating fast food, we won't be able to pay for our health system in future".

Vocabulary help

The conclusion of all this is that …	Die Schlussfolgerung ist …
All in all one can say …	Alles in allem kann man sagen, dass …
It is by no means certain that …	Es ist keineswegs sicher, dass …
Obviously / Doubtless it is wrong / right to say that …	Offensichtlich / Zweifellos ist es falsch / richtig zu sagen, dass …
You can take from this that …	Als Ergebnis kann man festhalten, dass …
Weighing up the pros and cons, one comes to the conclusion …	Wenn man das Für und Wider abwägt, kommt man zu dem Schluss, dass …
The result / consequence of this is that …	Das Ergebnis / Die Folge ist, dass …
In short …	Kurz gesagt, …
To put it in a nutshell …	Um es auf den Punkt zu bringen …
Summing up, it can be said that …	Zusammenfassend lässt sich sagen, dass …

Connectors Satzverknüpfungen

To show time / Um zeitliche Abläufe hervorzuheben			
at first	als erstes	next	als nächstes
first	zuerst	after	danach
second	zweitens	afterwards	nachher
as / when	als	before	zuvor / vorher
while	während	at that time	zu der Zeit / jener Zeit
since / for	seit	soon	bald
later	später	previously	vorher, früher
then	dann	finally	schließlich
at last / lastly	zum Schluss / zuletzt	also / in addition	auch / zudem
To point at something / Um auf etwas hinzuweisen			
as far as	soweit	with regard to	im Hinblick auf / mit Blick auf
as to	um zu	regarding	im Hinblick auf / mit Blick auf
To express purpose / Um eine Absicht auszudrücken			
in order to / to	um zu	so that	sodass
To express reason / result / Um einen Grund / ein Ergebnis (Folge) auszudrücken			
because	weil	for this reason / for these reasons	aus diesem Grund / diesen Gründen
because of	wegen		
due to	aufgrund / infolge	the reason for this is	der Grund dafür ist
since / as (am Satzanfang)	weil	as a result of	als ein Ergebnis von
therefore	deshalb	as a consequence	als Folge / folglich / somit
thus	dadurch / deshalb	in consequence / consequently	als Folge / folglich / somit
so	so / also		
caused by	verursacht durch		
To express an unexpected result / Um ein unerwartetes Ergebnis auszudrücken			
however	jedoch / allerdings	though / although	obwohl
in spite of	trotz	despite	trotz
nevertheless	trotzdem	even so	allerdings
To give an example / Um ein Beispiel zu geben			
for example / for instance	zum Beispiel	such as	so wie / wie etwa
To explain something / Um etwas zu erklären			
that is / that is to say	das heißt / nämlich	in other words	mit anderen Worten / anders gesagt
namely	nämlich	to put it in another way / in a different way / differently	mit anderen Worten / anders gesagt
To express similarity / opposition / Um Gleichheit / Ungleichheit auszudrücken			
in the same way / manner	in gleicher Weise	by contrast / in contrast	im Gegensatz dazu / hingegen
similarly	ebenso / gleichermaßen	but	aber
likewise	ebenso / gleichermaßen	on the contrary	im Gegenteil

Unregelmäßige Verben

Infinitive (1. Verbform)	Past Tense (2. Verbform)	Past Participle (3. Verbform)	
(to) be	was (sg.), were (pl.)	been	sein
(to) beat	beat	beaten	schlagen
(to) become	became	become	werden
(to) begin	began	begun	beginnen, anfangen
(to) bite	bit	bitten	beißen
(to) bleed	bled	bled	bluten
(to) blow	blew	blown	blasen
(to) break	broke	broken	brechen, zerbrechen
(to) bring	brought	brought	bringen, mitbringen
(to) build	built	built	bauen
(to) burn	burnt	burnt	brennen
(to) buy	bought	bought	kaufen
(to) can	could		können
(to) catch	caught	caught	fangen, ergreifen
(to) choose	chose	chosen	wählen
(to) come	came	come	kommen
(to) cost	cost	cost	kosten
(to) cut	cut	cut	schneiden
(to) deal (with)	dealt	dealt	sich kümmern, sich beschäftigen mit
(to) do	did	done	machen, tun
(to) draw	drew	drawn	zeichnen, malen
(to) dream	dreamt	dreamt	träumen
(to) drink	drank	drunk	trinken
(to) drive	drove	driven	(Auto) fahren
(to) eat	ate	eaten	essen
(to) fall	fell	fallen	fallen
(to) feel	felt	felt	fühlen
(to) fight	fought	fought	bekämpfen, kämpfen
(to) find	found	found	finden
(to) fly	flew	flown	fliegen
(to) forget	forgot	forgotten	vergessen
(to) forgive	forgave	forgiven	vergeben, verzeihen
(to) freeze	froze	frozen	frieren, gefrieren
(to) get	got	got	bekommen, kommen
(to) give	gave	given	geben
(to) go	went	gone	gehen, fahren
(to) grow	grew	grown	wachsen
(to) have	had	had	haben
(to) hear	heard	heard	hören
(to) hide	hid	hidden	(sich) verstecken
(to) hit	hit	hit	schlagen, stoßen
(to) hold	held	held	halten, abhalten
(to) hurt	hurt	hurt	(sich) verletzen
(to) keep	kept	kept	behalten, halten
(to) know	knew	known	wissen, kennen

Infinitive (1. Verbform)	Past Tense (2. Verbform)	Past Participle (3. Verbform)	
(to) lead	led	led	führen
(to) learn	learnt	learnt	lernen
(to) leave	left	left	verlassen, abfahren
(to) lend	lent	lent	leihen, verleihen
(to) let	let	let	lassen
(to) lie	lay	lain	liegen
(to) lose	lost	lost	verlieren
(to) make	made	made	machen, anfertigen
(to) mean	meant	meant	bedeuten
(to) meet	met	met	treffen, begegnen
(to) pay	paid	paid	bezahlen
(to) put	put	put	setzen, legen, stellen
(to) read	read	read	lesen
(to) ride	rode	ridden	reiten, Radfahren
(to) ring	rang	rung	klingeln, läuten
(to) rise	rose	risen	aufstehen
(to) run	ran	run	rennen, laufen
(to) say	said	said	sagen
(to) see	saw	seen	sehen
(to) seek	sought	sought	suchen
(to) sell	sold	sold	verkaufen
(to) send	sent	sent	senden, schicken
(to) shake	shook	shaken	schütteln
(to) show	showed	shown	zeigen
(to) shut	shut	shut	schließen
(to) sing	sang	sung	singen
(to) sit	sat	sat	sitzen
(to) sleep	slept	slept	schlafen
(to) smell	smelt	smelt	riechen
(to) speak	spoke	spoken	sprechen
(to) spend	spent	spent	verbringen, ausgeben
(to) stand	stood	stood	stehen
(to) steal	stole	stolen	stehlen
(to) swim	swam	swum	schwimmen
(to) take	took	taken	nehmen, mitnehmen
(to) teach	taught	taught	lehren, unterrichten
(to) tear	tore	torn	zerreißen
(to) tell	told	told	erzählen
(to) think	thought	thought	denken
(to) throw	threw	thrown	werfen
(to) wake (up)	woke	woken	aufwachen
(to) wear	wore	worn	(Kleidung) tragen
(to) win	won	won	gewinnen
(to) write	wrote	written	schreiben

Alphabetische Vokabelliste

s. th. = something s. o. = someone

A

ability	Fähigkeit
(to) accept	akzeptieren
accident	Unfall
(to) accompany s. o.	jmd. begleiten
(to) achieve	erreichen
(to) adapt	anpassen
adaptation	Anpassung
(to) add	hinzufügen
addict	Süchtige(r)
addiction (to)	Sucht / Abhängigkeit von
administration	Verwaltung
(to) admire	bewundern
admission	(Krankenhaus-) Aufnahme
admitted	hier: eingeliefert
advancing	fortschreitend
adventure	Abenteuer
advice	Hinweis, Ratschlag
Advocat	Eierlikör-Marke
(to) affect	beeinflussen, hier: angreifen, beeinflussen
affectionate	(sehr) emotional
age suit	Anzug, der das Alter simuliert
alert	aufmerksam, wach
alongside	neben, Seite an Seite
amount	Menge
anger	Wut, Zorn
ankle	Knöchel
anorexia	Magersucht
antidepressants	Antidepressiva
apathetic	apathisch, regungslos
appearance	Aussehen, Erscheinungsbild
(to) appreciate	zu schätzen wissen
apron	Schürze
area	Bereich
around the clock	rund um die Uhr
(to) arouse interest	Interesse wecken
(to) arrive	(an-)kommen
art	Kunstunterricht
arthritis	Arthritis, Gelenkentzündung
assessed by	hier: festgestellt von
(to) assist	helfen, begleiten
assisted living	Betreutes Wohnen
at a slower pace	in langsamerem Tempo
at their weakest	im schwächsten Zustand
attention	Aufmerksamkeit
attentive	aufmerksam
authorised	autorisiert, befugt
available	verfügbar, hier auch: ansprechbar
average	durchschnittlich
(to) avoid (+ing-Form)	vermeiden

B

back and fro	hin und her
bacteria	Bakterien
bad-tempered	übellaunig
balance	Gleichgewicht
balanced	ausgewogen
balcony	Balkon
bandage	Bandage, Verband
barrier-free	barrierefrei
bathing	Baden
bathroom	Badezimmer
bathtub lift	Badewannenlift
(to) be able (to)	fähig sein zu
(to) be attached (to)	an etwas hängen
(to) be available	hier: vorrätig sein
(to) be behind schedule	hinter dem Zeitplan zurück sein / liegen
(to) be convalescent	auf dem Weg der Genesung sein
(to) be disabled	eine Behinderung haben
(to) be divided into	aufgeteilt sein in
(to) be equipped with	ausgestattet sein mit
(to) be firm with s. o.	gegenüber jmd. entschlossen / bestimmt bleiben
be furnished with	möbliert sein mit
(to) be interested in	sich interessieren für
(to) be limited	eingeschränkt sein
(to) be mentally strong	psychisch stark sein
(to) be off sick	wg. Krankheit fehlen
(to) be on call	abrufbereit sein
(to) be on watch	hier: Nachtwache haben
(to) be overwhelmed	überfordert sein
(to) be reminded	erinnert werden
(to) be responsible for	verantwortlich sein für
(to) be transferred (to)	(über-), eingewiesen werden
bean bags	Bohnensäckchen zum Jonglieren
(to) bear s.th.	etwas ertragen
bed linen	Bettwäsche
bedridden	bettlägerig

bedside locker	Krankenbettspint
(to) behave	sich verhalten
(to) bend	beugen, bücken, vorbeugen
(to) lean forward	nach vorne beugen / lehnen
(to) benefit	profitieren
benefit	Vorteil, Nutzen
(to) benefit from	Nutzen ziehen von, profitieren von
bin	Mülleimer
biography	Biografie, Lebensgeschichte
bipolar	manisch-depressiv
bite	Biss
blindness	Blindheit
blinds	Rolladen, Jalousie
blood pressure	Blutdruck
blur	Unschärfe
(to) bob up and down	rauf und runter bewegen
boiled egg	gekochtes Ei
bones	Knochen
book of condolence	Kondulenzbuch
borderline personality disorder (BPD)	Borderline-Persönlichkeitsstörung
boring	langweilig
bottom	hier: Po
bowl	Schüssel
(to) brainstorm	hier: Ideensammlung
(to) break into a sweat	in Schweiß ausbrechen
bricklayer	Maurer
bride	Braut
bridesmaid	Brautjungfer
brilliant	strahlend
brittle	porös
bruise	blauer Fleck
(to) build relationships	Beziehungen aufbauen
(to) build strength	Kraft aufbauen
(to) build up reserves	Vorräte anlegen
(to) build up strength	Kraft gewinnen
bulimia	Bulimie, Ess-Brechsucht
bust / chest	Brust
button	Knopf

C

caffeine	Koffein
calcium-rich	kalziumreich
calf	Wade
call button	Notrufknopf
(to) calm down	(sich) beruhigen
(to) calm sb. down	jmd. beruhigen
cancer	Krebs (Krankheit)
canteen kitchen	Großküche
care assistant	Pflegehelfer/-in, Gesundheits- und Pflegeassistent/-in
care coordinator	Pflegekoordinator
(to) care for	sich kümmern um, jmd. pflegen
care worker	Pflegekraft
carer	Person, die sich um die Pflege kümmert
(to) carry out	durchführen
case	Fall (eines Patienten)
catheter bag	Katheterbeutel / Urinbeutel
cattle	Vieh
(to) cause	verursachen
cell	Körperzelle
cerebral palsy	spastische Lähmung
(to) chair	leiten, den Vorsitz haben
chair exercise	Stuhlübungen
chairman	Vorsitzende, Vorsitzender
challenge	Herausforderung
(to) change bandage	Verband wechseln
(to) check	kontrollieren
cheek	Wange
(to) cheer up	aufmuntern
cheerful	fröhlich
chest of drawers	Kommode
(to) chew	kauen
child with special needs	Kind mit einem besonderen Bedürfnis, Kind mit einer Behinderung
children's home	Kinderheim
chiller cabinet	Kühlregal
chin	Kinn
choir	Chor
(to) choke	ersticken
(to) choose	auswählen
chore	Hausarbeit
chores	Haushaltspflichten
chromosome	Chromosom
(to) clench fist	Faust ballen
cliché	Klischee, Floskel

clubs	Gymnastikkegel
clumsy	ungeschickt
coffee maker	Kaffeemaschine
cognitive decline	geistiger Verfall
colleagues	Kollegen
(to) collect	abholen, (ein-)sammeln
(to) commit suicide	Selbstmord begehen
communication skills	kommunikative Fähigkeiten
competitive	konkurrierend
(to) complain	sich beschweren
concern for	Sorge um
condition	Zustand
confidential	vertraulich
(to) confirm	versichern, bestätigen
confusion	Verwirrung, hier: Verwirrtheit
(to) connect (to)	vermitteln, zusammenführen
(to) consider	in Betracht ziehen
consoling words	tröstende Worte
constructive	konstruktiv, hilfreich
(to) consult	konsultieren, sich besprechen mit
consultation	Konsultation, hier: ärztliche Behandlung
(to) contain	beinhalten
(to) contribute (to)	beitragen zu
convalescence	Genesung
cooperative	kooperativ
(to) cope	mit etwas fertig werden, etw. verarbeiten
(to) cope with	umgehen mit, auch: ertragen
corridor	Flur
cottage cheese	Hüttenkäse
(to) counsel / advise	beraten
counselling service	Beratungsdienst
(to) count as	zählen / gelten als
countless	zahllos
cradle	Wiege
(to) create	erstellen
(to) create a barrier	eine Barriere aufbauen
crisis service team	Krisenberatungsteam
crisps	Chips
(to) criticise	kritisieren
(to) cross arms	Arme verschränken
cruel	grausam
crust	hier: Wundschorf
cupboard	(eingebauter) (Kleider-)Schrank
currently	derzeit, zurzeit
cutlery	Besteck

D

dairy products	Milchprodukte
(to) damage	zerstören
database	Datenbank
deaf	taub (Hörvermögen)
(to) deal with	sich befassen mit
(to) deal with death	mit dem Tod umgehen
decrease	Abnahme
(to) dehydrate	austrocknen
dehydration	Austrocknung
delay	Verzögerung
(to) delegate	delegieren / übertragen
dementia	Demenz
density	(Knochen-)Dichte
dental	adj. Zahn-…, zahnmedizinisch
(to) depend on	abhängen von, angewiesen sein auf
(to) develop	entwickeln
deviations	Abweichungen
diabetes	Diabetes, Zuckererkrankung
(to) diagnose with	diagnostizieren
diagnosing	das Diagnostizieren
(to) die	sterben
diet	Ernährung, auch: Diät
digestion	Verdauung
diluted juice	mit Wasser verdünnter Saft
disability	Behinderung, Unfähigkeit
(to) disappear	verschwinden
discharge	(Krankenhaus-) Entlassung
discomfort	Unbehagen
discounts	Rabatte
(to) discover	entdecken
(heart) disease	(Herz-)Erkrankung
disgust	Entsetzen, Ekel
disorientation	Orientierungslosigkeit
disoriented	desorientiert
disrespect	Respektlosigkeit
distracted	abgelenkt
distress	Verzweiflung
(to) distribute	austeilen, verteilen
diversity	Vielfalt
divorced	geschieden
dizzy	schwindelig
(to) do exercise / to exercise	(sportl.) Übungen machen

(to) do on the job training	Ausbildung am Arbeitsplatz
(to) do the lion's share	den Löwenanteil machen
doctor's appointment	Arzttermin
doorway	hier: Türrahmen
dose	Dosis
(to) draw s. o. in	jmd. an- / hereinziehen
(to) dress wounds	Wunden verbinden
dressing	hier: Verband
drug advice center	Drogenberatung
drug related crimes	Drogenbeschaffungskriminalität
drugs	Drogen
dumbbell	Hantel
(to) dust	staubwischen
(to) dye	färben
dying process	Sterbeprozess

E

ear muffs	Ohrenschützer
eating disorder	Essstörung
eating habits	Essgewohnheiten
effective	wirksam
efficiency	Effizienz
effort	Anstrengung
elasticity	Spannkraft
elbow	Ellbogen
emergency number	Notfallnummer
emotional impairment	emotionale Einschränkung
emotional stress	emotionaler Stress
emptiness	Leere
(to) enable	ermöglichen
(to) encourage	ermutigen
(to) encourage to	ermuntern zu
end-of-life care	sterbebegleitende Pflege
endorphins	Endorphine, „Glückshormone"
enriching	bereichernd
en-suite room	Zimmer mit eigenem Bad
(to) ensure	sicherstellen
(to) entertain	unterhalten
entirely	völlig, gänzlich
entrance hall	Eingangshalle
equal	gleichberechtigt
(to) evaluate	bewerten, auswerten
event	Ereignis, Anlass
(to) exchange glances	Blicke (aus)tauschen
exciting	aufregend
(to) exclude from	jmd. ausschließen von
exclusion from	Ausschluss von
(to) exercise	hier: sich bewegen, trainieren
experience	Erfahrung
(to) experience sensations	Empfindungen wahrnehmen
external	jemand, der von außen kommt
eyebrows	Augenbrauen
eye-catching	ein Blickfang sein

F

facial expression	Gesichtsausdruck
facial profile	Gesichtsprofil
fake	Attrappe
family album	(Familien-)Fotoalbum
(to) fasten	hier: zuknöpfen
favourite	Favorit
fear of failure	Versagensangst
fearful	ängstlich
features	Merkmale
(to) feed	Essen anreichen
(to) feel ashamed	sich schämen
(to) feel guilty	ein schlechtes Gewissen haben
fibre	Balaststoff
fibre-rich	balaststoffreich
final stage / s	Endstadium
fine motor skills	Feinmotorik
(to) fire	entlassen
first name	Vorname
flat	Wohnung
fluid intake	Flüssigkeitsaufnahme
food	Essen, Nahrung
food going the wrong way	sich verschlucken
food intake	Nahrungsaufnahme
foods	Nahrungsmittel
foot tapping	mit dem Fuß wippen
forehead	Stirn
forgetful	vergesslich
forgetfulness	Vergesslichkeit
(to) form a circle	einen Kreis bilden
fracture	Knochenbruch
(to) fracture the thigh bone	den Oberschenkelhals brechen
fractured	gebrochen

fragile	zerbrechlich
French Fries	Pommes Frittes
frequent	häufig
fresh	frisch
fresh dressing	frischer Verband
fried potatoes	Bratkartoffeln
from scratch	von Beginn an
fruit	Obst
fun fair	Kirmes

G

(to) gain experience	Erfahrung sammeln
(to) gamble	Spielen (um Geld)
gambling addiction	Spielsucht
gambling afternoon	Spielnachmittag
gang	Bande
GCSE General Certificate of Secondary Education	Mittlerer Schulabschluss
general practitioner	Arzt / Ärztin für Allgemeinmedizin
genetic	genetisch
gesture	Geste
get connected	Anschluss finden, Kontakt aufnehmen
(to) get lost	Orientierung verlieren / sich verlaufen
(to) get to know	vertraut werden mit
getting dressed	Ankleiden
(to) give a hug	umarmen
(to) give s. o. response	jmd. eine Antwort geben
gloves	Handschuhe
(to) go on binges	auf ein (Sauf- / Fress-) Gelage gehen
GP (general practitioner)	Allgemeinarzt / Allgemeinärztin
grateful	dankbar
grieving	trauernd, in Trauer
grieving relatives	trauernde Verwandte
grocery shop	Lebensmittelgeschäft
gross motor skills	Grobmotorik
(to) guess	raten
guilt	Schuld
guilty	schuldig

H

habit	Gewohnheit, Sucht
habits	Gewohnheiten
handicraft	Basteln
hardness of hearing	Schwerhörigkeit
hardship	Entbehrung, hier: harte Zeit
(to) harm	hier: schaden
(to) harm oneself	sich selbst verletzen
(the) harvest	(die) Ernte
(to) harvest	ernten
(to) haunt s. o.	jmd. verfolgen
(to) have a lie in	ausschlafen
(to) have in common	gemeinsam haben
(to) have meaning	Bedeutung haben
head	hier: Leitung, Leiter / in
headache	Kopfschmerzen
healer	Heiler
healing	Heilung
health	Gesundheit
health condition	Gesundheitszustand
health problems	gesundheitliche Probleme
hearing aid	Hörgerät
heart attack	Herzinfarkt
heart disease	Herzerkrankung
heart failure	Herzversagen
heel	Ferse
help yourself	bedienen Sie sich
herbal butter	Kräuterbutter
highs and lows	das Auf und Ab (des Lebens)
(to) hinder from	hindern an
hip bone	Hüftknochen
hips	Hüften
(to) hoard	sammeln, horten
home care service	häuslicher Pflegedienst, ambulanter Pflegedienst
home care worker	Pflegekraft im ambulanten Pflegedienst
hoop	Gymnastikreifen
hospice	Hospiz
hospital	Krankenhaus
hospital bed	Krankenbett
hospital ward	Krankenhausstation
hot-box	Warmhaltebox
housekeeping	Haushaltsführung
hug	Umarmung
human	menschlich
hurtful	verletzend
hygiene	Hygiene

I

icebreaker	Eisbrecher, hier: Kennenlern-Aktivität
(to) identify	hier: erkennen
ill	krank
illness	Krankheit
immune system	Immunsystem, Körperabwehr
impression	Eindruck, Wirkung
(to) improve	verbessern
in detail	im Detail, genau
in moderation	in Maßen
inactive	inaktiv, ruhig
inappropriate	unangemessen
inclusion	Aufnahme, hier: Inklusion
inclusive summer camp	integratives Ferienlager
(to) increase	zunehmen
independent living	alleine leben / wohnen
infection	Infektion, Ansteckungserkrankung
infectious	ansteckend, infektiös
influence on	Einfluss auf
ingredient	Inhaltsstoff, Zutat
injection	Spritze
injured	verletzt
injury / injuries	Verletzung(en)
(to) insert a catheter	Katheter setzen
(to) insult	beleidigen
integrated nursery school class	integrative Kindergartengruppe (Gruppe mit Kindern mit und ohne Behinderung)
intellectual deficit	intellektuelles (geistiges) Defizit, Mangel
intellectual difficulties	intellektuelle Schwierigkeiten
intensive care unit	Intensivstation
intimate	persönlich / intim
(to) introduce s. o.	jmd. vorstellen
(to) investigate	prüfen, ermitteln
(to) involve	beinhalten
(people) involved	Beteiligte
iron-rich	eisenhaltig
isolated	isoliert, ausgeschlossen

J

joints	Gelenke
juggling rings	Jonglier-Ringe
juggling veils	Jonglier-Tücher

K

(to) keep active	aktiv bleiben
(to) keep an eye on	die Augen offen halten auf / für
(to) keep occupied	beschäftigt bleiben / halten
(to) keep sb. comfortable	dafür sorgen, dass sich jmd. wohl fühlt
(to) keep sb. company	jmd. Gesellschaft leisten
(to) keep the project going	das Projekt in Gang halten
(to) keep to schedule	den Einsatzplan / Zeitplan einhalten
knee	Knie

L

lack of	Mangel an
language difficulties	Sprachschwierigkeiten
language exercise	Sprachtraining
large	groß
laundry	Wäscherei, Wäsche
lean	mager
learning disabilities	Lernbehinderung
left undone	liegen bleiben, nicht erledigt werden
leisure time	Freizeit
lentils	Linsen
lethargic	träge
level	Ebene, Stockwerk
life story	Lebensgeschichte
(to) lift	heben
lift	Aufzug, Lift
(to) lift out of bed	aus dem Bett heben
(to) lift / (to) raise	heben / hochheben
(to) limit	beschränken
limited movement	eingeschränkte Bewegung
listener	Zuhörer/-in
(to) live a full life	ein erfülltes Leben leben
liver	Leber
long-term care	Voll- / Langzeitpflege
long-term	Langzeit…
long-term memory	Langzeitgedächtnis
(to) lose appetite	den Appetit verlieren
(to) lose control of	Kontrolle verlieren
loss (of)	Verlust
(to) lower	senken
lunatic	verrückt
lung cancer	Lungenkrebs
lying down	liegend

M

magnifying glass	Vergrößerungsglas
(to) maintain	aufrechterhalten, erhalten
(to) maintain health	die Gesundheit erhalten
(to) make eye-contact	Blickkontakt herstellen
mashed potatoes	Kartoffelpüree
meadow	Wiese
meal tray	(Essens-)Tablett
meals on wheels	Essen auf Rädern
mealtimes	Mahlzeiten
meat	Fleisch
medical care	medizinische Pflege / Versorgung
medical equipment	medizinisches Gerät
medical file	Krankenakte
medication	Medikation / Tablettenversorgung
medication chart	Einnahmeplan / Medikamenteübersicht
medication management	Medikamenten-versorgung
medication plan	Medikamenten-verschreibung
medicine intake	Medikamentenaufnahme
memo	Notiz
memory exercise	Gedächtnistraining
memory loss	Gedächtnisverlust
mental	mental, geistig
mental disability	geistige Behinderung
mental health	geistige / mentale Gesundheit
(to) misuse	missbrauchen
mobility	Mobilität, Beweglichkeit
moderate	gemäßigt, mittelmäßig, moderat
(to) modify	ändern, modifizieren
(to) monitor	überwachen
monitoring	Überwachung
mood	Laune, Stimmung
mood swings	Stimmungs-schwankungen
moody	launig
(to) motivate	anspornen
mouldy	schimmelig
multiple	mehrfach
(to) mumble	murmeln, nuscheln
muscles	Muskeln
muscular weakness	Muskelschwäche

N

napkin	Serviette
nausea	Übelkeit
neat	ordentlich, adrett
neck	Nacken
neglect	Vernachlässigung
neurological	neurologisch
night commode	Nachtstuhl (Toilettenstuhl)
(to) nod	nicken
(to) notice	hier: erkennen
nourishment	Ernährung
numb	stumpf, abgestumpft, taub (im Gefühl), gefühllos
numbness	Taubheit, Gefühllosigkeit
nurse	Pflegefachkraft
nurse station	Stationszimmer
nursing assistant	Pflegehelfer/-in, Gesundheits- und Pflegeassistenz
nursing home	Pflegeheim
nursing intervention	Pflegemaßnahme
nursing profession	Pflegeberuf
nutrient	Nährstoff

O

oats	Haferflocken
obesity	Fettleibigkeit
obituary	Traueranzeige
(to) observe	beobachten
observed behaviour	beobachtetes Verhalten
occupational therapy	Beschäftigungstherapie
(to) offer	anbieten
oily	ölig, ölhaltig
ointment	Salbe
old people's day care centre	Tagespflege für Senioren
old people's home	Seniorenheim / Seniorenresidenz
on behalf	im Interesse
on your own pace	im eigenen Rhythmus
one-on-one-time	Zeit für den Einzelnen
open ended	offen (gestellte Frage)
openness	Offenheit
operation	Operation
operation scar	Operationsnarbe
operation theater	Operationssaal
opportunity	Möglichkeit
orders	hier: ärztliche Anweisung
organ capacity	Organleistung
organic	biologisch
originally	ursprünglich

out of breath — außer Puste / Atem
outraged — aufgebracht
oven — Backofen
overbed table — Rolltisch / Beistelltisch
overburdened — überlastet
(to) overcome obstacles — Hindernisse überwinden
(to) overdose — Überdosis, (sich) überdosieren
(to) overeat — (sich) überessen
overweight — übergewichtig

P

pain — Schmerz
painful — schmerzhaft
painkiller — Schmerzmittel
palm — Handfläche
pancake — Pfannkuchen
paperwork — Papier- / Büroarbeit
paramedic — Rettungssanitäter
participant — Teilnehmer
participation — Teilnahme, Beteiligung
parts of the body — Körperteile
(to) pass around — (herum-)reichen
(to) pass away — sterben
passing — das Ableben
patient — Patient/-in
peanuts — Erdnüsse
peas — Erbsen
pendant — Anhänger
people problems — persönliche Probleme
pep — Pepp, Schwung
(to) perform — hier: ausführen
(to) perform tests on s.o. — jmd. Tests unterziehen
performance — Auf- / Vorführung
personal hygiene — Körperpflege
personal profile — Personenbeschreibung, Steckbrief
personality — Persönlichkeit
pharmacy — Apotheke
physical — körperlich
physical disability — körperliche Behinderung
physical strain — körperliche Anstrengung
physical strength — körperliche Stärke
physical therapy — Physiotherapie
physically — körperlich
physically active — körperlich aktiv
placement — Praktikum
(to) plant — pflanzen
plaster — Gipsverband
pleasant — angenehm
positive feedback — positive Rückmeldung
(to) pot — eintopfen
(to) prefer — bevorzugen
preferably — möglichst
prescription — (ärztl.) Rezept
pressure sore — Druckgeschwür
(to) prevent — vermeiden
private rooms — Privaträume
produce — Erzeugnis, Produkt
productive — produktiv, schöpferisch
(life) prognosis — Lebenserwartung
proper — richtig, angemessen
protruding — hervorstehend, herausragend
(to) provide — zur Verfügung stellen
(to) provide so. with — jmd. versorgen mit
psychiatric ward — psychiatrische Station
psychological — psychologisch
psychotherapy — Psychotherapie
pulse — Puls
pulses — Hülsenfrüchte
pus — Eiter
(to) push aside — hier: verdrängen
(to) push s.o. — jmd. (zu etwas) drängen
(to) put on weight — zunehmen, Gewicht zulegen
(to) put yourself in the other person's shoes — sich in den anderen hineinversetzen
puzzled — verwirrt sein

Q

questionnaire — Fragebogen
(to) quit — aufgeben, beenden

R

(to) raise — heben, steigern
(to) raise money — Geld aufbringen
(to) range from … — (to) reichen von … bis
rapid — schnell, rapid
raspberry syrup — Himbeersirup
rational arguments — rationale / begründete Argumente
(to) reach for — greifen nach
reacher — Greifstock
reading glasses — Lesebrille
(to) recall — sich erinnern
recent — kürzlich, neulich
reception — Rezeption, Empfang
(to) recognize — erkennen
(to) recommend — empfehlen
(to) record — aufzeichnen, dokumentieren, aufschreiben

record of care	Pflegebericht
(to) recover	genesen, (sich) erholen / regenerieren
(to) recover from	sich erholen von
(to) reduce	reduzieren
(to) refer sb. to hospital	jmd. ins Krankenhaus überweisen
refreshed	erfrischt, hier: erholt
(to) refuse	(sich) weigern
(to) regain	wiedererlangen
registered nurse	examinierte Pflegefachkraft
regular care	ständige Pflege
rehabilitation clinic	Rehabilitationsklinik
(to) reinforce	bestätigen
reintegration	Reintegration, Wiedereingliederung
(to) reject	ablehnen
(to) relax (muscles)	lockern
(to) relax	sich entspannten
relaxing atmosphere	entspannte Atmosphäre
(to) release	abbauen, (frei) / (heraus) lassen
release	Erlösung, Befreiung
(to) release emotions	Gefühlen freien Lauf lassen
reluctant	widerwillig
(to) rely on	sich verlassen auf
(to) remember	sich erinnern
(to) repeat	wiederholen
repetition	Wiederholung
(to) report	berichten
(to) reposition	neu positionieren
repositioning	(Neu-)Positionierung
(to) require	brauchen, benötigen
resident	Bewohner/-in
resistance band	Gummiband
resolute	entschlossen
(to) respect	respektieren
respiration	Atmung
responsibility	Verantwortung
responsible	verantwortlich
responsive	ansprechbar
restlessness	Unruhe, Ruhelosigkeit
(to) restrict	begrenzen
restriction	Begrenzung
result	Ergebnis
ribbon	Band
rice pudding	Milchreis
risky	risikoreich
roast pork	Schweinebraten
(to) rock from side to side	Hin- und Herschaukeln
rude	beleidigend

S

safely (adv.)	sicher
safety net	Sicherheitsnetz
schedule	Einsatzplan / Zeitplan
(to) scold s. o.	mit jmd. schimpfen, jmd. beschimpfen
(to) screw up the forehead	„die Stirn runzeln"
seating area	Sitzbereich / Aufenthaltsbereich
seed	Saat
seizure disorder	Krankheit, die Anfälle verursacht
self-assured	selbstsicher
self-care deficits	Mängel in der persönlichen Pflege / Körperpflege
(to) self-harm	sich selbst verletzen
self-harm	Selbstverletzung
semi-private room	privater Raum mit geteiltem Bad
sense of humour	Sinn für Humor
sensible	vernünftig
sensitivity	Sensibilität, Feingefühl
sensory perception	Sinneswahrnehmung
serious	ernst
(to) set oneself goals	sich Ziele setzen
(to) set up an infusion	eine Infusion legen / jmd. an den Tropf hängen
sexual / emotional / physical abuse	sexueller / emotionaler / körperlicher Missbrauch
(to) shake hands	Hände schütteln
(to) shape	formen, hier auch: prägen
(to) shed tears	Tränen vergießen
(to) shop until you drop	kaufen bis zum Umfallen
shopping addiction	Kaufsucht
short-term care	Kurzzeitpflege
short-term memory	Kurzzeitgedächtnis
shower chair	Duschstuhl
showering	Duschen
(to) shut off	sich verschließen, sich abgrenzen
sign	Zeichen, Anzeichen
significant	bedeutend, sehr wichtig

(to) simulate	nachahmen, simulieren
simulation	Nachahmung, Simulation
(to) sit in an circle	im Kreis sitzen
skill	Fähigkeit
skilled	qualifiziert, erfahren
skills	Fähigkeiten
skipping rope	Springseil
slant	Neigung
sleeping position	Schlafposition
slice of bread	Brotscheibe
slight	hier: leicht
slovenly	heruntergekommen
smartly	adrett
snappy	treffend, flott
social volunteer	hier: jemand, der / die ein freiwilliges soziales Jahr macht
sole of the foot	Fußsohle
(to) sow	säen
soya beans	Sojabohnen
special care	besondere Pflege, -Fürsorge
splint	Schiene
(to) spoil	verderben
sport	Sportunterricht
sporty	sportlich
(to) squeeze	hier: drücken
staff	Mitarbeiter
staff meeting	Mitarbeiterbesprechung
staff panel	Mitarbeitertafel
staff room	Personalraum
staff support	Unterstützung durch Mitarbeiter
stairlift	Treppenlift
stairs	Treppe
stance	Körperhaltung
starchy	stärkehaltig
(to) stare at s.o.	jmd. anstarren
(to) starve	hungern, verhungern
(to) starve oneself	hungern, (sich) aushungern
(to) stay independent	unabhängig bleiben
steady	sicher, ruhig
(to) steal	stehlen
(to) stick to schedule	den Einsatzplan / Zeitplan einhalten
stiff	steif
(to) stir	(um)rühren
stockroom	Lagerraum
stomach	Magen
stomach pain	Magenschmerzen
store	speichern, verstauen
straight up	aufrecht
straw	Strohhalm
(to) strengthen	stärken, ausbauen
stress busters	Stresskiller
stress factor	Stressfaktor, Stressverursacher
(to) stretch	strecken, dehnen
(to) stroke	streicheln
stroke	Schlaganfall
stroke patient	Schlaganfallpatient
(to) struggle	mit etwas kämpfen, sich abmühen
subject	Unterrichtsfach
(to) suit	passen zu, gefallen
suitable	geeignet, qualifiziert, passend
supply	Versorgung
(to) supply with	versorgen mit
(to) support	unterstützen
surroundings	Umgebung
suspicious	verdächtig, argwöhnisch
(to) swallow	schlucken
(to) swing	kreisen lassen
swing stick	Gymnastikstab
Swiss ball	(großer) Gymnastikball
sympathy	Mitgefühl

T

(to) take blood	Blut entnehmen
(to) take frustration out on s.o.	Frustration an jmd. auslassen
(to) take s.th. personally	etw. persönlich nehmen
(to) take your mind off s.th.	auf andere Gedanken bringen
temperature	Temperatur
(to) tend	(to) neigen zu
(to) tense	anspannen
tension	Anspannung
terminal illness	tödliche Krankheit
terminal stage	Endstadium
the elderly	ältere Menschen; Senioren
the past	hier: das vergangene Leben
the present life	das gegenwärtige Leben
thigh	Oberschenkel
thigh bone	Oberschenkelknochen
thirsty	durstig
thrombosis stockings	Kompressionsstrümpfe

thumb	Daumen
(to) tick	ankreuzen, abhaken
time management	Zeiteinteilung
time pressure	Zeitdruck
timekeeping	Einhalten / Einhaltung der Zeit
to take a mouthful	einen Schluck nehmen
toes	Zehen
toilet	Toilette
(to) topple over	umfallen
torso	Oberkörper
(to) touch	anfassen
tour of the house	Hausrundgang
towel	Handtuch
trainee	auszubildende Person
tranquiliser	Beruhigungsmittel
transport	hier: Krankentransport
transportation	Transport
(to) treat a patient	einen Patienten behandeln
(to) treat s. o.	jmd. behandeln
treatment	Behandlung
trust	Vertrauen
(to) trust	vertrauen
trusted	bewährt
turning point	Wendepunkt
twice	zweimal

U

unbearable	unerträglich
(to) undergo	(sich) unterziehen
underweight	untergewichtig
unfulfilled	unerfüllt
unique	einzigartig
unpleasant	unangenehm
unstable	instabil
unsteady	unsicher (körperlich)
upright	aufrecht
upset	traurig
upwards	nach oben gerichtet

V

validity	Gültigkeitsdauer
value	Wert
variety	hier: Vielfalt
vegetables	Gemüse
vicious circle	Teufelskreis
vision	hier: Sehvermögen
vision problems	Sehstörungen
vital signs	Vitalzeichen
vocational training	Berufsausbildung
volunteer	Freiwillige Person, Person im Praktikum
(to) vomit (up)	erbrechen

W

waist	Taille
walker	Rollator
walker training	Rollatortraining
walking stick	Gehstock
ward	Pflegestation
wash basin	Waschbecken
(to) watch out for	aufpassen auf
(to) weaken	schwächen
wearer	Träger, die tragende Person
(to) weigh	wiegen
weight	Gewicht
what a burden	was für ein schweres Schicksal
wheelchair	Rollstuhl
wheelchair ramp	Rollstuhlrampe
whilst (=while)	während
whipped cream	Schlagsahne
wholegrain	Vollkorn-…
wide range	große Bandbreite
(to) widen	weiten, öffnen
wireless emergency system	drahtloses Notrufsystem
(to) withstand	standhalten, durchhalten
work independently	selbstständig arbeiten
work management	Arbeitsorganisation
(to) work out	(Muskeln) trainieren
work overload	Arbeitsüberlastung
working world	Arbeitswelt
wound management	Wundversorgung
wrinkles	Falten
wrist	Handgelenk
writing a nursing care plan	Pflegeplanung

X

x-ray	Röntgenaufnahme

Y

(to) yawn	gähnen
(to) yell at	anschreien

Bildquellenverzeichnis

123RF GmbH, Nidderau: S. 94/2 (Rob Marmion); 111/2 (Kasia Bialasiewicz),3 (Marcos Calvo Mesa)
dpa-Picture-Alliance GmbH, Frankfurt am Main: S. 8/2 (Patrick Pleul); 25/7 (Heiko Wolfraum); 32/4 (Fredrik Von Erichsen); 40 (Kurt Röhrig/Helga Lade); 49/8 (Stiftung_zur_Prävention_der_Arte); 76 (Karl-Josef Hildenbrand); 80 (Felix Kästle); 87/2 (picture-alliance /ZB); 98/1 (picture alliance /Klaus Rose); 111/4 (picture alliance / dpa),6 (picture alliance / Robert Schles),8 (picture alliance /ZB); 122/1 (picture alliance / JOKER),2 (picture alliance /Sueddeutsche)
F1online digitale Bildagentur GmbH, Frankfurt am Main: S. 45/1 (Creativ Heinemann RF imageBROKER); 49/9 (Jochen Tack RM imageBROKER); 50/2 (Brandon Sawaya RF Aurora); 52/1 (Ben Kepler Image Source)
Fiand, Ruth, Aachen: S. 67/1-11; 73/1-3
Illustrationsbüro Müller-Wegner, Hamburg: S. 18; 20/1; 27; 75/1-6; 93/1,2
iStockphoto, Berlin: S. 12 (AlexRaths); 16 (Horsche); 25/4 (Lisa-Blue); 39/2 (SolStock),3 (Antonio_Diaz),4 (Klubovy); 41 (NickS); 46 (4774344sean); 49/2 (Evgeny Sergeev),4 (OcusFocus),5 (Maica),6 (monkeybusinessimages),7 (ZoneCreative S.r.l.); 50/1 (KatarzynaBialasiewicz); 69 (EllenaZ); 94/1 (ajkkafe); 98/2 (AndreyPopov),3 (Dean Mitchell),4 (GBZero),8 (FredFroese); 104/1 (SolStock),2 (EVAfotografie); 111/7 (ozenli); 116/1 (Slonov); 121 (SilviaJansen); 124 (Robert Kneschke)
Mauritius GmbH, Mittenwald: S. 111/5 (mauritius images /Science Source)
Meyer, Rebecca, Wachtberg: S. 19
Produkt + Projekt Wolfgang Moll, Niederstotzingen: S. 58/1
Schmidt, Hartmut W., Fotografie, Freiburg: S. 1/4; 4
Shutterstock Images LLC, New York, USA: S. 1/5 (wavebreakmedia); 2/2 (Flashon Studio); 5 (Flashon Studio); 7/3 (Andrey_Popov); 20/3 (Morphart Creation); 29/3 (PathDoc),4 (RealPeopleStudio); 36/2 (Monkey Business Images); 39/1 (Stefano Cavoretto),6 (Jochen Schoenfeld); 49/3 (Nadino); 50/3 (jeanete_ehab),4 (Robert Kneschke),5 (Voronin76); 52/2 (JPC-PROD); 60/5 (Craig Russell); 88 (Photographee.eu); 98/7 (Halfpoint); 112 (Katrinshine); 115 (Photographee.eu)
Spehzies Illustration, Comic, Animation, Bernhard Speh, Hamburg: S. 29/5
stock.adobe.com: S. 1/1 (drubig-photo),2 (Monkey Business),3 (.shock); 2/1 (purplequeue); 7/1 (Daniel Ernst),2 (Phase4Photography); 8/1 (Peter Maszlen),3 (Tyler Olson); 13 (giorgenko); 15 (Kzenon); 20/2 (Morphart),4 (Morphart); 22 (Alexander Raths); 25/1 (Peter Maszlen),2 (Gina Sanders),3 (drubig-photo),5 (Kzenon),6 (Alexander Raths); 28 (Robert Kneschke); 29/1 (Axel Bueckert),2 (Axel Bueckert); 32/1 (pablocalvog),3 (pololia),5 (Andy Dean),6 (Firma V); 34 (Monkey Business); 35 (pathdoc); 36/1 (waxart),3 (giorgiomtb); 39/5 (kasto); 44 (Picture-Factory); 45/2 (Tyler Olson); 49/1 (Photographee.eu); 52/3 (Pavel Losevsky); 58/2 (Vladimir Voronin); 59/ (PrettyVectors); 60/1 (Birgit Reitz-Hofmann),2 (Ingo Bartussek),3 (PhotoSG),4 (Stephen),6 (Ocskay Bence); 62 (Robert Kneschke); 63 (Ingo Bartussek); 77 (Gina Sanders); 78 (rainbow33); 83/1 (dinostock),2 (volff),3 (Paulista),4 (Rostislav Sedlacek),5 (Joe Gough); 84/1 (michelaubryphoto),2 (Joe Gough),3 (mskphotolife); 85 (slavomir pancevac); 87/1 (Pixsooz); 94/3 (sabine hürdler); 97 (antikarium); 98/5 (sabine hürdler),6 (karelnoppe); 101 (shootingankauf); 102/1 (Jaren Wicklund),2 (Jaren Wicklund); 105 (Miriam Doerr); 111/1 (DoraZett); 116/2 (Jürgen Fälchle)
Thinkstock Deutschland GmbH, München (by ghetty images): S. 57 (TheaVector)
Walle, Andreas, Hamburg: S. 32/2

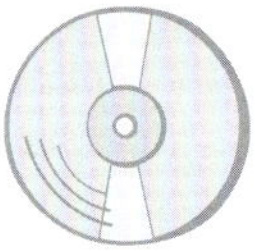

Zu diesem Buch sind Audio-Dateien (Best.-Nr. DA0901055) und ein Lehrerhandbuch (Best.-Nr. E16411) erhältlich.

ISBN 978-3-582-94908-0   Best.-Nr. 1671

Verlag Dr. Felix Büchner – Handwerk und Technik GmbH,
Lademannbogen 135, 22339 Hamburg; Postfach 63 05 00, 22331 Hamburg – 2022
E-Mail: info@handwerk-technik.de – Internet: www.handwerk-technik.de

Layout: Harro Wolter, 20253 Hamburg
Korrekturausführung: L101 Mediengestaltung, Julius-Pintsch-Ring 13, 15517 Fürstenwalde
Umschlagbilder: Fotolia Deutschland, Berlin , © www.fotolia.de: 1(Melpomene), 2 (Николай Григорьев), 3 (majivecka), 4 (Helder Sousa)
Druck: Grafisches Centrum Cuno GmbH & Co. KG, 39240 Calbe